The ADIRONDACKS
FULTON CHAIN – BIG MOOSE REGION

The
STORY
of a
WILDERNESS

The ADIRONDACKS
FULTON CHAIN – BIG MOOSE REGION

The
STORY
of a
WILDERNESS

By
JOSEPH F. GRADY

NORTH COUNTRY BOOKS, INC.
Utica, New York

The ADIRONDACKS
FULTON CHAIN – BIG MOOSE REGION

The
STORY
of a
WILDERNESS

Copyright, 1933
By Joseph F. Grady

SECOND EDITION
1966

THIRD EDITION
1972

FIRST PAPERBACK EDITION
2002

ISBN 0-932052-85-1

NORTH COUNTRY BOOKS, INC.
311 Turner Street
Utica, New York 13501

PREFACE

This preface must begin with the author's expression of gratitude to Miss Margaret L. Helmer, a helpful, patient and companionable critic. Her constructive interest in the story of a wilderness is a goodly part of the pages which follow.

Numerous sources of information have been explored to gather the facts of this brief narrative—too numerous to be set forth conveniently, if, indeed, the author could recall them all. Many good friends have contributed abundantly and kindly from their rich store of memories. But they, too, are numerous, and so are unnamed on this page. Let them not believe that because of this omission their splendid help has been forgotten. It is remembered, and they are remembered, with the heartfelt gratitude of the author.

*Dedicated to the Memory
of Joseph F. Grady and
Dorothy Thompson Grady*

THE AUTHOR

JOSEPH F. GRADY was a man with fine literary talent, accuracy in detail, a keen personal interest in people, dedication to the best interests of his community and a great capacity for leadership. He added to this a high degree of modesty which helped to make both his literary productions and his community efforts highly effective.

Joe was born in Davenport, Iowa, on September 17, 1891, the son of William J. and Marion Grady. He attended schools in Davenport and Iowa City, Iowa, where he was an outstanding student. His special interests were education, literature and drama. Upon graduation from high school, he taught for two years in rural schools where he became familiar with the problems and the hopes of growing farm boys and girls.

Following his venture in teaching, he attended the University of Iowa in Iowa City where he majored in Liberal Arts and Law. Courses in literature and writing were also of special interest to him.

With the entrance of the United States into World War I, Joe decided to spend some years in the service of his country and enlisted in the U.S. Navy on December 7, 1917, for a four-year term, most of which was spent on the Atlantic Coast, where the U.S. Navy kept a constant watch for German submarines.

Following his discharge from the U.S. Navy on September 30, 1921, Joe joined with his brothers as a partner in a large wholesale egg and poultry business. His particular responsibility was sales in New York City.

A breakdown in health in 1922 brought him from New York City to Old Forge in the Central Adirondacks where many other people had come in search of better health. This Adirondack Mountain area proved to be helpful and furnished the scene for an extended period of convalescence. It was during the latter part of this period that he wrote "The Adirondacks — The Story of a Wilderness."

As health and vigor returned, Joe took an increasingly active part in community activities in Old Forge. He joined with several other service men in the William Covey Post of the American Legion in putting on many interesting community programs.

An unusual opportunity for community service came in 1934 when he was chosen as Secretary-Manager of the Central Adirondack Association with headquarters at Old Forge. Joe led the young organization in an expanded program of service to the region which included the following activities:

He became personally acquainted with all of the resort hotel operators and business men of the Central Adirondacks and took an active interest in their program and achievements.

With the cooperation of the State Health Department, he launched an extensive program of publicity which established this area as a widely-known haven for hay fever sufferers.

Joe led the area in celebrating a number of outstanding events including "The George Washington Bicentennial" in 1932 and "Fifty Years of Conservation" in 1935.

These events and many other features of Central Adirondack life were widely publicized. His literary efforts included national coverage as an Associated Press correspondent and illustrated magazine stories, the most outstanding of which was a pictorial article on the Fulton Chain canoe trip appearing in *Look* magazine.

He concentrated on the development of Old Forge as a well-known winter sports center. To dramatize the movement, he introduced weekly "Snow Trains" which arrived filled with enthusiastic skiers.

Following his marriage to Miss Dorothy Thompson of Old Forge on August 13, 1938, the Gradys travelled throughout the south and southwest, returning to Old Forge in 1940 where he served effectively for several years as Secretary-Manager of the Central Adirondack Association and Director of Publicity for the Town of Webb.

In 1947 he resigned for health reasons and, after a period of travel and rest, Joe and Dorothy settled in Encinitas, California, in 1948. This led to a position as Secretary-Manager of the Cardiff-Encinitas-Leucadia Chamber of Commerce. Joe gave active leadership to these communities in a dynamic program of development and publicity. He was forced to retire from the Chamber of Commerce in 1957 because of ill health but continued for a time as acting secretary for the Encinitas Fire Department which he helped to organize on its present basis.

Following his death at the U.S. Naval Hospital in San Diego on October 31, 1962, the *Encinitas Coast Dispatch* gave the following tribute:

"The death last week of community leader, Joseph F. Grady, brought its measure of sadness to countless San Dieguito residents who counted him as their friend. He is remembered by the community for his quiet leadership in civic activities both in and outside of the Chamber of Commerce work."

Those who knew him through the years, as did the writer, remember Joseph F. Grady as a devoted citizen, a competent community leader, a Christian gentleman, and a real friend.

FRANK A. REED

CONTENTS

ILLUSTRATIONS

ILLUSTRATIONS

I
PROLOGUE

On a certain blustery November evening in the year 1930 two men chanced to meet at the intersection of village streets which is popularly known as the "busy corner" of Old Forge. Pausing to chat, they were joined by a third and, presently, by a fourth man. A sparse snow, hurried by the night wind, whipped downward past the arc of overhanging light to the glistening pavement where it swirled uncertainly into thin formations, then scurried away to the sheltering walls of the corner's modest business structures. The vanguard of Winter had descended upon the Adirondacks, and the wooded valleys and ridges surrounding the little village would soon be asleep under billowing mantles of snow. Heedless of the gusty elements, the four friends talked on, warmly concerned with a topic of common interest. They were weather-beaten, quiet spoken, unassuming men, inconspicuous in dress and manner, and all had passed life's meridian by several winters. The average of their ages bordered seventy years, yet the belligerent wind and whipping snow seemed to cause them no concern for they ignored the inviting refuge of a nearby doorway. They were discussing an incident of the mountains which had occurred nearly half a century in the past.

In the days of their youth the four had wandered into the Fulton Chain region. Gripped by the charm of rippling lakes and streams and seemingly endless stretches of mysterious forest, they remained. Their subsequent years were spent blazing new trails, learning new ways, gaining new understandings of nature. By dint of hard study and harder experience they, and comrades like themselves, had solved many of the problems confronting the forest dweller and had finally won the honest credentials of guides. At times their researches into the intracacies of woodcraft had been a trying course of study, for Nature, if not actually perverse, is an occasionally inscrutable and bewildering mistress of magic even to her most responsive apprentices.   But dogged courage and persistence had carried them on to surmount the peculiar difficulties attending their novitiates and, although success brought them neither wealth nor fame, their compensation, on the whole, had been satisfy- ing.   To a greater extent than the average of their fellow men they had been masters of their fates; they had followed con- genial careers cast in environments of their avowed choice; they had lived the lives they wanted to live.

In their boyhood years they had known old men who looked back from the sunset of life to recall their own youthful days when they roamed the Fulton Chain country, armed with muz- zle loader and powder horn, eager for its wealth of precious fur, its trails of wolf, moose and panther, and alert, too, for the possible ambush of an equally alert Indian.   But those days were far behind and now the four friends, themselves, were fast approaching the sunset of life; their own span of years had bridged the gap between the primitive and modern eras of the mountains.   Schooled in a rigorous but glorious country where daily necessities bred danger and hardship, they had witnessed its slow conversion to a beautiful land of comforts.   Yet the transition wrought in them no affection for the new order, no sense of achievement at the passing of the old, no exultance of the pioneer who beholds the fruition of his former hardihood. On the contrary, the innovations of the years had found and left them clinging hard and fast to their first and profoundest love—the Adirondacks as they had known them in the glad days of youth.   No alloy had ever found its way into that love. It had been the inspiration of their young careers.   Its warmth remained to comfort them in later life.

As they stood now amid the beat of the storm, conversing of the past, they formed a quietly dramatic, somewhat lonely group, representative of a fast vanishing type.   The swirling snow that hurried along the cold pathway of the street was not more foreign to their glowing memories than the hectic refine- ments of a new era that swirled along and left them—men apart and alone. One by one, their comrades of other years had dropped the rifle and the pack to follow the still trail into a dis' tant woodland. One by one, they had heard the far call, and had tramped onward to present their last credentials to the Master of all Woodcraft. Only a few remained; but the beauty and happy adventure of bygone years remained with them, and will remain until they, too, are summoned to lay aside their earthly concerns and make their camps upon a dis' tant shore.

*　　*　　*

Geologically, the Fulton Chain region takes its place among the oldest land areas of the earth. Historically, it is a land of comparative youth. Its story, like its fresh green face, bears no mellow imprint of age such as marks the chronicles of the major portion of eastern America. But despite its meager tradition and its brief existence as the scene of recorded human energies it is a fascinating sweep of lakes and woodland which merits a story more comprehensively and skilfully told than that which follows. As the plains and the sea weave curious enchantments that grip their people, so does a great forest cast a mystic spell over its dwellers. It is more than the spell of natural loveliness. It is a distinct atmosphere rising from an environment of leaf shadowed mystery, incomparable and unsearchable. To con' sider a forest as an incomparable division, as a land apart, is in no sense distortion even in times of swift communication that makes far places neighborly. It differs palpably from those in' tensively exploited areas which supply the country's economic vigor—the vast regions of tillable lands, the industrial centers and productive mining localities, and the populous cities of commerce. Its place in geography is distinct, and distinct, too, were many of its inhabitants whose peculiar inclinations led them into a wilderness frontier to lay the foundation of its history.

The Fulton Chain-Big Moose region lies in the westerly portion of the Adirondack Mountains, entirely within the mythical blue lines that encloses New York's immense natural park. Its political location embraces those portions of northern Herkimer and western Hamilton Counties which contain the hamlets of McKeever, Thendara, Carter, Big Moose, Eagle Bay and Inlet and the village of Old Forge. To say that it lies in the foregoing area is to deviate from strict accuracy, for, in reality, it rises more noticeably than it lies. The entire region is a rugged succession of wooded valleys climbing irrepressibly to the crests of ponderous ridges that wander away into an obscurity of forest. Its undulating contour is frequently levelled, and its succession of forest broken, by a network of lakes and streams. Except for these waterways and occasional clustered settlements, no clearings interpose to interrupt the awesome contiguity of wilderness. The most conspicuous of the waterways are the eight connected lakes of the Fulton Chain, extending east and west, and Big Moose Lake which lies amid scenic formations of peaks and ridges a few miles north of the Chain. Surrounding these picturesque bodies are scores of lakes and ponds, smaller but not less picturesque, gleaming like earthly satellites across a firmament of forest. The better known and more accessible of these include Limekiln, Little Moose, Twitchell, Dart's, Rondaxe, Moss, Cascade, Nick's, Old Forge and Okara Lakes. The whole area is drained by the North, South and Middle branches of the Moose River which converge into a single stream flowing west to join the Black River in Lewis County. For the purpose of geographical designation this area and the lake region adjoining on the east are styled the "Central Adirondacks" in local commercial literature.

During the past half century the region has passed from the domination of the hunter and trapper to acquire prominence as a resort area. Hunting, however, is by no means a forsaken pursuit, for game and fur bearing animals are numerous in the locality and the Adirondacks are bounteous providers of food and shelter for their creatures. But restrictive legislation now decrees that the huntsman pursue his avocation as a sport and an art rather than as a mingled business and science. Professional game killers have long since vanished from the scene. Their balsam-boughed shanties of the nineteenth century have given place to commodious twentieth century resort hotels which modern agencies of travel make easily accessible. In dispersing this predacious group of Nimrods, the law effaced a certain glamour from the personality roster of the woods, but compensation came in a more abundant survival of wild animal life.

A trip to the Adirondacks is now a convenient and popular means of recreation. It imposes no hardship or uncertainty, nor does it demand a knowledge of woodcraft to insure the traveller's comfort. But only a few brief decades have passed since visitors needed to be sportsmen or woodland adventurers of the more doughty type, inured to physical hardship, indifferent to the polite accessories of a civilization left behind, and whole-heartedly in a humor to pit cunning and endurance against any brusque reception an ill-disposed Nature might tender. Decade after decade has witnessed innovations which have affected the ways and fortunes of mountain dwellers. Change has followed change and new methods have supplanted the old with a persistence that may often cause the frontier-loving pioneer to consider dejectedly the environment of modernity which surrounds him. Happily, his situation is not lacking a goodly measure of solace. The encroachment of the modernizing process left no salient disfigurement in its train such as all too frequently results from human enterprise set foot free in virgin fields. Neither axe nor plow has marred the face of the region. It is the same continuity of shade and cool rippling water that it was generations ago: and being now the cherished ward of a nature minded commonwealth, it is not improbable that its deeply satisfying, natural, intimate beauty will remain forever unaltered.

II

INDIANS

THE first great families of the Adirondacks were roving bands of Iroquois. They were seasonal visitors, as great families are today, for their interests were diverse and often vital, and required their presence in other sections of the country. Before the shrewd tactics of the white race disloged them from preeminence in aboriginal affairs, they were the sovereign political group and the most formidable fighting clan east of the Mississippi. A singular faculty for government, shared by this racial family, inspired the formation of a five-tribe confederacy for purposes of mutual defense and the general advancement of the Iroquois fortunes. This confederacy, or league, unique in its day, became known as the Five Nations of the Long House. Its march to supremacy was swift and its authority absolute, achievements which demonstrated the expedience of its political conceptions and earned for the Iroquois a notable place in the history of American aborigines. The Long House was subsequently enlarged to include Six Nations through an eighteenth century alliance with the Tuscaroras, an Iroquoian branch whose unbridled savagery had led to its expulsion from North Carolina.

Among the tribal subdivisions of the Long House were the Mohawks, a versatile group of unsurpassed cunning in the business of war and the chase, whose settlements extended westward from near the present site of Albany. A locality just east of the city of Utica is believed to have been the site of their first permanent village. With the Moose River Valley's abundance of game and fur so enticingly at hand, the Mohawks and kindred tribesmen naturally designated that area as Iroquois territory. They claimed and utilized it as a sort of private hunting preserve long before the wary white man first challenged the solitude of the Adirondacks. At the dawn of its historical period, roving bands of the Five Nations were incessantly on the move through the region, and rare was the summer's dusk that failed to settle upon at least one company of savage hunts-men snugly encamped on the shore of the Fulton Chain. Their assertion of mountain ownership by no means referred to the Moose River Valley only. Moderation in the acquisition of empire was not an Iroquois trait. They annexed the entire Adirondack wilderness and labelled it the "Couchsachrage," which means "The Beaver Hunting Grounds of the Iroquois." It was the first proper name of record applied to the region and, its implication being starkly manifest, it proved to be an effec-tive one. With the equivalent of a Long House *no trespass* sign posted, few rival braves dared impugn the integrity of title to the extent of poaching or counter-claiming, and the widely feared Iroquois met with feeble opposition in enforcing their interdiction.

Of secondary importance to its value as a game preserve, the Moose River and Fulton Chain region offered a partial water route to Canada, the home of the northern division of Algon-quins. Iroquois and Algonquins were traditional rivals, and the former engaged in frequent raiding expeditions against the enemy settlements beyond the St. Lawrence. Many of these hostile excursions were nothing more than petty sallies con-ducted by a few spirited tribesmen in a passing mood for mis-chief, and were not the mobilization of the entire confederacy or even of an entire tribe. The more favored route to the north led the dusky warriors through Lakes George and Champlain, but seasonal inclemencies of weather could lash those waters to such fury that even the hardy Mohawk, skilled waterman that he was, had little taste at such times for the discomforts of that expansive course. Thus it chanced that occasional war parties headed northward along the more sheltered pathways of the Adirondacks. Entering the Moose River Valley, they followed its tree-cloistered lane to the Fulton Chain of lakes. The abundance of game encountered on the way offered an oppor-tunity of combining business with pleasure by testing their archery against the swift flanks of moose and deer. When satiated with the sport, and amply provisioned with venison, they resumed the watery warpath, intent, once more, upon the spicier prospect of a man hunt.   Leaving the Fulton Chain, they proceeded through Raquette Lake and thence by a choice of routes to the St. Lawrence and whatever of fortune awaited beyond in the form of scalps and plunder.

It so happened, at intervals, that parties of Algonquins— particularly the nomadic and improvident Montagnais tribes- men—made their way southward along the identical route then being followed by an Iroquois expedition.   The results were fatal, for sooner or later the two were bound to meet.   When they did, grewsome episodes of the mountains' history were enacted as attackers and attacked whooped and hacked their ways to a bloody conclusion respecting the ownership of the Adirondacks.   The Iroquois, of course, triumphed in a majority of such combats.   Only the employment of flawless stratagems or pronounced numerical superiority enabled the Northerners to overcome their rivals, or even to reach their homes after an encounter.   There they related the details of their unpleasant experience; dolorous tidings, they were, that served to augment the already stupendous prestige attached to the name of Iro- quois.   Terror of the Mohawks, alone, became so intense and far-reaching that the approved military tactics of certain enemy tribes degenerated to nothing more subtle than fleeing the dread presence as fast and as far as quaking legs could be induced to function.

They were startling outbursts of savagery which thus broke upon the customary quiet of the region.   An Indian war cry is a terrifying phenomenon in the realm of sound.   It is especi- ally terrifying when projected into a realm of nearly absolute silence.   Both Algonquin and Iroquois were psychologists enough to esteem its demoralizing effect upon an enemy, and both were capable of extracting from its utterance a maximum of military value.   Its fearful crescendo signalized the savage war scene—the glint of arrows streaking their ways to targets of human life—the tomahawk, circling to descend with cleav-

ing violence upon a savage head—savage arms embracing as
their owners lurched and rolled and grunted in a death grip
from which but one would emerge alive. Signal smokes, too,
rising from adjacent peaks, had their part in the drama, and so
had the ghastly torture fires that mirrored themselves in the
guileless face of the lake chain. How often and of what magnitude were scenes thus enacted is conjectural. They were
frequent enough and bloody enough, however, to bring the
region into bad repute even in localities remote from the
Adirondack foothills. Eventually, the length and breadth of
the Couchsachrage became known as "the dark and bloody
ground" and timorous natives shunned its forbidding recesses as
a place of certain doom.

It was the feud between Iroquois and Montagnais that
resulted in the name "Adirondacks" being applied to the mountains. Unlike their Long House foes, the Montagnais were not
agriculturists. They preferred to subsist on the spoils of the
chase rather than on the fruits of the harvest and were constantly on the go in quest of game. They were not always
aware of their destination, but as long as they were on their
way they seemed to be satisfied. At times the hunt proved
woefully unproductive and the hungry Northerners were reduced to the necessity of munching roots and twigs to avoid
starvation. The Iroquois, aware of their enemies' frequently
recurring diet of wood, contemptuously referred to them as
"Ha-de-ron-dah," which means "eater of trees." In the guttural
enunciation of the Iroquois the term sounded like "Adirondack," and the Montagnais tribesmen became known to early
white traders as "Adirondacks." In 1837, Professor Ebenezer
Emmons, a New England geologist, scaled the heights of Mt.
Marcy in the interest of a geological survey undertaken at the
request of the New York Legislature. He named that peak in
honor of William L. Marcy who was then serving his third
term as governor of the state. The following year his report,
submitted to the legislature, referred to the range of which Mt.
Marcy is the most prominent peak as the *Adirondack Range*.

This name, he explained, would serve to perpetuate the memory of the wandering Indian tribe that roamed the mountains in years gone by. Popular application of the name was at first restricted to the range and its locale designated by Professor Emmons. But gradually it superseded such widely known generic terms as *The Wilderness, The Brown's Tract* and *The Northwoods* and by 1875 it had grown into common usage in designation of the state's entire northern wilderness. In the meantime, *Couchsachrage* had passed from memory. Along with a miscellany of other linguistic unutterables, it had found its way to the happy hunting grounds of Indian nomenclature. But forty years after Professor Emmons had completed his survey, the forgotten name was resurrected into a brief Indian Summer of popular interest through the efforts of Sylvester, the historian. In an interesting work on the subject of New York's frontiers, Sylvester deplored the current use of *Adirondacks* to the inconsiderate and utter exclusion of *Couchsachrage*. In substance, he contended that the latter name refers directly to the Iroquois, the first acknowledged owners of the mountains as well as the most famous of their inhabitants, while the former term connotes a tribe whose relative unimportance is inconsistent with the perpetuation of its memory by so colossal a monument as several thousand square miles of rugged woodland. Sylvester's attitude was, of course, obviously rational. It was warranted by fact and founded on a scrupulous sense of justice and historical propriety. But influence other than historical determined the matter; particularly the ponderous influence of pronunciation. *Adirondacks* comes trippingly from the tongue, while *Couchsachrage* emphatically does not. Its syllabic joints are anything but nimble. Following a course of least resistance in fashioning speech is a universal trait, and Sylvester's was but one voice of authority among many which the mass tongue has glibly defied merely as a matter of lingual convenience. Had the mighty Iroquois cultivated the art of prophecy as intently as they groomed their talent for coining derision perhaps a foreknowledge of posterity's averseness to unwieldy language would have inspired them to rhetorical habits better calculated to immortalize themselves rather than their enemies.

It is improbable that any permanent Indian settlements ever existed in the Central Adirondacks or in any other locality within the Adirondack foothills. Abundant evidence has been unearthed, however, to tell the story of recurring Indian activity along the region's principal waterways. This evidence invariably relates to such aboriginal employments as hunting and warfare rather than to the routine affairs of established community life. Deposits of stone implements have been uncovered along the shores of all the Fulton Chain lakes, and at the head of Fourth Lake, Oliver Phelps, a gardner, added to his summer earnings a number of years ago by supplying vacationists with Indian relics hè had unearthed during the spring digging. The Hotel Arrowhead at Inlet commemorates in its name the interesting fact of the Phelps excavations.

In the year 1492, there occurred an event of gloomy portent for the aborigines. Three little ships pushed their inquisitive noses westward across the Atlantic. They were pudgy little vessels, mere specks of humanity-laden timber tossed by an endless sea, and very uncertain of their whereabouts, but their spread of canvass was vast enough to shadow the complexion of Indian destiny. Other ships followed. Land-hungry, freedom-hungry Europeans responded to the allurements of a new continent so glowingly described by returned voyageurs. In 1609, Samuel Champlain and Henry Hudson encountered the Mohawks on sharply contrasted terms of social relationship, and there was finally injected into the tense affairs of Iroquois and Algonquin a third human factor—the white man. Lo, and alas, the poor Indian! His doom impended: his fate was sealed. Too late he would realize that a word of flattery, a genial handclasp and the baubles of a new civilization are but pitiful compensation for the loss of an empire; especially a mountain empire of fair lakes and gracious trees, where gay streams splash and sing, or pause in their wanderings to murmur friendly greetings to the forest creatures that drink from their pools at twilight.

III

JOHN BROWN

THE first of a series of episodes in the long drawn out task of colonizing the Fulton Chain region found John Brown, a Providence, Rhode Island, merchant, taking a lone and reluctant hand in the rude affairs of the Adirondacks. This first (and for John Brown the last) episode was brief and futile. Nothing tangible survived the attempt locally except the good name of the Providence merchant which, today, is affixed to the region as securely as the name of a later John Brown is to the annals of the anti-slavery crusades.

The eighteenth century was drawing to a close when the region first appeared in the speculative spotlight. It had been a century of variegated experience for colonial America, of pioneering and culture building, of high hopes and deep dejections; it had hearkened to spirited trans-Atlantic controversies and to many daring pronouncements anent the theme of liberty; finally, it had witnessed the triumphal climax of the Revolution. The Adirondack wilderness had become part and parcel of an infant republic. White men were begining to penetrate its fastness on methodical itineraries; to harvest its treasure fields of fur and game. From white settlements dotting the Mohawk valley they struck northward to the Moose River and followed its age-old course to the Fulton Chain, as the Iroquois had been doing for centuries. The latter race had sometimes referred to the river as "Te-ka-hun-di-an-do," meaning "to clear an opening." They were adventurers of a pioneering era, these white men, as they entered the forest clad in the serviceable fur, leathern, and homespun garments of the eighteenth century trapper. Across their backs were slung bundled traps and rolled blankets; twin necessities, powder horns and bullet pouches hung from their deerskin belts as did the vitally important hatchets and hunting knives. Simple items of ground meal, salt, and tea constituted the total of their rations, for trusty flint locks and fishing tackle could be depended upon to balance the diet. Of necessity, caution was the watchword. Resentful Indians still prowled the region and Death could stalk the white trapper as intently as the trapper stalked the moose and beaver. The men thus roaming the wilderness were few and exceptional at that period. But little was known of the Adirondacks and not many persons cared to know more at the cost of personal observation. The average valley settler pic' tured the area as an interminable jungle of alternating swamps and peaks, the severity of its tempests and climate inimical to health, and the ferocity of its brute inhabitants an actual men' ace to life. In fact, the beautiful Adirondacks were snubbed and ignored as a piece of totally undesirable property.

But a smaller and more remote group—the land speculators —did not share in its entirety the valley settlers' unflattering conception of the wilderness, or if they did they discreetly avoided mention of it. They at least paid the region the mer' cenary compliment of appraising its turnover value. Flint locks and trap lines were no part of their equipment. Their's was bigger game than lead or steel could lay low. They were sophisticated denizens of the large seaboard cities, beaver-hatted gentlemen of finesse and persuasive eloquence who scented the fortunes to be made in catering to a national appetite for cheap agricultural lands. On any occasion and in any society they could produce from the pockets of their greatcoats prodigious maps revealing hundreds of square miles of virgin territory available to prospective investors at a shilling or two an acre if taken in large tracts—and if taken promptly. They were hard at it on both sides of the Atlantic, tracing out boundary lines, computing acreage, intriguing avid listeners as they ex' pounded in language of finance the possibilities of America's wide, unpeopled frontier. Fashionable homes and the sanctums of prosperous business houses knew them well; so did coffee houses and taverns of the better sort and other elegant haunts of the moneyed class where suave promotors found it profit' able to hold forth. Land was the speculative staple of the times as stocks and bonds are today, and there existed no dearth of investors who were willing to take a fling at the frontier in the hope of lavish profits.

With post-war land booms vigorously under way, the Adirondacks could not for long escape the advances of promotion. On paper they looked like salable merchandise; certainly they appeared as fertile and as congenial to home making aspirations as any other map tracts, especially when the map gazer lived several hundred or several thousand miles away. The first enterprising gentleman to cast an appraising eye upon the region was one Alexander Macomb, an Irish immigrant, fur dealer, and shrewd soldier of fortune, who had spent several years knocking about America and Canada on more or less profitable business missions. Being in straitened circumstances at the time of taking the Adirondacks into his calculations, he persuaded two wealthy acquaintances to join in his somewhat visionary project of acquiring for purposes of speculation a huge portion of what was then known as New York's "waste lands." The territory involved in the transaction was a contiguous tract lying in seven counties (Herkimer and Hamilton included) and embracing more than three and one-half millions of acres. The two acquaintances who, with Macomb, formed the buying syndicate were William Constable and Daniel McCormick. Both were men of business and social prestige in New York City. The handsome Constable home built in 1820 by a member of that family at Constableville, Lewis County, still survives as an impressive, well preserved example of the period's architecture and the family's prosperity. The first of a series of patents, conveying title to a portion of the foregoing area, was issued by New York State to Alexander Macomb in 1792, and the final patent was issued in 1798. The consideration of eightpence an acre called for an approximate payment (on the installment plan) of six hundred thousand dollars. The deferred payment provision enabled the syndicate to re-sell part of the tract as a means of financing the whole transaction. Although Macomb's interest terminated soon after the first patent was issued, the entire area of more than five thousand square miles conveyed by patent during the six years became known, and is still known, as "Macomb's Purchase."

Following the issuance of the 1792 patent, public interest in the Adirondacks quickened considerably, and huge mountain sites came tumbling down upon metropolitan realty marts as daily offerings in the trade. Fortune or disaster awaited successive buyers according to their ingenuity in unloading on other gullible purchasers before their own frail equities should perish in the ever lurking foreclosure proceedings. Most of the transactions, of course, were map sales. The average purchaser would have contemplated a journey to the North Pole with hardly less relish than he would have considered a trip to the Adirondacks. The distance was not prohibitive, but the way was rough and popular conceptions of the region's vast interior were of a kind to discourage city bred investors from making inspection tours in that direction. As that parcel of territory which later became known as the Brown's Tract (a portion of the original 1792 patent conveyance) is especially pertinent to our story, the remainder of this chapter will be confined to its history.

In June, 1792, Constable acquired title to Macomb's holdings which the latter had obtained from the State less than six months before. This comprised an area of 1,900,000 acres in Jefferson, Lewis, Herkimer and Hamilton Counties. It lay in the western and southwestern section of Macomb's Purchase and was designated as Great Tracts IV, V and VI. The abstract of title records the consideration as fifty thousand pounds. In December of the same year Constable sold to Samuel Ward, of New York, 1,280,000 acres of this tract for one hundred thousand pounds. The seller gained fifty thousand pounds by the transaction, in addition to which he still held title to 620,000 acres. He was one of the very few who profited extensively through ventures in the public waste land. In November, 1794, Samuel Ward and his wife, Phebe, conveyed by warranty deed 210,000 acres of their tract to James

Greenleaf for 24,000 pounds. This acreage lay in the Moose and Beaver River Valleys and included First, Second, Third and Fourth Lakes of the Fulton Chain, a part of Big Moose Lake and the sites of a number of future settlements extending from McKeever to Big Moose. Spruce trees were popular delineators of its boundary lines: one tree, listed in the title instrument, bore the carved initials W.I. C. B.; another "standing in a swamp" was marked C B 1794; a small beech tree "on the westerly side of a spruce mountain" was blazed with the notation W C 1793. Soon after purchasing this tract, Greenleaf apparently became pressed for ready money for the abstract reveals a mortgage dated July 29, 1795, recorded in favor of Philip Livingstone. For the next three years no facts are available pertaining to the fate of the land, its owner or its mortgagee. Greenleaf was probably unable to meet his obligations and both his and Livingstone's affairs became enmeshed in litigation. At all events, the title search reveals John Brown receiving on December 29, 1798, by virtue of a suit in Chancery, a Master's deed to the entire 210,000 acres.

The circumstances involving John Brown in Chancery proceedings were not of his making or to his liking, nor did he regard the favorable outcome of the suit as a legal triumph which would clear the way to a profitable colonizing venture. During the feverish land boom years he had remained aloof from the mob of visionaries who were reaching out in quest of quick fortunes to incredible distances beyond the young republic's flimsy outposts of civilization. He preferred to deal in the more tangible and immediate realities which he encountered in the prevailing tide of social and commercial affairs. Yet he by no means lacked the constructive attribute of vision. He possessed it abundantly—practical, sanguinary vision—the kind that is considerate of needs and probabilities, and that bases itself on the good foundations of reason and experience rather than on ephemeral enthusiasms or motives of unqualified self consideration. His methods were uniformly direct and unostentatious, and, as a rule, successful. No sharper contrast to his orderly approach to the realization of objectives is to be found than that revealed by the stormy career of his celebrated namesake of Harper's Ferry renown, who now lies buried at North Elba, Essex County, in the Adirondacks. No kinship existed between the two John Browns beyond the affinity inherent in high purposed minds. Both were men of wholesome ideals and flawless courage, and both pursued their ideals with iron resolve and a fine disregard for personal jeopardy. The abolitionist, however, chose his weapons and tactics with a showman's eye to their effect of up-stage glitter, instead of to their fitness for the stubborn battle at hand. He sallied forth from his Torrington, Connecticut, birthplace into a world of slavery that stirred to the utmost his righteous anger and his imagination—but not his intellect. Nobly intent upon the extinction of the time's cruelest social inequity, he ignored the political and constitutional processes which good government holds at the disposal of reform bent citizens, preferring instead, to deal with the evil in terms of physical violence which bluntly expressed the degree of his loathing for it. His resort to arms and his guerrilla skirmishes were the gestures of a well meaning fanatic who permits his infatuation with methods to obscure his goal. Depending on viewpoint, he was a saint or a simpleton, or something between, but not a straight thinking man who wins his battles by tempering proceedure with expedience. When loving hands bore him to his mountain grave, a self made martyr to an eminent cause, no link in slavery's chain had yet been broken, and, pathetically enough, no break loomed on the drab expanse of the negro's horizon.

Similarly impelled by a motive of principle, the John Brown of our story also had recourse to arms on a certain historic occasion. But he employed strategy with a view to results regardless of style, and was cautious to escape the glorified role of martyred hero in the aftermath. The occasion was the capture and destruction of England's war schooner *Gaspe* in 1772 which historians commonly credit to the leadership of Captain Abraham Whipple. It was the first maritime affray in the colonies' long struggle for immunity from British exploitation, and it is celebrated in history as the primal ancestor of all American naval engagements which followed. Its heartening success prompted the Colonial Assembly of Rhode Island to recommend to the Colonial Congress at Philadelphia the imme' diate building of an American fleet as a means of preserving the liberty of the colonies.

Prior to its destruction, the *Gaspe* had been patrolling Amer' ican harbor waters to enforce the payment of import duties imposed by England. In June, 1772, she ran aground in a stretch of shallow water in Narragansett Bay, near Providence. News of the mishap quickly reached the city where it caused general rejoicing. It was an exceptionally welcome bit of glad tidings to the colonists who heartily disliked every adjunct of Britian's tax gathering agency, and as heartily wished them all at the bottom of the sea. But while they gloated over the plight of the stranded vessel, several of their townsmen were plotting its complete destruction. John Brown had gone about the city, quietly mustering a company of sturdy young patriots who were willing to undertake a dangerous enterprise for the sake of partially avenging their aggrieved country. Under cover of darkness, they set out for the *Gaspe* in a tiny fleet of rowboats, with John in the lead. His Majesty's seamen were asleep in their bunks as the conspirators crept softly over the side and overpowered the watch. After a short tussle the surprised crew was subdued and transferred to the small boats alongside, then the ship's hold was fired, and the raiders departed with their captives—well satisfied with the outcome of the expedi' tion. In the morning, nothing was left of the *Gaspe* except the charred remnant of a hull that rose in dismal outlines above the sparkling surface of the bay. The daring coup aroused America's admiration and England's ire, and for obvious rea' sons John and his compatriots prudently refrained from expos' ing themselves to either. Conniving friends shielded them from the vengeance of Crown authorities, but an oppressive period of time elapsed before the shadow of the gibbet passed entirely from their paths.

At the time of his participation in the foregoing drama, John Brown was well established in the commercial life of the colonies. Two generations of his family had spent their lives in Providence, and he was born there in 1736. Unknown to him at the time, that famous little city was then observing the one-hundredth anniversary of its founding by Roger Williams, the practicing advocate of religious liberty. John's grandfather, Chad Brown, had won distinction as a preacher in the first Baptist Congregation established in America, which was founded in Providence by twelve men, including Roger Williams, in 1639. John's education was received in the common schools of his native city, where he excelled in his studies to a degree that astounded his teachers without stifling the lively outdoor enthusiasms of normal boyhood. His father, James, died prematurely; so an uncle, Obadiah Brown, supervised the business training of John and his three brothers. Seemingly, Obadiah made a thorough success of this delicate art, for all the brothers attained prestige and affluence in their respective callings, and all became favorably known throughout the several colonies.

An early astuteness exhibited by John in his attention to business matters, developed uninterruptedly until it had brought the young man to an enviable position in New England commercial life. In time, his ships sailed the seven seas bearing cargoes between Europe, Asia and America. During the Revolution, he placed these ships and their cargoes at the disposal of the colonies, for his allegiance to the cause of American independence was sincere enough and deep enough to affect his pocketbook as well as his emotions. He was a personal friend of Washington and of many other prominent Americans, all of whom evaluated his counsel highly in economic, and even in military, matters during the long struggle for liberty.

Despite his pronounced business success, John's interests were not money-bound. They ranged the fields of politics, religion, education and philanthropy with the same directness and fruitful results that invariably marked their adventuring into the realm of trade. He served several terms in the Rhode Island Assembly and the National Congress; in fact, it was while serving as a member in the former body that he led the memor- able attack against the *Gaspe*. The sympathy of several mem- bers of the Brown family with the ideals of higher education manifested itself through their cooperation in the movement to found Rhode Island College in 1764. For many years John served as treasurer of the institution, and in 1804 its name was changed to "Brown University" as an expression of gratitude to the family whose benefactions had materially aided its early growth.

The ingrained virtues that formed the well balanced struc- ture of John's character were oddly contrastive with his physical appearance. Although his height did not exceed aver- age, his weight, in the later years of his life, reached the astonishing total of three hundred pounds. So unfortunate a lack of bodily symetry was bound to impose a serious handicap on his physical movements, and to offset the restriction, at least in part, he had a specially designed gig constructed for his per- sonal use. This was a low built vehicle of great tensile strength in which he drove about the city on his numerous business mis- sions. On more important social and political occasions he used a coach and four. In September, 1803, he was fatally injured when the gig overturned as he was driving into the yard of his Providence home.

His plunge into Adirondack affairs came late in life and was precipitated from an unexpected quarter. Of his four children, James, Abigail, Alice and Sarah, none were potential successors to his high place in commerce. James had no taste for business whatever and, to his father's disappointment, blankly refused the offer of a partnership in the house of Brown. But Abigail supplied a partner for both herself and her father by marrying John Francis, a personable though impecunious young Philadel- phian. Francis was hardly more inclined to a business career than James professed himself to be, and probably was no better

fitted for one, but he was affable enough to accept the invitation of his father-in-law to a junior partnership in the prosperous firm of Brown and Francis. The elder man was not misled
into the belief that he was getting a sterling business partner.
He suspected the young man's ineptitude, but relied on the
family connection to spur him on to a fair mastery of business
tactics.

For a while all went well, and the partnership enterprises
prospered. The senior member shouldered the major responsibilities, while the junior attended to the less significant details
which his limited experience enabled him to grasp. Between
times, the latter continued to indulge his taste for the festive
boards of gay society, a source of entertainment whose fascination for him easily outweighed the obscurer attractiveness of
commercial life. But a time came when the elder partner found
it necessary to invest his son-in-law with a weighty responsibility. One of John's ships, having cleared an Asiatic port
some months before, was momentarily expected to reach New
York. It was laden with Oriental merchandise valued in excess of 200,000 dollars, and John deemed it expedient to send
Francis to New York to superintend the unloading and delivery
of the cargo, and to bring back the proceeds. Not at all averse
to a sojourn in the lively metropolis, brief though it might be,
Francis set out upon his journey, well fortified with instructions
concerning the performance of his mission. He arrived safely
at his destination, and in the interim before the ship reached
port he sought diversion in the companionship of a number of
congenial acquaintances. It proved to be costly diversion for
the firm of Brown and Francis. Apparently, an ulterior motive
lurked behind the congeniality of some of these acquaintances
as an unfortunate turn in affairs subsequently indicated.

In due time, the awaited vessel came to anchorage in New
York Harbor, and Francis promptly turned his attention to the
business entrusted to his care. He checked the manifest and
lading, attended to customs requirements, delivered the merchandise, and collected the money—210,000 dollars. In fact,

he was commendably punctilious in the observance of his father-in-law's instructions with the exception of one important detail—returning with the funds. When he reached Providence he carried not a penny of the sum realized from the sale of the cargo. Instead of returning to his home with a draft for 210,000 dollars, he returned with a questionable title to 210,-000 acres of land which lay tucked away in the remote wilds of the Adirondacks. The purchase price of the land equaled to a farthing the selling price of the cargo.

Among the acquaintances whom Francis had cultivated in New York, and who had cultivated him, incidentally, were Aaron Burr, James Greenleaf, Philip Livingstone and a man named Morris. All were shrewd, impressive men of affairs, alert to the foibles of their moneyed acquaintances and clever in taking advantage of them, and all were involved in Adirondack land deals. Possibly they composed a syndicate of super-salesmen at the time, with their attentions centered on the genial visitor from Providence; possibly the visitor himself soberly conceived what he regarded as a master speculative stroke that lay in his power to encompass and that would redound to the credit of his hitherto undiscovered business acumen; or it may have been the roseate influence of a famous vintage that animated him to unwittingly conclude a thoroughly bad bargain with a view to advancing the fortunes of his firm. At all events, he handed over a goodly fortune in exchange for an imperfect deed to the tract of land which has been previously described in this chapter.

Needless to say, the duped young agent's penniless homecoming gave no occasion for family rejoicing. His account of the New York transaction was a somber revelation to John Brown who needed the money to finance an insurance company and a bank he had recently organized. But he received the bad news cheerfully enough and, to his son-in-law's gratification, gave vent to no outburst of angry admonitions then or afterward. He cherished the fond hope, however, that his erratic partner would attempt to retrieve his past mistakes by a close application to practical business methods in the future. In this hope he was doomed to disappointment, for Francis remained a discouraging liability until his death which occurred a few years after the time he negotiated the deal cited above. He left one son, John Brown Francis, a bright, lovable youngster, who became a special favorite of John Brown, his grandfather, and a source of daily comfort to him. His cheerful companionship amply repaid the old gentleman for the grievous trials he had undergone at the hands of his irresponsible soninlaw. In later life, this son rehabilitated the family name in Rhode Island. He became a man of excellent character and enterprise, and served two terms as governor of the state. For many years he owned the John Brown's Tract, but a knowledge of his relatives' tribulations in connection with the tract restrained him from serious attempts to develop it.

To make the best of a bad bargain John Brown resolved to undertake the colonization of his Adirondack land, and he instituted legal proceedings at once to clear the title. Had he cared to exploit his reputation for integrity and sound business judgment, he could have disposed of the tract to an unsuspecting buyer at a figure approximating its cost to him by merely affixing his personal recommendation to such a transaction, and thereby have saved himself considerable trouble and added expense, but this he refused to do. His wholesome repute had not been nurtured on a diet of mythical virtues. Sharp business practices—misrepresentations, the taking advantage of trusting friends or of others' ignorance—had no place in his category of trade methods. He shouldered the burden of his losses manfully, and his attempts to recoup were fashioned in like pattern. Nearly two years passed before legal action establishing an incontrovertible title to the tract was concluded. In the meantime, anticipating the favorable termination of his suit, he laid plans to develop the tract into a profitable colony. Inquiries directed to Old Fort Schuyler (Utica) concerning the character of the region brought no encouragement. By all accounts the region was rough, heavily timbered, sandy, rocky and cold—

not well adapted to agriculture. Water was plentiful, however; so were good mill sites, and the presence of valuable ore was suspected though not actually determined. John's interest in the tract seems to have been impartially divided between its agricultural and mining potentialities according to the two letters which follow:

Providence, June, 2nd, 1798.

Mr. John Hammon,

Sir:

I observe by yours of the 3d of April 1797 that you have discovered iron oar and copper on the tract of land I have mortgages of, say eight Townships in all—210,000 acres and that you wish to do any surveying I may have to do. Pray what season will be the best to survey it and what will be the expense to survey the whole, lay it out in quarter mile squares, describe the rivers or the kind of land or rivers in every division, with what kind of wood and whether much wood or less and mention the iron oar, lime rock salt springs, the kinds of timber on every piece or No. How did the copper oar turn out that you sent to New York for trial, what quantity of copper does there appear to be and what extent of Iron Oar and what kind, whether Bog Oar, rock oar or Mountain Oar, or whether it is on dry level ground or in swamps or mountains and what appearance—how far distant on the Moose River did you discover a plenty of Iron Oar. If the mill seats are good and the Iron Oar is good it appears to me that the land must be valuable, the soil may not be rich and proper for raising wheat, but is the whole 210,000 acres so generally bad as not to afford any wheat or corn farms; as you yourself and three of your family are surveyors I suppose you will undertake to survey it with accuracy for a reasonable sum as you may do it at leisure and miss no other employment, please to mention the lowest price you'll do it for to give me a particular description of every quarter mile square affixed to its number, say from No. 1

to 1200 or 1300 which will comprehend the whole tract.
I am Sir your Kind Servant,

JOHN BROWN

John Hammon, Esq.,
Schuyler,
State New York.

The next letter, written ten months later, indicates a more pronounced disposition on the part of the writer to develop an extensive farming community:

Providence, March 31st, 1799.

Elder John Hammon, Sr.:

If you have concluded to survey on the same terms as Mr. Arnold Smith and Mr. John Allin have, I desire you'll begin the business immediately. Indeed I hope you'll be at work on the ground before this letter reaches you—as I wrote Mr. Bellews some time past, that I told your son at East Brayton that I would give you the same as I gave them. You'll be very particular in your Field Book and note everything of importance so as to give me the value of every town as near as possible by its number. You'll be sure to note every mill place, every good place for a compact town, the iron oar, the salt spring if any, the kind of timber, the laying of the ground whether good or bad or indifferent, whether broken or even or whether large or small hills and every other observation you think worthy of my knowing.

I shall be on the ground in all April, and if you and I both like I may continue you at surveying until the whole tract is laid out into four rod roads within one mile of each in every town, and the roads at right angles within two miles and every farm to be laid half mile square and fronting one of said roads, and of course one half the farms will lay on two roads.

I am Sir your humble servt,

JOHN BROWN

P. S. If not convenient for you to begin immediately I

shall not want you at all.

Apparently it was convenient for Elder John Hammon to begin immediately, for he surveyed the land, rendered his bill and received his pay. (Honorable William J. Thistlethwaite of Old Forge now holds the receipted bill in memory of the completed transaction.) However, the ambitious program sug' gested in the closing paragraph of the foregoing letter was never carried out: to this day, the John Brown's Tract has not been crisscrossed with a network of four-rod roads. It is likely that after spending the month of April on the tract John de' parted for home retaining but scant hopes for the success of an extensive colonization project, and that he concluded to let road construction await the current needs of settlers. He built one road giving access to the tract from the northern border of Remsen Patent, near Forestport. According to Mr. Charles E. Snyder of Herkimer in his excellent historical pamphlet, *John Brown's Tract*, this road was about twenty-five miles in length and its construction must have been a costly undertaking. It entered the Old Forge vicinity at a point south of the present Town of Webb school structure and continued to the river approximately along the same route now followed by the high' way leading to the state dam. This road which is now partially incorporated in the Nick's Lake Trail extending southward from the village, became known as the "Remsen Road."

At the time these preliminary operations were progressing, practically all the region's lakes which empty into any of the Moose River branches were commonly referred to as Moose Lakes, and what is now the Fulton Chain was then a consecu' tively numbered series of eight Middle Branch Moose Lakes. Old Forge Lake was no more than a slender stream, a continua' tion of the middle branch of the Moose River which carried the water of the eight lakes to its confluence with the North Branch. Across this slender stream, on the site of the present state dam in Old Forge, John Brown caused a log dam to be constructed which created a waterfall of sufficient force to power a sawmill and gristmill. A sawmill was then located beside the dam on the left bank (downstream) and a gristmill was erected on the opposite bank slightly below the dam. Thus deepened and harnessed to perform man's will for the first time in its long, inscrutable history, the river was re-christened "The Mill Stream," and as such it was known for many years thereafter. Apparently it pondered its novel situation with leisurely thoroughness before submitting, meanwhile permitting its channel below the dam to become dust dry in the summer sunshine, for, according to Mr. W. W. Benchley of Newport, three months were consumed before the oncoming water reached the top of the dam. But it did reach it, finally, went over, and tumbled swiftly down, and the wheels of industry began to turn in a new born mountain village. Nearby this little cluster of industrial plants, a house and barn were erected for the use of John's resident agent and workers, also a roomy wooden building which functioned as a retail store and supply depot. Prospective settlers began straggling into the rude community, beguiled by the attractive offers of free homesteads made by John's persuasive land agents, and soon the persistent strokes of axe against wood sounded in the forest as homeseekers chopped from dawn to dusk in hurried efforts to bring their lands under cultivation. A log bridge was built across the Mill Stream near the dam and a short road cut eastward through the woods as a means of making additional farms available to settlers. It has been estimated that by the year 1800 a score of clearings had been effected in the region, and that as many families, housed in rude wooden cabins, were struggling to adjust themselves to the harsh environment of their new homes. The sawmill provided cheap lumber for their construction needs, the gristmill stood ready to grind such grain as could be harvested from the homesteads' thin, virgin soil, and in the settlement store a variety of food, tools and clothing could be purchased on reasonable credit terms. All in all, the whole formed a rather pretentious little colony which, considering the initiative and money cost involved, merited a far better fate than that which soon befell it.

In the meantime, surveyors had plotted the entire 210,000 acres into townships numbered from one to eight. To each of these townships John Brown applied a proper name selected from a program of virtues which he had long been known to practice. Township 8, which he christened Regularity, lies in the southeastern section of the tract, and included Second, Third and Fourth Lakes of the Fulton Chain and a part of Big Moose Lake. To the west lies Economy (Township 7) which now contains Old Forge, Thendara and the sites of John's major development operations. A departing settler once paused in dreary reminiscence to proclaim Economy an appropriate title for the Township inasmuch as only the strictest practice of the virtue enabled a dweller therein to survive. Southwest of Economy lies Industry (Township 1) extending into Lewis County and including Copper Lake and a picturesque length of the Moose River. Enterprise (Township 2) bordering on the north contains Big and Little Otter Lakes and is drained by Pine Creek. Adjoining its eastern border is Sobriety (Township 6). Beaver River is beyond Sobriety (pun not intentional) to the north, and its drainage area is divided into two townships, Unanimity and Frugality (Townships 4 and 5). Directly south of Unanimity is Perseverance (Township 3) which is drained by Independence Creek. Having applied this last appellation, John's land holdings became exhausted, though not his knowledge of noble virtues. He continually practiced liberality and sympathetic cooperation in his dealings with settlers on the tract, many of whom were without means upon their arrival—or became so shortly after.

All the original homestead clearings in Township 7 were situated within three miles of the Mill Stream dam. Plantings of rye, barley, oats, hay, peas and potatoes were made, but the short and sometimes unfavorably cool growing seasons rendered the yields uncertain in quantity and the harvest time often a season of disappointments. Game was plentiful, however, and rod and gun eked out the inhabitants' humble subsistence. The gun's contributions were welcomed with especial heartiness for the sense of retaliation against ravaging night prowlers which they afforded. Moose, deer, bear, wolf, fox and other creatures of the forest, being no respecters of property rights, made disconcerting inroads on ripening grain, livestock and sapling fruit trees.

White and Indian trappers passed through the clearings. Occasionally they accepted the overnight hospitality of a cabin before plunging deeper into the wilderness where they spent a few evenings, at least, before their lonely camp fires, musing on the settlements' slashing invasion of the woods. If it continued it would hurt their business—perhaps end it. But the invasion was shortlived. In 1803, John Brown's useful life came to a close. Through his resident agent on the tract he had dealt generously with the impoverished settlers with a view to encouraging them to remain, but the incentive of his personal interest ended with his death. Slowly but unceasingly, an atmosphere of depression drifted across the colony and enveloped its inhabitants. The odds of cold and loneliness were great against them, the soil was of grudging fertility, the channels of social intercourse laborious, and in despair they envisaged a future which bore scant promise of improvement. Thoughts of returning to the valley abodes which they had deserted a few years before cheered them, and eventually took shape in a general exodus. One by one they packed their meager belongings into ox carts and departed, abandoning the settlement to the quiet forest which had been despoiled to give it place. Twin parasites, briars and decay, ever ready to trespass upon an absent man's property, closed in upon the tenantless homesteads and the once busy clearings soon presented a picture of desolation and ruin. Civilization's first mass attack against the Fulton Chain thus became an historic failure.

In his will, executed one year prior to his death, John Brown bequeathed Townships 1, 2 and 3 to his wife, Sarah; Township 4 to his daughter, Abigail Francis; Township 5 to his daughter, Sarah Herreshoff; Township 6 to his daughter, Alice Mason; Township 7 to his grandson, John Brown Francis, and Town ship 8 to his son James. In a schedule of assets annexed to the will he valued Township 7, consisting of 23, 180 acres and improvements, at $29,180, or at $1.25 an acre. His total money investment in the 210,000 acre tract probably exceeded $300,-000. The son-in-law, John Francis, who was responsible for the entire unfortunate investment, preceded John Brown in death, but his name also is mentioned in the latter's will, a portion of which follows:

"I give and devise to my grandson, John Brown Francis, on his arriving at the age of twenty-one years, his heirs and assigns on this express condition, that his deceased father's relations never make any demand on me as the surviving partner of the late firm of Brown and Francis or on my heirs, or executors in consequence of such partnership, as they can certainly in justice have no claim for one shilling by reason of said partnership as John Francis, my late partner and father of John Brown Francis, never put any property into the company stock and from his almost constant sickness and our bad fortune during the partnership I do not think my estate was worth as much, including the whole stock, at the expiration of the partnership as at its commencement, the following estates, particularly described in the schedule annexed viz.:

21—The township No. 7 containing twenty-three thousand one hundred and eighty acres on which are good improvements of cleared land, etc., a house, barn, good sawmill and gristmill with a great plenty of the best pine timber, so that white pine boards may be procured at the mill for two and one-half dollars per thousand, being part of my aforesaid tract of 210,000 acres of land in New York, and annexed on the schedule marked No. 21, 29,180 dollars. And described below in No. 21 in schedule referred to as follows:

The township No. 7 called Economy, quantity 23,180 acres, through which the large and fine river called the Moose River runs and on which I have made great improvements of a grist mill, saw mill, house, store, etc. On this town is the best pine timber which may be floated to the mill and sawed into the best pine boards very cheap."

Thus ended the final, material influence John Brown could ever exert upon the mountain tract which now bears his honest name and retains the memory of his many virtues. In time, other men would come on the tract, would toil there, some complacently hopeful, some joyous, some in grief and desperation, but none would contrive a more fortunate outcome of their labor than the empty failure its former owner had struggled in vain to avert. They were industrious and brave enough, these men who followed John Brown, yet their efforts were doomed to unconditional defeat, for only the slow drift of many years was destined to reveal the rich deposit of treasure which is the endless glory of the Fulton Chain.

IV
HERRESHOFF AND THE OLD FORGE

CHARLES FREDERICK HERRESHOFF, the man whose futile endeavor to conquer the Brown's Tract gave Old Forge its name, travelled a curious path in life to reach his station of prominence in Adirondack history. It was an amiable, wandering path that took its way through congenial fields of social and intellectual interests, and led its traveller pleasantly onward until it halted with tragic abruptness before an obdurate mountain of rock. In several respects Herreshoff was conspicuously ill equipped to attempt an Adirondack development project. In many ways, too, his was the most pathetic and disastrous, and yet the noblest enterprise of that nature to be attempted in the early history of the mountains. His connection through marriage wth the family of John Brown first brought the region to his notice, and a subsequent impairment of his wife's inheritance, partly due to his own administrative shortcomings, inspired his active interest in it. Mortified at his failure to manage the inheritance wisely, and eager to restore it to its former ample proportions, he turned to the wilderness, hoping there to carve out an empire of tenanted farms or to blast a fortune from its rocky hills which rumor hinted were impregnated with a wealth of valuable ore. His scheme was visionary and, of course, it profited nothing. Where the practical, resourceful John Brown could not succeed it was inevitable that a less skilful fortune seeker would fail.

Herreshoff was born at Minden, Prussia, in 1763, one hundred and ten years before the German Empire was founded. His parents, though not of the nobility and though possessed of only moderate resources, were people of some distinction in Prussian society. The mother was a gentlewoman of marked culture and personal beauty: the father, an officer in the Potsdam Giant Guard and a man of splendid physique, was well educated and on terms of intimacy with several German intellectuals. Both parents died before the son was five years old, and the orphan's training and education were left to a Berlin professor, an old friend of the Herreshoffs who guided the boy through his adolescent years with the zeal and devotion of a father. As a young lad, Herreshoff was sent to the Philan- thropin, an exclusive school at Dessau, Prussia, which he attended until he reached the age of twenty. The Philanthropin was patronized chiefly by scions of the nobility; its curriculum, conducing to a knowledge and appreciation of the arts and kindred polite matters which were deemed the cardinal intel- lectual requirements of the peerage, gave but passing notice to youths of lesser station whose mental equipment might event- ually be called to the test in the world of commerce. In this school Herreshoff applied himself diligently and attained high scholastic honors. During his years of study—which were per- haps the pleasantest of his life—he was privileged on several occasions to meet and converse with Frederick the Great, Prussia's reigning monarch. These meetings, which were no more than informal chats between the two, are said to have delighted the king, who openly expressed his admiration for the boy's vivacious intellect and prepossessing appearance. This celebrated ruler, although renowned as an exceptionally capable strategist in marshalling Prussian arms against a hostile Europe as a means of enhancing the political prestige of his kingdom, remained a steadfast patron of literature and the arts during the forty-six years of his reign. Intellectuals of all Europe were in constant attendance at his court, and his cultural influence on German youths was notable. It was his deep seated interest in scholarly effort and his direct, personal response to excellence in that branch of endeavor that gave the orphaned student entree to the royal presence.

Upon being graduated from the Philanthropin, young Herr- eshoff faced the world with no precise knowledge of what to do with it. He resolved, therefore, to see it first and to reach a conclusion later, whereupon he set out on a leisurely itinerary through the principal countries of Europe. Neither counting-house nor army attracted him as the starting point of a desirable career. His vision had been deflected from mercenary employ-ments by education and schoolboy associations, yet his exceed-ingly modest income demanded that he engage in some kind of gainful occupation as soon as possible. What this would be, or how he would undertake it, he hadn't the fragment of an idea.

For three years he wandered aimlessly across Europe, accom-plishing nothing, and coming no nearer to a solution of his individual employment problem than he had been at school. Finally he sailed for America, hoping the new land would pro-vide the economic adjustment he sought. He reached New York in the summer of 1786, a handsome, straightforward young immigrant, one among thousands who were seeking social and economic re-adjustment in America. He was then twenty-three years old, six feet four inches tall, well propor-tioned physically and of an engaging personality. In New York he met two German acquaintances who were on quests similar to his, and the three formed a business partnership cater-ing to their countrymen's needs with importations from Ger-many. This partnership lasted more than ten years, although it met with but indifferent success.

While living in New York, Herreshoff found easy access to successively higher levels of society. His distinguished appear-ance and intellectual charm gave him entrance to the homes of many of New York's prominent families, and in the circle of his most intimate friends his fine sense of honor and genial, wholesome companionship inspired profound admiration. In business circles, however, his attainments were less pronounced. Competition, the reputed life of trade, was Herreshoff's despair. The fundamental proceedure of making close, accurate calcula-tions usually essential to the profitable outcome of commercial ventures seems never to have come within the scope of his understanding. It was all too sordid and practical, too lacking in academic character to pique his curiosity and stimulate his unpractical mind. But he did assist the partnership materially by his fluent command of English, if by no other means. Upon arriving in America he immediately began the study of the new language. This was a scholarly pursuit which challenged his mental faculties and intrigued his interest, and in a compara' tively short time he acquired a nearly perfect mastery of Eng' lish. His oral and written use of it displayed hardly a trace of his mother tongue which he had learned so thoroughly in Prussia.

Herreshoff's acquaintance with the Browns of Providence came about through a business transaction with the firm of Brown and Francis in which he represented the New York partnership. His meeting with John Brown's daughter, Sarah, was a mutually enjoyable occasion which resulted in Herres' hoff's making return trips to Providence more often than were warranted by mere business interests. Sarah was a comely, gracious hostess and had the added attractiveness of being a learned woman in her own right. So unusual a combination of social and intellectual graces was bound to charm the cul' tured New Yorker, and he embraced every opportunity of enjoying the hospitality of the Brown home, which at that time was the most palatial mansion in New England.

Admiration soon blossomed into love, and for several years Herreshoff advanced his suit in the approved manner of local and long distance courtship in vogue among eighteenth century suitors. Sarah approved of his affectionate advances, and as affectionately bestowed her heart, whereupon he approached John Brown to ask for her hand. If the father interposed ob' jections they were not serious ones, for the two were married at his home in July, 1801, and a new chapter in Herreshoff's excursive career was begun.

The New York partnership was dissolved within a year after the wedding and the Herreshoffs took up their residence in Providence. Possibly the husband would have entered into a partnership with his father-in-law, but the latter died suddenly in 1803, leaving his affairs in excellent shape but with none of his heirs or sons-in-law fitted to hold them together and manage

Ruins of the Herreshoff Manor near Thendara.   Photo of 1892.

them as a going business concern.   It will be recalled that his
wife, three daughters, son and grandson, were named as the
principal beneficiaries of his will.   This document bestowed
a bulky accumulation of wealth: when the estate was liquidated
and divided among the six heirs it provided each with a comfortable fortune.   Finding themselves happily settled in life
with the means of gratifying their refined inclinations, the
Herreshoffs betook themselves to the country estate at Point
Pleasant which John Brown had purchased and improved soon
after the close of the Revolution.   It contained a commodious
dwelling house, stables, barns, and other useful and ornamental
structures, and its wide expanse of partially wooded, rolling
land overlooked Narragansett Bay near the site of the *Gaspe*
raid.   The farm is still in the possession of Herreshoff's grand-
sons, the boat builders of the same name whose craftsmanship
has contributed notably to America's yachting supremacy.

Six children were born at the Point Pleasant home, Anna,
Sarah, John, Agnes, Charles Frederick, and James.   The swift
years slipped along blissfully for the growing family; for the
parents, life on the estate chrystallized into a prolonged honeymoon.   They entertained, indulged their artistic tastes, effected
extensive improvements on the place, and undertook various
horticultural and landscaping projects with a view to beautify-
ing their surroundings.   Between times, Herreshoff engaged in
practical farming with negligible results, his chief outdoor interest, of course, being centered in pastoral activities befitting a
cultured gentleman of landed estate.

Meanwhile, the family fortune dwindled with the years in
direct proportion to the family's mounting enjoyment of life.
The shrinkage was gradual at first and barely perceptible, but
by the year 1810 the once ample legacy had contracted to an
alarming state, and the Herreshoffs became pinched for ready
money with which to meet their fixed obligations.   They had
neglected to exercise proper caution in selecting their investments, and in safeguarding them after they were selected;
moreover, Herreshoff's farming operations had harvested noth-

ing but deficits which, added to the family budget, exceeded the yearly income by an appreciable sum. An immediate re- duction in their scale of living and a philosophic acceptance of the change would have saved them future disappointments and heartaches. Enough assets remained to insure their living in comfort if not in luxury, but apparently that mediocre prospect was too bleak, and Herreshoff cast about for means of restoring the fortune. It was at this time that he conceived the idea of colonizing the Brown's Tract. The idea eventually proved to be tragic and ruinous, but it presented itself at the time as a sure and rather attractive way out of the dilemma; so he carefully laid his plans to attempt it. By using a portion of the assets remaining in his wife's inheritance and receiving aid from other members of the Brown family he believed that he could finance the undertaking until it progressed to the dividend-paying stage. Accordingly, in 1811, he took leave of his family and moved to Township 7 of the tract. The land belonged to his young nephew, John Brown Francis, but the latter, who was very fond of his Uncle Charles and Aunt Sarah, readily agreed to the project and even expressed a desire to accompany his uncle. He was disappointed in this ambition. Because of his youth, the family thought it best that he remain at home, so his uncle started off alone.

Herreshoff immediately set men to work repairing the Mill Stream dam, the sawmill and gristmill, and improving the de- serted cabins to a habitable condition. Partially overgrown clearings were re-cleared and made ready for the anticipated influx of settlers, and agents once more scoured the valley settle- ments beyond the Adirondack foothills to coax pioneering homesteaders into the new development. A few settlers strag- gled in, bearing their scanty possessions and questionable hopes, and community life on the Brown's Tract again greeted the cynical gaze of trappers who continued to plod through the clearings. Herreshoff planned, as his father-in-law had done nearly fifteen years before, to establish an agricultural colony of sufficient size and economic vigor to enhance the value of the surrounding land. To speed the growth of the colony he offered the 160 acre lots at extremely low prices and on attractive credit terms, together with certain material aid gratis to the first dozen or so of settlers who cared to take advantage of a temporary bargain. In the meantime, the hamlet of Boonville, twenty-five miles away, which was founded in 1796, was growing into a thriving settlement which would soon become a sort of civic foster father to the Fulton Chain region. A steady tide of immigration was moving northward to build homes in the valley of the Black River and to engage in agriculture and related industries that would bring prosperity to the little hamlet and to the valley as a whole. Roads had been opened, traversing the valley north and south, some of them skirting the western and southern edges of the Brown's Tract. To facilitate transportation to and from the tract by way of Boonville, Herreshoff cut a road from the southeastern corner of Lewis County through the forest to his development thirteen miles away. Beginning at a point beyond the Moose River, several miles west of McKeever, the road pursued a northeasterly course to the site of Thendara, where it again crossed the Moose River by means of a rude log bridge. Over the river, it curved upward to the left and converged with the older Remsen Road about one mile south of the Mill Stream dam. This new highway became known as the "Brown's Tract Road." It served usefully for a number of years, and became somewhat famous in time, although it also became a distinctly unpleasant memory to countless wilderness travellers who had bounced their painful way over its rutty surface.

The new road did not bring the hoped for rush of settlers, and it soon became evident that the task of sprinkling a farming population over a considerable area of Township 7 would be a long, tedious task. The tract was noticeably less productive than other agricultural regions then awaiting settlement, and no rumors of prosperity drifted to the outside world to spur homeseekers on to the place. On the contrary, the entire section was fast acquiring an unsavory reputation for hardship and poverty through reports bruited about by trappers and former settlers, all of which increased the difficulties to be contended with in building an attractive community. Some of these reports were highly colored inventions spread by imaginative tattlers who enjoyed the telling of a good story, but their effect was hurtful nevertheless.

To make his stay on the tract more comfortable and more in harmony with his accustomed standard of living, Herreshoff built a substantial dwelling house with lumber sawed at his mill. It was a two story structure with six large rooms and a wide veranda which extended the length of the house. This became known as the "Herreshoff Manor." It stood on a slope overlooking the Moose River and the intervening expanse of level land on which the hamlet of Thendara is situated. For more than eighty years it occupied this prominent site, slowly crumbling before the onslaughts of neglect and weather, a gloomy, unkempt relic that arrested the traveller's attention and brought to mind its former owner's unfortunate story. Toward the close of the century it became a menace to children playing near its walls, and Dana Fraula, of Old Forge, burned it to the ground, leaving only the inconspicuous cellar depression to mark its location. This may still be seen about one hundred yards west of the Thendara Station. The sloping land has been partially cut away to accommodate railway tracks and the state highway, and a sharp declivity of sand obtrudes between the cellar and the road.

Housed in his comparatively luxurious Manor, Herreshoff continued to attack the baffling problem of colonization. Three hundred merino sheep in a single flock were herded to the tract from Rhode Island, and a rough shed, two hundred feet long, was erected for their shelter. Wool raising then added variation to local husbandry, but it brought no profit. The region was not suited to the grazing of so many sheep in a compact flock. The animals subsisted for a time but finally disappeared, leaving the record of their brief stay to be recorded as one more discouraging entry on the wrong side of the ledger. Added incentives were offered to potential homesteaders in the hope of stimulating migration, and Herreshoff, himself a novice in the ways of the forest, constantly encouraged dwellers on the tract to remain. His advice on their problems was probably of slight help to the settlers, most of whom had a more comprehensive working knowledge of agriculture than he possessed. But his attractive personality, his sympathetic interest and unquestion-able honesty inspired them to a genuine affection for him and a loyalty which held to the end of his career. These were the only dividends the harassed promoter was destined to collect from his investments in the wilderness.

After he had spent five fruitless years on the tract, a ray of hope appeared which temporarily brightened his prospect of success. Workmen, engaged in removing stone for building purposes from a long wooded ridge near the Manor, discovered traces of iron which seemed to indicate the presence of exten-sive deposits of the ore deeper in the ridge. Rock samples were gathered and sent out for analysis, and the assayer's report led Herreshoff to believe that a profitable smelting and forging industry could be established locally. The possibility of de-veloping a business of this kind on the tract had been uppermost in his mind for several years, but hitherto a favorable oppor-tunity had not presented itself. Accordingly in 1817, he opened a mine at the base of the ridge about a quarter of a mile north of the Manor, and arranged charcoal pits nearby to pro-vide fuel for the smelting. He then erected a building a few rods below the Mill Stream dam to house the forge and other necessary equipment. This building stood at the water's edge on what is now the State Hatchery lawn, about a rod below the highway which now crosses the Middle Branch of the Moose River at that point. The ponderous iron forge and hammers were hauled into the woods over several highways, including the Brown's Tract Road, and observing residents of the Mo-hawk and Black River Valleys fell to speculating anew regard-ing the outcome of activities in the wilderness.

As Herreshoff had long since exhausted his personal resources, this new venture, like his other development projects, was financed by his wife and by certain affluent members of the Brown family whose sympathy had been enlisted by the decline of their relatives' fortune. Funds to supply his needs continued to arrive for a time, but in decreasing amounts and at longer intervals, and his mining operations often neared collapse due to a shortage of capital. The Browns had lost faith in his ability to convert the region into an income producing estate, and were plainly reluctant to throw good money after bad. But he struggled on as best he could, bravely facing the many difficulties that beset him, firmly resolved to fight it out until success or failure should definitely mark his efforts. From time to time the mine caved in; water flowed in from unexpected sources to flood the shaft; thin deposits of ore vanished quickly, and substantial deposits never appeared. Nothing developed to encourage him in the hope that a fortune lurked beneath the inscrutable face of the rock cliff, but he continued to bore in with dogged persistence, hoping against hope with every sunrise that the new day would bring success.

Two of his letters, written during his last year on the tract, are of especial interest here for the light they throw upon him and his activities during the closing period of the development project. They were originally published in Alfred E. Donaldson's excellent two volume work, "A History of the Adirondacks," and are reprinted here through the courtesy of Mrs. Donaldson and the Century Publishing Company of New York.

Brown Tract, 5th Sept., 1818.

MY DEAR WIFE:

I had secretly determined not to write to you till I could give you the pleasing intelligence that my forge was in full operation. But though I cannot give you such good news yet, I will not let this day pass by without some token of remembrance. I should at least have answered your letter, so full of pleasing information, were it not so much against my inclination to write in an unhappy mood.

How true what some celebrated author says, that the best human conjectures are but weak.

When I arrived here on the last day of June, I found myself unexpectedly farther remote from the accomplishment of my plan than on parting. From a misunderstanding of my orders my overseer had set the rock blowers to work in the mine three weeks before my return. I found to my surprise that things had taken such a turn that I could not proceed without danger that the expense of getting the ore would far exceed my calculations, nor did I see any prospect of arriving at a certainty for the future. I therefore determined upon a bold and tedious, but decisive maneuver, the result of which must either realize all my hopes to the fullest, or at least prove them to be out of my reach under present circumstances. I calculated it would take me about three months to accomplish that object: I have already entered the third without having gained any great degree of certainty. The appearances, however, keep increasing in my favor, in my judgment.

Everybody who sees this piece of Herculean work exclaims what a grand affair it would be if I succeeded, but to tell the truth, not one single soul has the smallest belief in a favorable issue. That however operates rather as a spur than a discouragement upon me. I am still full of faith, or else infatuation, that I shall come off triumphantly in a short time.

Like all the rest of the world we have had a most glorious season, fine weather all the time, even during haying, when generally here we are favored with copious showers. I have made one hundred tons of hay, and have left grass uncut. We might this summer have raised as good corn as any of our neighbors, if any had been planted. Of all the fine weather, however, I enjoyed but little else than the satisfaction the storms did not interrupt my work in the quarry; there I have spent all my hours from morning to night, Sundays not excepted.

Once however I have been out as far as Trenton, 18 miles beyond Boonville, to stand my trial in the suit of that villain Joy, before Referees under rule of the supreme court. Though it lasted a part of two days, it remained undecided, and an argument of the lawyers on both sides is to take place this very day in Utica, which will bring the business to a close. It will make a difference of about 900 dollars to me whether I gain or lose the case, but I shall feel horribly mortified to have that ungrateful monster triumph over me. So far the case stands entirely in my favor.

Our daughter, Anna, I suppose is so absorbed in her studies that she never thought of me. How different last year; how grateful I felt then for her frequent letters. I love her more I imagine than I was ever conscious of before.

Sunday 27th September.

I have let several opportunities go by to send out the above. I was constantly in hopes that by waiting a few days longer I might be able to say something rather more decisive in regard to my iron prospects. I can at least tell you that all is well. I am now only waiting for my blowers who stand ready to repair hither at my call, but are at present 120 miles from here. The moment they arrive I shall set the hammer in motion, not to rest again very soon I hope. I have also gained victory over old Joy, to his great grief.

Several letters addressed to John Francis have arrived at Boonville; he had not made his appearance here last Thursday. Our summer is over; the nights turn frosty and the woods pale, I keep however no fire yet in my room. You shall soon hear from me again. Give my love to our dear children and believe me,

Affectionately yours,

C. F. HERRESHOFF

The next letter, written the following year, is addressed to his favorite daughter, Anna, and was penned during what undoubtedly was the bitterest period of Herreshoff's life.

Brown Tract, 8th October, 1819.

My Dear Daughter Anna:

And would you really leave so many dear friends, give up all your pleasures and comforts, to go into the wilderness to be a comfort to your poor old father? Heaven bless you. Surely I am better off yet than the poor old wretch of a king who cried in the agony of despair: God help me, my own children have forsaken me!

I have yet what a crown cannot buy: a heart that remains true to me through all the vicissitudes of life. Remain where you are, my dear child; make the best of your present time; such opportunities for improvement will never come again. Enjoy the innocent pleasures of your age; the days in which you shall find no pleasure will come without your seeking. I understand your sister Agnes is now with you. She learns with such ease whatever she feels interested in it must give you pleasure to assist her in her studies. Her chief aim, I hope, will be to deserve the love of her friends by an amiable conduct. Be kind to her my dear Anna, that she may be inclined to take advice from you; let those little explosions of a quick temper never make you for a moment forget that she is your sister, your own blood; nay, to speak the truth, they ought to remind you of it.

Winter is again approaching, and you are not one of those, I know, who hail its grim visage. I never thought much of the heart of young people who prefer winter on account of parties, balls, etc. They ought to be sent to Siberia without benefit of muffs or tippits. The sociable shade of a tree is to me as far before your sociable fireside, as the sun is before the moon. People who have lost their hearts and are out of their heads, I believe always love the fireside and the moon, and they should be excused.

The season with us has been the finest I ever witnessed here; we raised no large crops of any kind, but what we raised was remarkably good, as rye, wheat, corn, peas and potatoes. Though we had much heat yet we never suf- fered in the least from drought, which has been very harmful in some places of our neighborhood; neither have we been visited by hailstorms, tornadoes, floods nor earth- quakes, and of mosquitoes and flies we had no more than our usual crop. In fact the whole season from May until now has been like one fine summer day, nor have the rude winds yet encroached upon it. Even today, one would think it were mid-summer, walking through the woods if it were not for the pale and tumbling leaves that drop at every breath of the breeze. They are the tears of a parting friend, mingled with smiles, as if saying: We shall meet again! That we too may meet again, my dear daughter, is the ardent wish of

Your ever affectionate father,

C. F. HERRESHOFF

The father's ardent wish was not gratified, for he never again met Anna or any other member of his family, nor did they ever again hear from him directly. Success, with her laurels of wealth and honor, remained forever aloof, and Herreshoff could have penned no additional messages without including a dis- heartening echo from his bleak environment of failure, and this he was unwilling to do. During his earlier years on the tract he had often returned to Providence to visit his family, but the visits ceased entirely during the last eighteen months of his stay. Either the operations in the mine and forge required his constant attention and prevented his journeying to Rhode Island, or he had secretly resolved never again to appear in the family circle without bearing the tidings of success which he felt pledged to carry.

At the time the foregoing letter was written, the ore output of the mine had cost about one dollar a pound to extract and reduce, and Herreshoff foresaw the certain ruin that faced him unless his workmen could uncover an iron deposit far richer than any yet discovered. Loyal to the end, his men obeyed his urging to haste in desperate hopes that the long awaited wealth of the underground would reveal itself. Drafts drawn by Herreshoff on the family at Providence had been returned unpaid, and no further assistance from them could be expected. In the dim cavern of the mine lay his sole chance to stem the approaching tide of disaster, but it proved as fruitless as the many other hopes he had cherished during his eight years in the wilderness.

On the morning of December 19, 1819, workmen brought news to the Manor that water from an unexpected source had again flooded the mine, and months of expectant labor had once more come to naught. Almost unbelieving, Herreshoff hurried from the house and over the short trail leading to the mine. The men were not mistaken. From a slender crevice in the rock wall a stream of spring water flowed downward through the cavern, and the lower shaft was flooded with a deep expanding pool that gleamed malevolently in the quiet gloom of its new found home. In silence, the heart broken man surveyed the watery grave in which he knew his last hope lay buried forever. Then he turned, and slowly retraced his steps to the Manor. On a table in his study lay a loaded pistol which he sometimes used for target shooting. With this in his hand, he walked from the house to the crest of the slope overlooking the snow covered expanse of cleared land and the fringe of woods along the Moose River.

It was Sunday, and as usual on that day Herreshoff was dressed immaculately in his finest apparel as a mark of respect for the Sabbath. As he paused, alone on the slope, his outward bearing was still that of the elegant, commanding figure of other years which had won the lasting respect and admiration of countless friends on both sides of the Atlantic. But inwardly he was a lonely, broken man, staring wistfully across white fields that lay as barren and lifeless as his hopes. Nothing in the bleak prospect that came within range of his vision could hearten or console him.   Unoccupied cabins tinged the land-scape with that peculiar atmosphere of gloom which emanates from deserted homes.   Many of the fields had not been tilled for several seasons, and briars and underbrush were already creeping out from the rim of woods to root themselves in the clearings and bear future witness to his failure.   The sublimest period of the Christian calendar, the Christmas season, was at hand, bearing its manifold gifts of good cheer, peace and hap-piness, but they were not for him.   Rather, the thought of the season added to his melancholy.   Old friends of his boyhood, men of prosperity and distinction, would be making merry in far off Prussia.   In Providence and New York, family and friends were preparing to observe the enduring old customs and enjoy the happy fellowship which attends the season the world over, but from all these he felt himself forever excluded.   It was this sense of self-imposed ostracism from family hearth and the companionship of his kind that crushed him unresisting to the depths of utter despair, and yet steeled his will to accom-plish the last design of his career.

It is said the workmen who hurried to the scene cried bitterly as they raised their dead leader from the ground and bore him tenderly to the house.   Distinguished by so profound a tribute at the moment of his passing, Herreshoff's life was far from the failure he had assumed it to be.   If human affection, loyalty and trust are in reality jewels of their reputed worth, he carried a mighty treasure to the storehouse of eternity.   The men carried his body through the woods to the coroner at Russia Corners for inquest, and at the request of a number of Boonville citi-zens it was taken to their village and buried in the old cemetery at that place.   The following epitaph was inscribed on the hum-ble stone which marked his grave: "Charles Frederick Herres-hoff, Obiit Dec. 19, 1819. Aetat 50." The epitaph erred by six years, for Herreshoff was fifty-six at the time of his death. Forty years later, when the Boonville Cemetery was re-estab-lished in its present location to make way for a proposed railroad, his body was exhumed and sent to Providence for burial beside his wife and children.

Herreshoff's nephew, John Brown Francis, the owner of Township 7, continued the attempt to colonize the tract for some time after his uncle's death. He offered a homestead of 160 acres, ten sheep and a cow to the first ten new settlers who would make their homes on the tract, but he was no more successful than his two predecessors had been. The region's reputation was too ill-flavored to support a third colonizing project, and the few gullibles who moved to the tract experienced the same vicissitudes that had made life miserable for its former inhabitants. One commentary at the time described the Brown's Tract as "a region so barren that a crow would shed tears of sorrow while flying over it." Mr. Donaldson tells of a Lewis County judge who warned a frequent offender that he would be sentenced to a year on the Brown's Tract if he appeared in court again. The frightened culprit left hastily for parts unknown, and was never seen thereafter in Lewis County.

The economic imprint resulting from the various attempts to colonize the region was negligible, and to this day the entire area is regarded with disfavor by agriculturists. A certain historical prominence attaches to the attempts, however, for the very reason that they failed. At that time productive lands as far west as Illinois were beckoning the race of homeseekers, but the tide of migration warily avoided the Adirondacks. Hostile forces of climate, topography and loneliness were in array to combat the encroachment of civilization within the foothills.

A brief glimpse in perspective into the personalities and activities of the unsuccessful Brown's Tract colony is of some interest here. Major Abiathar Joy, a native of Vermont and a veteran of the Revolution was one of the early settlers. His 160 acre lot bordered the Brown's Tract Road near its junction with the Remsen Road, and today, bordering Old Forge on the south, it is known as the "Joy Tract." He settled there in 1814, cleared about one-fourth of his land, and remained for some time after Herreshoff's death.   Later, he settled on a farm near Remsen. He was "that villain Joy" to whom Herres-hoff referred in his last letter to his wife.   A Johnson family occupied a clearing on the Remsen Road near Nick's Lake. An orchard which had been set out there during John Brown's ownership of the tract enabled the Johnsons to trap a great many bears that visited the clearing during the fruiting season. Years after the Johnsons had left the vicinity their place was still known as the "Johnson Lot."   The Wilcox family settled on land near the log dam, and their cabin stood on a clearing near the site of the present school building in Old Forge. Nicholas Vincent, a metal worker, came to the tract to make nails at the forge.   He also made love during his stay, for he courted and wed Major Joy's daughter, Elizabeth.   According to Mr. Snyder, this was the first marriage ceremony performed on the tract, but there is no record disclosing the identity of the official who pronounced the couple into happy servitude. The affair took place in the Joy cabin on the clearing and, no doubt, the Major and his wife were hosts to the entire popula-tion of Township 7 who declared a holiday to enjoy the attend-ant festivities.   There is no record of a white child having been born on the tract prior to the birth of Joanna Arnold, daughter of Otis and Amy Arnold, who first saw the light of day in the Herreshoff Manor in 1838.

Another wedding which blossomed from a wilderness court-ship took place soon after the Vincent-Joy nuptials, with Emmiline Sperry and David Sweet in the amatory roles of bride and groom.   Emmiline was a young school teacher and, when weather permitted, gathered the Brown's Tract children in an untenanted cabin for instruction in the three R's.   David was a strapping young farmer lad, and apparently a handy man about the tract.   In addition to performing his daily routine of labor, he often accompanied teacher to her home after school hours, thus assuring her safety against the menace of wild beasts of the forest.   It seems that even in those good old days prim and proper young lady teachers were not at all disposed to reject the shielding arm of a stalwart escort.

David Sweet was the eldest of five children who were brought to Township 7 by their parents, Caleb and Sarah. Though poor in worldly possessions, the family was of excellent character and in high repute among the settlement folk. Caleb was an industrious farmer of deep religious convictions and stern ethics, something of a spiritual and social leader in the community, but markedly ungifted in the function of getting ahead in the world. In making his home on the tract he had been prompted by the double incentive of a low priced home-stead and the opportunity of rearing his children amid the morally unsullied associations of the forest. The moral factor proved all that could be desired by a zealous parent, but the low priced homestead was also low in productiveness, and as the family could not subsist entirely on the morals of the situation, Caleb eventually returned to the valley settlement he had for-saken. His fervent piety led to his commendable habit of addressing frequent confidences to the Deity; and although, on the whole, he considered earthly affairs to be of comparatively trivial significance, he rarely failed to return thanks for every phenomenon, good or bad, that affected his lot. If the occur-ence were a fortunate one, he was thankful for the blessing; if unfortunate, he was grateful for its being no worse. His fourth child, a daughter, he named "Thankful," but whether the name signified an exalted spiritual state on that occasion is not known. Being the unprosperous head of a growing family at the time, he may have bestowed the appellation as an expression of his relief that the infant came as a single personality rather than in the form of twins.

While living on the tract, he often presided over gatherings of his neighbors who met for public worship on the Sabbath. During winter months these meetings were held in one of the larger cabins, and in seasons of mild weather they were held in the open, under an arch of evergreens along the Moose River or beside the Mill Stream Pond. No clergyman was available to conduct the services, but the worshippers expressed their wholesome sentiments of reverence in a hearty program of song and prayer. These services, though conducted with rustic simplicity and lacking the inspiration of beautiful music, helped to alleviate the discomforts of poverty and to fortify the settlers against the harsh, profitless rounds of toil which faced them. Caleb's voice, whose ringing sincerity and solemnity coincided with its owner's firm moral constitution, invested the devotions with a goodly measure of sanctity despite the fact that his song selections were among the most melancholy of the hymnal. In his time, popular compositions of a religious or moralizing character usually embodied a somber theme designed to suppress human buoyancy to a minimum by insisting to all and sundry that life, at best, was a very dubious proposition, and that it should be valued only as a thoroughfare to immortality. Such was the following, a gravestone octave set to a dead march accompaniment for purposes of mortifying the flesh: it was a favorite of Caleb's, and its gloomy message of frustration was often sung at the Brown's Tract gatherings:

"Hark! from the tomb; a doleful sound,
Mine ears attend the cry.
Ye living men, come view the ground
Where you must shortly lie.
Princes, this clay must be your bed
In spite of all your towers.
The wise, the high, the reverend head
Must lie as low as ours."

While the concluding sentiment was hardly appropriate for rendition by people on a mountain top, the verse as a whole echoed a raw truth which may have cheered the singers with the thought that there existed at least one condition more to be dreaded than the fate of a Brown's Tract farmer.

Other settlers included Gardiner and John Joslin and their families, Ephraim Justin, who married Gardiner Joslin's sister, Margaret, while living on the tract, Silas, Lewis and Isaac Thomas, Jabez Morgan, Robert Pritchard, a blacksmith, and Green White. White, who will be mentioned again, was also

Herreshoff Mine near Thendara

a blacksmith, but he speedily renounced his craft upon coming to the woods in favor of the spicier vocation of hunting and trapping. A settler named Gibbs located near the small lake which now bears his name. Clearings were made along the North Shore as far as First Lake, but these, like many of the other homesteads have long been overgrown and are now reforested beyond recognition.

Community gatherings, aside from those dedicated to religious worship, were infrequent. On certain holidays picnic parties rowed up the lakes to spend a leisurely day fishing and bathing along the shore of Fourth Lake. Hunting and trapping furnished some excitement and a little profit but were not extensively engaged in by the agriculturally minded residents. Wild animals were sometimes captured alive, and the captors enjoyed the companionship of creatures thus taken and trained as pets. Caleb Sweet and his son, David, captured a calf moose which had wandered from the cow to the Sweet cabin. After a few weeks' confinement, the ungainly little fellow browsed contentedly about the clearing with a resounding cowbell suspended from its neck. On one occasion, Caleb's daughter, Lydia, having lost her way in the woods, was guided safely home by this musical calf which had strayed from the clearing in quest of succulent herbage.

On the whole, however, the forest offered but few diversions that could lighten the settlers' burdens. They had come to the wilderness, not in search of health or scenic charm, or to find surcease from exactions imposed by a former environment, but for the prosaic and altogether grim purpose of winning their daily bread. The mountain beauty that captivates visitors today barely gained their notice as they struggled for a livelihood against the natural handicaps of the region. The hungry wolf packs howling nightly beyond the borders of their clearings were omens of an uncertain future which could not be disregarded with complacency, and the tenants' uneasiness increased with the passage of time and with their repeated failures to realize their modest ambitions. Neither Herreshoff nor

John Brown Francis were able to hold more than an insignificant group on the tract at a given time, and at the former's death the colonizing structure collapsed beyond his nephew's power to rebuild.   One by one the settlers took their prudent depart- ure toward lands of greater promise, leaving their forsaken neighbors more discouraged than before and eager to follow their retreating footsteps.   Mr. Snyder informs that toward the end the abandoned forge had become a plaything for chil- dren who delighted in opening the sluice gates to set the slow moving hammers in motion.   The gristmill remained in service to the last, grinding the hard earned grain the settlers had gleaned from their final planting, but a full century has passed since its crude stones ground the product of an Adirondack harvest.

After the last settler had departed, the disused forge assumed the function of an "X" in modern journalism.   It marked the spot.   Hunters and trappers, in referring to their wilderness itineraries, stated that they were going up to "the forge" or had come by way of "the forge."   Years passed, and the dilapidated structure and its rusting contents became known as "the old forge," still marking the spot and calling attention to Herres- hoff's ill-fated enterprise.   In 1930, several iron parts of the forge, together with the one surviving mill stone, were assem- bled on the state hatchery lawn and marked with an inscription designed to perpetuate the memory of the region's past and of the origin of the name "Old Forge."

The mine, which yielded so meager an output of ore and so abundant a portion of grief, still gapes from the wooded rock cliff as it did in the final despairing moment of Herreshoff's life. It opens at a point in the ridge within a quarter of a mile north of the New York Central Station, and may be reached by a short trail leaving the highway near Thendara.   The spring still flows from its cavernous inner walls as it flowed more than a century ago when its sudden appearance washed away Herres- hoff's last faint hope of success, and the quiet pool of water still gleams from its rocky depths.   It became known as John

Brown's Well, and for many years served as a water source for residents of Thendara who prized its clear, cold liquid for drinking purposes.   Buckets in hand, the thirsty made daily pilgrimage to its refreshing presence, and the pathway worn by their eager feet may yet be followed by visitors of inquiring minds who wish to inspect this redoubtable relic of the Fulton Chain's woeful past.

V

EARLY NAMES AND NIMRODS

DURING the years elapsing between John Brown's earliest connection with the Fulton Chain and Big Moose region in the
closing decade of the eighteenth century, and Herreshoff's final
gesture of despair more than twenty years later, game hunters
continued to frequent the locality in increasing numbers. They
composed a straggling caravan of whites and Indians, nomads
of the wilderness, in which the former race predominated:
Indians were becoming less and less in evidence with the passing
years. An outward semblance of peace prevailed between the
two groups, but racial distrust still lurked deeply enough in
both to engender open hostility and bloodshed. There remained
old scores to settle; rankling memories of old friends, victims of
physical violence, to be avenged; new enmities to be incurred
over disputed spoils of gun and trapline. The forest was a
matchless locale in which to bring smoldering feuds to a decisive conclusion. It offered an endless choice of sheltered
arenas, suited to ambuscade or open combat, in which men
could kill or be killed with impunity: the law could not penetrate its dense thickets, nor were prying witnesses likely to be
at hand who would carry fatal testimony to remote constabul-
aries.

Such feuds were not entirely the result of racial feeling.
Members of the white brotherhood of forest rangers were sometimes fired by greed or rancorous sentiment to engage in
internecine conflict among themselves. Many hunters entered
the woods in those days and never returned, leaving a knowledge of their fate shrouded in mystery to all but a few uncommunicative woodsmen. Jeptha R. Simms, the historian of
nearly a century ago, relates the details of such a happening in
his *Trappers of New York*.

According to Simms, two brothers, George and Joseph
Benchley of Newport, with two hired men, extended a line of

marten traps along the Fulton Chain and on to a point beyond the eastern shore of Raquette Lake in the late fall of 1819. The four men had established their headquarters in a bark shanty at the head of Third Lake, and had erected smaller brush shanties for temporary shelter at intervals of a few miles between Third Lake and the eastern terminus of their trapping route. George, having completed the final inspection of the lines to the east, was prevented from returning to headquarters with his furs by a deep, unseasonal fall of snow which held him to his shanty with only a limited supply of provisions on hand. Neither he nor his comrades at Third Lake had snowshoes, and his brother Joseph felt serious concern for his safety. Two days later, a hunter named Morgan arrived at the western shanty on snowshoes and assured its occupants that George was safe, that he had set out for Newport by way of Lake Pleasant as the snowfall had been much lighter through that section of the mountains. Thus assured, the three men started for home soon after, satisfied that George would arrive in good time and that no mishap had befallen him. But George did not return, nor, it seems, had he even started toward Lake Pleasant. In the spring, his body was found in the eastern shanty, which had collapsed during the winter, but his pack of furs was missing. He had died slowly from the effects of several wounds, and the hunting knife in his hand, together with a few chips hacked from a slender spruce upright, told the story of his feeble efforts to nourish the dying camp fire as he vainly awaited the arrival of a searching party. Morgan, whose reputation was generally unsavory, was immediately suspected and accused, but he stoutly averred his innocence, and as no convicting evidence could be adduced against him, the identity of George's slayer was never legally determined.

Many place names applied to Central Adirondack localities during the eighteenth and nineteenth centuries, or before, still survive in popular usage. Some are terms of Indian origin, coined before white men first penetrated the Adirondacks; others were supplied later, during the heyday of professional game slaughtering when celebrated marksmen and trappers were pursuing moose and beaver and other wild prizes to premature extinction. The Moose River and Moose Lakes owe their names to the Algonquin Indians. This great race of aborigines employed the terms "mos" or "moos," (meaning "he eats off") to designate the huge, antlered mammal whose capacity for devouring foliage from standing timber is one of its well-defined traits. The prevalence of this species in the Moose River country led to the name being applied to the region's lakes and streams, and finally to the entire region. The Fulton Chain of lakes was then designated First Lake, Second Lake, Third Lake, etc., of the Middle Branch Moose River, while Rondaxe, Dart's and Big Moose Lakes were known as First, Second and Third Lakes of the North Branch Moose River. Collectively, the two groups were distinguished by the terms "Middle Branch Moose Lakes" and "North Branch Moose Lakes." Both were consecutively numbered from their downstream extremities because a majority of travellers entered the region from the west and, in consequence, encountered the lower lake bodies before proceeding eastward on their journeys.

The term "Middle Branch Moose Lakes" gradually gave way to the name "Fulton Chain" during the first half of the nineteenth century. The latter appellation derives from a survey of the region made by Robert Fulton, of steamboat fame, in 1811. In addition to being internationally prominent as the builder of the steam vessel *Clermont* which successfully navigated the Hudson River in 1807, Fulton was known as an outstanding authority on the mechanics of canal transportation. He had spent several years in Europe engaged in an exhaustive study of inland waterways and, upon returning home, had applied his knowledge to the solution of problems connected with the extension of the domestic canal system. In 1811, the New York Legislature appointed him to membership on a commission created for the purpose of investigating the practicality of establishing a direct water route between the Hudson River and the Great Lakes which would penetrate the Adirondacks. During

the course of his inquiry into the proposal, he explored numerous lakes and rivers in the mountains, concluding, finally, that
the inclusion of the Adirondacks in the plan would be inexped-
ient except as a source of water supply. His written and oral
reports on this phase of the investigation, however, included a
glowing description of the beauty and potential utility of the
chain of eight Moose Lakes on whose shores he had tarried. So
graphic and enthusiastic were his accounts of the region and its
most conspicuous waterway, that current newpaper references
to his reports coupled his name with the lake chain by terming
it the "Fulton Chain of Lakes." The name survived and found
its way into common usage, but a knowledge of the facts concerning its origin faded to almost complete obscurity. In 1845,
Simms, the historian, in writing of the Fulton Chain, confessed
his ignorance of the source of the name, thus making it apparent that Fulton's connection with the region had not survived
for long in popular memory.

The most prominent topographical feature adjacent to the
Chain is a rambling, tree-covered formation of rock that flings
itself skyward to a commanding height from the lower North
Shore, and which is known as "Bald Mountain." It rises to a
lesser altitude than several other noted Adirondack peaks, but
due to the peculiarity of its formation and position its bald
summit affords a long range view which compares favorably
with panoramas surrounding the peaks of greater magnitude.
During periods of favorable visibility, the distant blue outline
of Mount Marcy can be sighted from its summit.

Considering the immutable physical character of this huge
pile, and its unfailingly good natured tolerance of hordes of
mountain climbers who have clambered to exalted heights on
its rugged back, its admiring public has exhibited singular
caprice in subjecting it to indiscriminate christenings. A century and a half ago it was called "Pond Mountain" by white
hunters and trappers because of its towering aspect high above
the lower lakes of the Fulton Chain. During the next fifty
years this name was gradually discarded in favor of "Bald

Mountain," a more truly descriptive term which was suggested by the outcroppings of bare rock on its summit. Several years before the outbreak of the Civil War, a group of campers on First and Second Lakes took it in hand, brushed it clean of all former appellations, and in a formal ceremony atop its loftiest knob, re-christened it "Mount St. Louis" in honor of their native city, the flourishing metropolis of Missouri. This gesture of civic loyalty and pride had its effect for a quarter of a century thereafter. Several maps of the region, some published as late as 1880, designate the mountain as Mount St. Louis, but this name does not appear on maps of later date. In the meantime, the stolid old crag had fallen prey to a miscellany of imaginative sponsors who dubbed it a variety of pet names, more or less logically chosen, none of which held the popular fancy for an appreciable time. One traveller-writer, flourishing his hero worshipping pen across a manuscript of Adirondack lore, denominated it "Foster's Observatory." In this name he hoped to perpetuate the memory of Nat Foster, a noted Adirondack woodsman of the early nineteenth century, who delighted to scale its heights to view the far reaching prospect of the wilderness. (Incidentally, Foster's favorite body of water was Seventh Lake of the Fulton Chain, which he often referred to as "the noble Seventh.") After undergoing a succession of nominal embellishments, the picturesque mount eventually regained its former name, and as "Bald Mountain" it has been known ever since. The observation tower erected on its summit by the Conservation Commission nearly resulted in the old name being abolished a few years ago in favor of the more exclusive term "Rondaxe Mountain." Many localities in the Adirondacks and throughout the state have lofty rock formations of considerable prominence to which a name, incorporating the word "bald," is applied. To obviate the possibility of confusion resulting from a similarity of titles, the Commission denominated the Bald Mountain observation station "Rondaxe Station," and mapped the mountain itself as "Rondaxe Mountain." The word derives from the pronuncia-

tion of the final two syllables of the word "Adirondacks."
Heeding the importunities of Fulton Chain residents, however,
the Commission soon resumed the mountain's older and better
known appellation, although it continued to designate the station as "Rondaxe Station."

Old Forge Lake, at the foot of the Fulton Chain, came into
existence with the building of the log dam across the Moose
River in 1799.   Prior to that time it was no more than a narrow stream which could be forded conveniently except when
spring freshets were abnormally high.   After the completion of
the dam, the stream widened to the dimensions of a pond and
became known as the "Mill Pond" or the "Pond."   Subsequent
construction and heightening of the dam by the State spread
the pond farther across the landscape until it attained the dignity of a lake; and under the more pretentious though less
endearing name of "Old Forge Lake" it now tumbles, none the
less merrily, over the concrete barricade that raised it to its
present high estate as a member of the Fulton Chain lake family.

Casual incidents often served to attach permanent names to
islands farther up the Chain.   Dog Island, which rises from the
waters of First Lake near Little Moose Landing, was so named
more than a century ago when a hunting party found a deserted
dog howling mournfully on its shore.   Grass Island (now submerged) near the head of Third Lake was known as Benchley's
Island for some time because the two brothers, George and
Joseph Benchley, usually shantied nearby while on trapping
expeditions.   The island was an object of morbid curiosity for
several years after George's mysterious death, and in consequence of the notoriety attending it the family name was also
given to Alger's Island in Fourth Lake for a time.   This latter
island, like Bald Mountain, has been encumbered with a variety
of titles.   In John Brown's time it was called Deer Island.
Later, it became "Big Island" because of its comparatively large
area; and more recently it acquired the family name of its owners, Mort and Ollie Alger, father and son who, between them,
have occupied it as a summer home for more than forty years.

Above Alger's island there rises a small rocky bit of land

that has long been known as Elba Island. No less a world figure than Napoleon Bonaparte inspired the christening of this tiny lump. Prior to the year 1831, a solitary pine tree about fifteen inches in diameter flourished there, the only plant life on the island. Its desolate situation, isolated by a formidable expanse of water from the forest that bordered the North and South Shores, recalled Napoleon's exile on the isle of Elba off the coast of Italy—hence the name. According to a letter written eighty years ago by one John Stillwell of Herkimer, the tree was wantonly chopped down in the spring of 1831. Its loss was mourned by fishermen who habitually frequented the locality, but chips from the cutting served handily as dinner plates for a few seasons. In the summer of 1830, a lively drama of the animal kingdom was staged on the island, which had as its finale a totally unexpected last act catastrophe for the villain. A party of fishermen, occupying two boats, were angling nearby when a deer plunged from the North Shore woods into the lake and swam frantically toward the island. A moment later, a large panther bounded from the forest and swam in pursuit. The deer proved to be the faster swimmer, and reached Elba several rods ahead of its pursuer. Without pausing to rest, it crossed the island and, entering the water again, continued its rapid flight to the South Shore. In the meantime, the fishermen maneuvered their small craft to force the panther to land on the island. There it scaled the lonely pine tree to the topmost limb, and lashing its tail and snarling in fury, glared balefully down at its enemies. Undaunted by this show of ferocity, the men took careful aim, and a single volley brought it tumbling to the ground, riddled with lead. Several years later the skin was donated to a Utica museum, and exhibited with a written account of the animal's capture.

Cedar Island, near the head of Fourth Lake, was known as Bear Island more than a century ago. Dollar Island still bears the significant title conferred in John Brown's time, but happily its value has not been subjected to the cycle of fluctuations which marked the economic career of its silver prototype during the intervening years.

Seventh Lake, ever a gem to gladden the hearts of buckskin clad pioneers, contains a large, heavily wooded island which its enamoured habitues referred to only as "Seventh Lake Island." Simms, in his Trappers of New York, called it White's Island because it was the favored shantying place of Green White, a well known trapper who plied his vocation in the region during the early nineteenth century. Beyond Eighth Lake to the east lie the beautiful Raquette, Blue Mountain and Long Lakes, formerly accessible from the Fulton Chain only by the narrow, tortuous stream known as the "Brown's Tract Inlet," which rises near the western extremity of Raquette Lake. Each of these localities is draped with romantic history of sufficient length and fascination to merit volumes of biography, but the limitations of space forbid the inclusion of their stories here.

*   *   *

Reference has been made to the picturesque garb of hunters and trappers who frequented the Central Adirondacks a century or more ago. They composed a distinctive and distinguished group of frontiersmen, colorful, not alone in their modes of attire, but in personality and ways of life as well. The peculiar traits of character which led them from the settlements to follow their callings in the seclusion of the uninhabited wilderness marked them among their fellows as men apart; and not a few have deservedly found a place in fictional and historical literature. While the pursuit of their craft brought monetary gain, their selection of the craft itself was made from a choice of gainful employments primarily because of its natural associations. With few exceptions, their devotion to the remote solitude of the forest and its wild, virgin beauty was a crude but real expression of a smoldering aestheticism which held them to their trade.

Jonathan Wright was one of the earliest of the celebrated Adirondackers whose exploits have enlivened the pages of frontier literature. "Jock," as he was known to his friends, served in the colonial army during the Revolution, and after the war sought further excitement in roaming the wilderness. He was a famous marksman, scout, hunter and tràpper and, when occasion demanded, an intrepid Indian fighter, although his relations with the red men were usually friendly. He often mingled with them socially, and counted several of his staunch-est friends among their number. His jovial disposition and entertaining manner made him a favorite in numerous village taverns where, between expeditions into the wilderness, and stimulated by frequently replenished tankards, he regaled his friends with vividly told stories of his adventures. One of these stories had to do with his discovery, and his half jocular, half serious claim to ownership of Honnedaga Lake, a large, radiant body of water which lies in the southwestern section of the Adirondack Park, about fifteen miles south of Old Forge. In the telling of this exploit, Jock meticulously avoided mention of the lake's whereabouts despite his friends' persistent question-ing on the subject. Instead, he delighted to pique their curi-osity the more by describing in superlatives the refreshing quality and transparency of Honnedaga's water, the variety, size and flavor of its fish, and the surpassing loveliness of its setting. No matter how swift the flow of foaming ale, or how choice the quality, its benign influence never loosened his tongue or mellowed his mood to the point of revealing the loca-tion of his cherished find.

Jock discovered the lake during one of his excursive Adiron-dack rambles about the year 1785, or shortly before, while idly tracing the northerly course of a brook to its outlet. As a rule, one lake more or less meant nothing to him, of course, for he knew the location of hundreds of watery beauties sparkling across the immense face of the wilderness. But this was a pre-viously unknown lake, and its very newness increased its value a hundredfold in the estimation of its finder. No white man had ever fished its waters or explored its shores, and Jock re-solved to keep the secret of its existence to himself, and to enjoy its exclusive hunting and fishing rights as long as he could. Being thus elevated to the proprietorship of so large a private preserve, he could not refrain from good-naturedly flourishing his domain, in a verbal manner, before his envying acquaintances. They in turn, while speculating among themselves as to its location, referred to it as "Jock's Lake"; and this name, applied at long range by persons who had never even glimpsed the locality, quickly took root in popular usage. Despite his sphinx-like reticence regarding directions and distance, Jock's luxurious privacy endured but a short time. Within a year or two after the discovery, other woodsmen came trudging to Honnedaga's enchanting shores, either by chance or on a premeditated tour of exploration, and the secret went back with them. Jock's name, however, remained connected with the lake for more than a century after he had carried the story of its natural wonders to the settlements. The Adirondack League Club, soon after its organization in 1890, purchased the lake and a large acreage surrounding it, and annexed the whole to their private club preserve of two hundred thousand acres. Desirous of employing a name more expressive of the water's beauty, they discontinued the appellation "Jock's Lake" and applied the Indian term "Honnedaga" to signify its transparency. Thus was poor Jock deprived of immortality on the map of the forest, as he had been deprived of a monopoly of the lake a century before, by the arrival of newcomers upon the scene of his magnificent discovery.

Nicholas (Nick) Stoner, a contemporary of Jock's, was born about 1762. His adventurous disposition asserted itself early in life, and at the age of fifteen he shouldered a musket in the ranks of the Continental army. For the next six years he fought his way to several promotions and a great deal of distinction in the struggle for independence. Although only twenty-one years old at the close of the war, he was famous throughout northern and central New York for his many deeds of daring under fire. He served his country again with like valor in the War of 1812, during which he rose to the rank of

Major. Between wars he acquired a masterful knowledge of woodcraft, and a reputation as an Indian killer which aroused the savage hatred of the vanishing red men. His aversion to the aborigines was life-long. It began in boyhood when his father was slain in an Indian massacre, and the bereaved lad swore vengeance against the offending race. From all accounts, this oath remained uppermost in his mind, and he seldom over-looked an opportunity of discharging its bloody obligations.

Like his good friend Jock, Nick was a tavern favorite and a hearty imbiber from the flowing bowl. What with wars and woodcrafting he had experienced a variety of adventures which made thrilling fireside narratives, especially when the telling was punctuated at not too great intervals with fresh libations from the taproom. During the course of these convivial gath-erings, Nick's implacable hostility towards his red brethern sometimes expanded to a perfect fury of rage. Woe to the unsuspecting Indian who, in a moment of alcoholic bravado, chanced to cross him at such a time with an intrusive remark. Nick's fists, his hunting knife, and even his pistol were brought into play with such rapidity and determination that the ensuing uproar could be quelled only by the flight of his antagonists or the stout hearted interference of mine host and his guests. On one occasion he seized a red hot andiron and swung it with fatal effect upon the head of a boastful Indian who professed a first-hand knowledge of the elder Stoner's death. For this display of choleric energy he was lodged in the Johnstown jail over-night. Being a Major, however, and a citizen of distinction in the community, while his victim was no more than an insig-nificant savage, he was promptly released in the morning amid the vociferous plaudits of his fellow villagers. The dwindling race of aborigines, at that time, had not sufficiently neared the vanishing point to merit recognition as human beings, or to be exalted with the endearing term "the noble red man" which is now lavished upon him in retrospection by his fondly appre-ciative vanquishers.

Nick's far reaching fame by no means rested only on his

prowess as a tavern parlour lion. His Adirondack woodsmanship was unexcelled by any of his contemporaries, and even
unrivalled by any except his two friends, Jock Wright and Nat
Foster. He was a tireless ranger of the wilderness, an expert
marksman and an exceptionally successful hunter and trapper.
The fact that he lived to the ripe old age of eight-eight, in the
face of repeated attempts on his life made by revengeful
Indians in the forest, attests his invincible prowess as a woodsman. He hunted occasionally with contemporaries, sometimes
with Wright or Foster, but more often alone. His fur and
game hunting expeditions brought him into the Fulton Chain
and Big Moose country regularly, as well as into the eastern
sections of the mountains.

During one of his solitary excursions through the Central
Adirondacks, soon after the close of the Revolution, he added
a new feat to his growing list of achievements—that of discovering a formerly unknown lake. By deviating from his
customary route through the region, he came upon Nick's Lake,
a shimmering, forest-walled expanse of water that lurks in the
pleasant woods three trail miles south of Old Forge and one
mile from Thendara. There he often fished in lonely contentment, and the lovely lake, with equal contentment, promptly
accepted his name as her own. Nick kept the secret of its location to himself long enough, and discoursed on its unparalleled
virtues eloquently enough to bring the lake into popular knowledge as his favorite retreat and as a place of considerable
mystery. It became known as "Nick's Lake" among his contemporaries before they were aware of its location. Nick's
jovial boasting of his discovery spurred other woodsmen to
undertake tours of exploration in quest of its waters, and it
soon became public property. Today it is one of the very few
Central Adirondack lakes which retain their original names.

In addition to his other adventurous tendencies, Nick was
also a marrying man. At the age of twenty, while still under
arms in the Revolution, he surrendered his heart to a companionable girl of his own age with whom he dwelt happily for

forty years. Death ended this congenial partnership, and find-ing himself a sorrowing widower at the age of sixty, Nick married again—a buxom widow somewhat younger than him-self. Fifteen years of blissful wedlock followed, but again the Grim Reaper appeared, this time to claim his second bride. Nick was then seventy-six, and thoroughly accustomed to matrimony. After tenderly committing his departed helpmate to the mothering arms of the earth, he looked about for an-other, and spied a gracious lady of Johnstown, very much younger than seventy-six, who was wrapped in the melancholy mantle of her second widowhood. Meanwhile, the exacting years had deprived Nick of his old time physical vigor and agility, but he still possessed the same dauntless, unflinching spirit that had carried him to innumerable conquests through half a century of frontier dangers. His face was stern, his jaw set defiantly against the attacks of Time, and his step, though slow, was steady and determined. He was a marked figure about the village, attired in a somber suit with long coat, pol-ished boots, a high collar snugly wound with a bulging black stock, silver watch chain, and the whole topped off with an upstanding squirrel cap. Invariably, even on tranquil Sabbath days, there hung from his fine leather belt the implements of his beloved vocation, pistol, hatchet and hunting knife. Thus armed and equipped, as though to stalk a plump doe in the sylvan remoteness of the Adirondacks, he advanced upon the latest and last object of his affections. Seemingly, the lady was taken by storm. Nick beguiled the evenings of a whirlwind courtship with thrillers chosen at random from the life book of his adventures. He explained the intricacies of a far flung trap line, revealed the best methods of removing the hides of slaughtered animals, cautioned the lady against Indian am-buscades, advised how to circumvent the evil designs of the red men, and, in short imparted much valuable advice concerning the ways of the wilderness and how to garner profit for soul and body from its multiple resources. Of course the good woman would not for worlds have thought of setting foot in the forest, but she listened attentively, for long practice had made the distinguished old woodsman an engaging conversationalist as well as a persuasive wooer. In due time she succumbed to his several arms and arguments, and Nick, in the last recorded triumph of life, proudly guided her, a bride once more, into the happy realm of matrimony. With her he spent his declining years in that blissful contentment which descends like a benediction to bless the mellow old age of a well spent life. He died in Fulton County, N. Y., in 1850, and was laid to rest in a cemetery near Johnstown, with notables from many walks of life attending his obsequies. He had survived the shot and bayonets of two wars, the hazards of the forest, the discovery of a lake, and the dangers of many an Indian feud and tavern brawl—to say nothing of three wedding ceremonies. If ever mortal man deserved the luxury of a long and peaceful sleep that man was Nicholas Stoner.

Green White easily possessed the most colorful name of all the early trappers, and, by way of contrast, the least colorful personality. He was born in the lower Mohawk Valley about 1765, and as a youth learned the blacksmith's craft in Schenectady. After a few years spent in a smithy of that thriving village, he abandoned the anvil and its sooty accessories and betook himself to the Brown's Tract to begin the career of a woodsman. He first ranged the tract about 1795, shortly before it was named. Occasionally he returned to his hammers to forge traps which he designed for his personal use. His forte in woodcraft was trapping. He had a pronounced talent and fondness for this art which he developed to a highly lucrative profession. Early in his career he gained the reputation of being able to trudge back to the settlement trading posts with more pelts taken in a given time than could be acquired by any other woodsman of his day.

Green was a quiet, uncommunicative individual, even when indulging his abnormal appetite for strong liquor. His taciturn, unsociable disposition corresponded somewhat to that of a confirmed hermit, and prompted other woodsmen to avoid him as often as possible; but their aversion caused him no loss of sleep at all.   The proximity of talkative persons irritated him, and in the wilderness he openly resented fellow trappers' making camp within sight of his own.   He was as ill favored in appearance as in disposition: short, though powerfully formed, of swarthy complexion, shrewd, piercing gray eyes which were as unsmiling as his grim, tight-lipped mouth.   Indians feared him greatly, several of whom he was reputed to have killed in the forest.   A portentious, oft repeated saying of his was "Indians never steal my furs but once," but he never enlightened his listeners regarding any possible tendency on his part to steal the Indians' furs.   Perhaps his averseness to loquacity overcame him before he could reach that topic in the course of his brief monologues.   He usually headquartered in a bark shanty on Seventh Lake Island from which point his trap lines extended for miles in various directions, like the spokes of a carriage wheel. Because of his preference for Seventh Lake the island in it became known as "White's Island."   He generally disposed of his furs at the nearest settlement trading post which boasted a well stocked tap room, and the proceeds, ranging from one hundred to three hundred dollars, were spent on a huge diet of rum which he absorbed to the last drop before returning to the woods.   At the end of his debauchery, and his money, (both circumstances being of simultaneous occurrence) he packed his meager supplies and trudged away to the forest, to re-appear in another month or two with the bulging pack and the inevitable thirst.

For thirty years or more Green White continued to plod his solitary way through the wilderness, probing its secret recesses in quest of furs, turning the furs into dollars and the dollars into rum and the rum into himself, growing ruder, grimmer and more hermitical with the swift march of the seasons, never a penny richer for the arduous labor of his sober periods, and never a whit remorseful over the fact.   In time, popular dislike gave way to the nobler emotions of mingled curiosity and sympathy, unexpressed in his presence of course, and the stolid, unsociable old trapper became something of a famous mystery and a living legend. His career ended suddenly about the year 1830 through one of those inadvertent acts of nature which have taken toll of many woodsmen's lives. While returning to Boonville, laden with the spoils of his trap lines, he camped at evening near Copper Lake, several miles west of Thendara, with a companion whom he had encountered on the way. During the night a high wind toppled a partially decayed tree across the brush shanty in which the two men slept, and Green's leg was broken. After a hurried trip to Boonville, his companion returned with help and the injured man was carried back on a stretcher. A surgeon was summoned from Utica, but despite his efforts, a gangrenous infection proved fatal and Green bid a sullen goodbye to his lonely world of game and grog.

Nathaniel (Nat) Foster, commonly acclaimed the deadliest marksman and shrewdest all around woodsman of his time, was the last of the Adirondack supermen to ply his trade in the Fulton Chain area. He looms heroically in the region's history as the slayer of the last Indian known to fall in the long series of feuds that have added bloody romance to the historical literature of the mountains. This fatal drama was in reality a commonplace action on the part of the white man, one of many in which he had triumphed, for it occurred at the conclusion of his forty years of adventuring which had raised him to the pinnacle of Adirondack fame. One Indian enemy, dead or alive, was of slight consequence to him in his subtle reckoning of the human factor of the forest; but popular interest, with its eager attachment to the tragic, has enshrined him primarily because of just one unfortunate red man who fell victim to his infallible marksmanship.

Nat, as he was known to his friends, was born in Vernon, Vt., in 1767. His father, a pioneer by instinct, engaged moderately in agriculture and extensively in hunting, but never at all in the enterprise of sending his boy to school. The lad grew to manhood with neither the advantage nor the impediment of book learning, and not till he reached the age of forty did he set himself to master the rudiments of reading and writing. He did learn, however, to shoot fast and straight, to bait an effective trap, to paddle a canoe with Indian-like precision, and to take excellent care of himself in the complex maze of the wilderness. At the age of twenty he was a renowned rifle and pistol shot, imbued with an insatiable love of frontier life, and self-reliant to a degree that was noteworthy even in a time when self-reliance was an ordinary virtue. While still a youth, he moved with his parents to Johnstown, N. Y., and from there to a farm near Salisbury, Herkimer County. In 1791 he married Jemima Streeter, a daughter of New Hampshire, and the pair settled on a small farm near the homestead of the elder Fosters. Nat paid for his place with the income he derived from hunting and trapping in the winter months of the first two years of his married life. In a single season he killed 76 deer, 35 bears and 25 wolves, in addition to gathering a harvest of mink, beaver, marten and otter furs. He also hunted moose which were plentiful at that time, and occasionally engaged in the less exciting and less profitable sport of panther hunting. His yearly earnings with gun and traps sometimes exceeded a thousand dollars, and in time he centered his attention on this source of income to the exclusion of his farm work. He always kept the farm, however, renting it to impecunious husbandmen on shares or hiring labor to cultivate it.

As game became scarcer in the Mohawk Valley he extended his trap lines deeper and deeper into the Adirondacks until his operations were confined entirely to the mountains. Each succeeding year added greater prestige to his name, and his feats of woodsmanship became absorbing topics around the camp fires of his less distinguished contemporaries.

Nature had lavished a good deal of attention on Nat in conforming his physical equipment with his predilection for a strenuous vocation in the wilderness. Six feet tall, weighing one hundred and eighty pounds, lean and powerfully muscled, he possessed seemingly unlimited powers of endurance. He could travel through the forest a full day and night in swift unbroken strides without exhibiting a sign of fatigue, and his uncanny skill as a wrestler provided many surprising upsets for the Mohawk Valley's strong men who were famed for their prowess in the art. In facial appearance he was less conspic' uous, except upon close observation. His unassertive sandy complexion and mild blond hair disclaimed the vigor of his sinewy frame, and the clear gray eyes that sparkled with honest friendliness gave no hint of the penetrating alertness they dis' played in the quick scrutiny of any significant detail that might lurk within shooting distance of their owner.

As a marksman Nat was never known to have met his equal. His favorite rifle was a "double shotter," and so accurate was his aim at a moving target that his admiring fellow woodsmen often remarked "Nat's rifle never told him a lie." The cavities at the base of his strong, prehensile fingers formed veritable bullet pouches in themselves. Between the four fingers of each hand he carried six leaden balls conveniently placed for sleight' of'hand insertions in the muzzle of his gun. Without restrict' ing the free use of his hands in any occupation, this method of carrying bullets obviated the necessity of handling his bullet pouch and greatly expedited his firing when rapidity became an important factor in the business at hand. Starting with his gun empty, he could load and fire six times in less than a min' ute, with each of the six shots boring its target with unvarying precision. Jeptha R. Simms, in his *Trappers of New York*, describes Nat's rifle as follows:

"The rifle with which Foster usually hunted would carry two balls as well as one; and when he desired to render the death of large game doubly sure, he loaded with two bullets. Foster and Stoner had each a rifle at one time made after the same pattern by Willis Avery, of Salis' bury, and called "double shotters." They were made with a single barrel with two locks, one placed above the other far enough to admit of two charges, and have the upper charge of powder rest upon the lower bullet. The locks were made for percussion pills, and when the pick which crushed the pill at the first lock was down, there was no danger to be apprehended in firing the lower charge. These rifles cost about seventy dollars each."

During the War of 1812, Nat added to his reputation in a friendly shooting match with a southern sharpshooter. A company of South Carolina riflemen, enroute to northern New York, encamped a few days near Salisbury when Nat happened to be sojourning on his farm. The company commander, Captain Forsyth, being justly proud of the marksmanship of one of his men who was celebrated for his fast and accurate rifle fire, challenged Nat to a contest for a small wager. Always glad to test his skill in competition, Nat accepted the challenge and presented himself, rifle in hand, at company headquarters. Two targets, identical in size and design, were set up at a distance of about two hundred feet. Starting with empty rifles, the men were to load and fire six times as rapidly as possible upon signal by the captain. Nat's sixth ball completed a perfect circle of six perforations about the center of the target as his opponent was dropping the fourth ball into the muzzle of his gun. Mohawk Valley residents who witnessed the match were not at all surprised at the outcome, but Captain Forsyth and his man, though philosophical enough in defeat, were noticeably crestfallen over the wide margin of the Northerner's superiority.

Nat's growing prestige and fame did not mar the wholesome simplicity of character or habits which he seems to have possessed from childhood. He used liquor sparingly, and seldom joined the convivial gatherings that frequented the cozy tavern barrooms. He was a friendly man, modest, charitable and scrupulously honest, and his generosity to the needy was a matter of comment among his neighbors. No one in distress, friend or foe, red man or white, hesitated to appeal to him, and none were refused. During severe winters and in times of economic hardship he quietly went about the countryside distributing the products of his farm to the poor. To overcome the deficit in his income resulting from these acts of beneficence,

he usually applied himself with added diligence to the cultivation of his trap lines.

Nat's one reputed foible was the impetuous conduct of his
trigger finger whenever Indians of suspicious character lurked
in his vicinity.   This trait had its origin in his younger days
when his sister, Zilphah, was abducted by a raiding band of
Algonquins.   The raiders were soon overtaken by a posse of
white frontiersmen, and the girl restored unharmed to her family, but the incident instilled in Nat an early distrust of the
race which influenced his attitude toward them throughout his
entire life.   His hatred was not as implacable or all-embracing
as Nick Stoner's.   He performed many acts of kindness to
alleviate the distress of deserving red men.   But he rigidly insisted upon honesty and fair dealing on their part, particularly
in their attitude toward the contents of his fur traps which
some members of the race were inclined to regard as legitimate
plunder.   Rumors were current that many personal feuds between Nat and dishonest or hostile Indians had been settled to
the former's satisfaction in the quiet byways of the forest. The
truth of these rumors he neither affirmed nor denied, but occasionally he took delight in relating the details of an exciting
episode in ambiguous language with the deliberate intention of
mystifying his friends.

On a certain expedition his traps along the Fulton Chain
shores were being mysteriously relieved of their contents by
some unknown agency.   An investigation revealed the presence of two Indians in the locality who were slyly prowling the
shore line, removing the trapped animals, and carefully avoiding the white man's vicinity.   To end their depredations, Nat
employed a clever stratagem which he based on the assumption
that, if the opportunity presented, the thieves would take his
life as readily as they had been taking his furs. Abandoning his
camp which was hidden in the deep woods, he built an open
brush shanty, thinly screened with trees, on a prominent point
near the head of First Lake.   Inside the shanty he draped his
blanket around a log to simulate the figure of a man composed

for sleep, and at dusk kindled a blazing camp fire to attract the attention of his unseen neighbors. Later in the evening as the unreplenished fire was slowly dying down, he concealed himself, gun in hand, to await his expected visitors.

The ruse worked to tragic perfection. About midnight Nat heard the soft scraping of a canoe as it slid gently upon the sand beach of the little cove in front of his camp. A few moments of silence followed, then two armed Indians stepped ashore and stealthily approached the shanty. When within a few feet of its open end they paused, took careful aim, and fired at the six foot length of blanketed wood. Nat concludes the story:

> "And this transaction so excited me that I yelled in my excitement, and my dog bayed with a vengeance, and sometimes I've thought that I must have fired twice right in the direction of them Indians, but I was so excited I don't exactly remember. But anyhow I know I discharged my gun and I've always been of the opinion it had the desired effect."

Nat had no "opinion" of the matter whatever. He knew for a certainty, and so did his friends. He was a deadly rifleman, especially when stakes were high, and excitement never unsteadied his nerves in the face of danger. Any belligerent Indian who exposed himself to the fire of that celebrated double shotter exposed himself to nothing less than instant death.

In 1832, after many years' wandering among the mountains, Nat moved his household from Salisbury to the Herreshoff Manor. He was then sixty-five and considerably less agile than in former years, but his spirit was as mettlesome as ever and his shooting eye as keen, and he wished to spend his declining days following his old vocation in the region he loved best. The Manor and the adjacent lands had been leased as a hunting preserve by John Brown Francis in 1830 to Caleb Lyon, of Lyonsdale, and his two neighbors, Solomon and David Maybee. Caleb Lyon acted as agent for Francis, and had charge of his entire land holdings in Township Seven. Nat purchased an assignment of the lease in January, 1832, and with his wife, his son David and the latter's wife, he moved to the manor in February of the same year.   But the son and daughter-in-law found life on the tract too lonely and moved away a few months after their arrival.

At that time there were seven persons living in the locality. Three of them were bachelors, William Johnson, William Wood and David Chase, all temporary residents who spent several months of each year hunting and trapping along the Fulton Chain.   They were housed in the cabin formerly oc- cupied by Major Joy which stood on the eastern edge of the Joy Tract overlooking the future site of Old Forge lying to the north.   Less than a mile farther along the overgrown road lead- ing to the dam stood the crumbling old Wilcox cabin, near the site now occupied by the Town of Webb school structure in Old Forge. In this cabin lived Peter Waters, a St. Regis Indian, commonly known as "Drid," with his wife and two children.

Drid was a good woodsman but a bad Indian.   His pro- pensity for mischief and his evident incorrigibility had led to several warnings from tribal chieftains, and finally to his ex- pulsion from the tribe.   An exile from his people, he wandered westward across the Adirondacks to the foot of the Fulton Chain and settled there with his family about two years before Nat Foster took up his residence in the Manor.   He was a tall, strongly built young fellow, twenty-seven or twenty-eight years old, a skillful hunter and trapper, and very jealous of his repu- tation as the possessor of vast knowledge of woodcraft.   His disposition was variable as the winds, sometimes sullen and vindictive, sometimes amiable, but always ugly and boastful during his frequent periods of intemperance.   The adulation lavished on him by amateur sportsmen visiting the region had swelled his normally exalted opinion of himself to intolerable proportions, and he clearly resented any like expressions of praise for his rivals in woodcraft.   In appearance he was hand- some, although his intelligent face was marred somewhat by an expression of sullen cruelty; he spoke English fairly well.   His dress conformed more or less with the prevailing mode of his tribe. He affected bright colors, carried a tomahawk among the several implements of his trade, and occasionally sported a jaunty crest of eagle feathers in his hair. In Indian fashion, also, he never forgot a real or imagined insult, and he bore his grudges long and venomously.

Squaw Waters—or squaw Drid—was a winsome young woman, and like her husband, a full blooded Algonquin of St. Regis parentage. Constrained as she was to a life of complete subjection to Drid, her lot was a hard one. She bore it with stoic fortitude, as she did the marks of beatings her irritable spouse administered from time to time, possibly to prove him-self the masterful big chief of the dusky household. Drid felt no compunction in leaving his family unprovided for while he squandered his earnings for drink and indulged his appetite for braggadocio at the settlements, but woe to his gentle little squaw if he thought her remiss in her domestic affairs or lack-ing solicitude for his personal comforts.

Needless to say, Nat Foster and Drid were never friendly. The old hunter tranquilly pursued his calling in the vicinity of his new home and made slight effort to conceal his dislike for Indians in general, and for Drid in particular. He ignored the latter as much as the circumstance of their proximity permitted, but at intervals a spirited exchange of personalities passed be-tween the two. Drid's vanity could not submit to the ignominy of being ignored, the most degrading of all affronts to the mortal ego, and he retaliated with a campaign of abuse which included a series of overt acts of hostility. Nat's wider fame and superior woodsmanship quickly undermined the prestige Drid had enjoyed for two years as the only permanent Fulton Chain resident, and visitors who had paid the latter's unrivaled prowess the compliment of their laudations began to confer the bulk of their admiring eloquence upon the white man's genius. This added fuel to the flames of Drid's rage. To be thus relegated to the shade of another's greatness was more than he could endure, and he publicly announced his intention of killing "that dam ole Foster."

About a month after Nat moved to the tract, Drid, without asking permission, took his boat from its moorings and after using it for the day, left it beached a mile downstream from where he had found it. Nat recovered the boat, and in the presence of several amused witnesses caustically rebuked Drid and warned him under penalty of harsher treatment not to repeat the offense. Stung by the public reprimand, the Indian retorted with a threat against Nat's life, but as the older man's pistol protruded menacingly from his belt he decided, with manifest prudence, to await a more favorable opportunity. Twice he appeared at the Manor to execute this threat but in each instance was balked by his intended victim's absence. Nat appealed to justice Joshua Harris, of Lewis County, but the magistrate, reluctant to place his own life in jeopardy by incurring the Indian's rancor, refused to issue a warrant for Drid's arrest.

In the meantime, Drid's domestic habits showed no sign of improvement. He continued to leave his wife and two children to shift for themselves at intervals while he remained away on various missions more congenial to him than the drudgery of fulfilling his conjugal responsibilities. During his absence the Fosters supplied the wants of the neglected family from their own ample store of provisions. Nat kept a cow and a thriving flock of chickens on his place which produced more abundantly than his small household could consume. The surplus, with venison and meal added by way of good measure, the elderly couple gave to their dusky neighbors in that friendly, unostentatious manner that had characterized their charities at Salisbury.

Drid's hatred and malicious conduct continued unabated for more than a year. Nat's failure to dispose of him at an early opportunity caused a good deal of amazement among white trappers, for reports of his unusual predicament had been carried far and wide among members of the craft. His reluctance to do so, however, is easily explained by the fact that, like many unlettered men of his time, he harbored a profound respect for the mysterious power of the law. Shooting it out with an enemy behind the impenetrable curtain of the forest was one thing, but staging a like drama near the populous three-family settlement on the Fulton Chain was an entirely different affair. Evidence could be gathered leading to a harrassing court procedure and possibly a long term of imprisonment, either of which ordeals loomed as a discomforting prospect to the man who had spent a lifetime in the freedom of the wilderness. The better chance lay in watchful waiting and the hope that the future might effect a more reasonable attitude on the part of his neighbor. But matters did not mend, and as time passed Drid became so menacing that Nat concluded one or the other must take the long trail, and naturally he resolved it would be the other. The climax and the end of the feud came soon after —on September 17, 1833.

On the evening of September 16, four men from the Town of Leyden, Lewis County, arrived at the Manor, intending to go trout fishing on Fourth Lake the next day. Nat planned to accompany them, and as the two bachelors, Wood and Chase, were going also, arrangements were made for the party of seven to travel in company. Early in the morning Nat and his friends left home, equipped for the day's fishing expedition and armed with rifles in the hope of encountering a deer on the way. They crossed the log bridge spanning the Moose River near the site of Thendara, and climbing the Brown's Tract Road that curved upward to their left, reached the Joy Lot clearing. Leaving his friends to wait outside, Nat entered the cabin to inquire if the other members of the party were ready to proceed. He found the two bachelors seated at breakfast, and Drid, pipe in mouth, squatted on the floor before the open fireplace. The Indian did not change his posture or expression, but continued to amuse himself by blowing smoke into the flames, seemingly unaware of the newcomer's presence, or unwilling to favor him with a glance of recognition. Nat returned the compliment by ignoring him as usual and confining his attention to the belated breakfasters. He talked briefly with the two men and was turning to leave the cabin when Drid sprang to his feet.

"Foster, you ole cuss," he shouted harshly, "what for you call me a rascal the other day?"

"Because I was a mind to," came the cool answer.

Without further parley, Drid rushed and the two men grap-pled. Nat still retained his old time wrestling skill, if not his strength, and with an adroit movement of his foot and shoulder flung his adversary heavily to the floor. As the enraged Indian arose he was seized by Wood and Chase who feared the enact-ment of a bloody tragedy if the quarrel were allowed to con-tinue.

"You want to pick a quarrel with me this morning, do you, you black — —?" asked Nat, as he turned to go.

Again the younger man sprang at the older, unexpectedly evading the grip of his captors, a long bladed hunting knife clutched in his upraised hand. The surprise attack bore his opponent to the floor, and Nat would undoubtedly have been an immediate victim to the ugly weapon but for the quick in-tervention of Wood and Chase.

"Foster, you ole cuss," exclaimed Drid with blasphemous emphasis, "you no live till Christmas!"

"And you'll do damn well if you live to see another moon," replied Nat evenly.

The ominous quiet of his tone startled the two bystanders, and even reduced Drid to speechlessly glaring his hatred. For a moment the two foes faced each other in tense silence, but there was no misunderstanding between them. Each would be fair game for the other, and one must soon die. The white man had never before threatened to kill his enemy except in self-defense, nor had he ever been known to utter boastful or idle threats.

Excusing himself from participation in the scheduled fishing trip, and urging the others to proceed, Nat regained his rifle from outside the cabin door and made his way back down the road toward the bridge. After he had disappeared in the woods, the seven men on the clearing heard two shots ring out in quick succession and they assumed Nat had fired at a deer, but they were mistaken. He had merely discharged his rifle to re-load it with special care. Dangerous game crouched on his trail, and the wise old hunter would not stalk it unprepared.

Instead of crossing the log bridge leading to his home, Nat turned to the right, and walking swiftly through the forest, arrived at the Mill Stream dam several minutes ahead of the fishing party. There he crossed to the opposite bank and following the stream's easterly channel continued his rapid pace to the foot of First Lake. At that place a small triangle or point of wooded land extended into the water from the North Shore which narrowed the river to a width of thirty or forty feet. This projection, which has long been known as "Indian Point," lay to the left of upstream voyagers, and its leafy thickets offered a place of concealment from which to view the progress of boats in either direction. It is now entirely submerged, except in seasons of very low water, due to the erection of the state dam. A submerged boulder lies at its extreme tip on which rests a weighted barrel maintained as a channel marker for lake craft of large displacement. On this point Nat took his stand, rifle in hand, to await the oncoming party.

The four friends from Leyden appeared first. They were pulling at the oars of a large rowboat. A few rods behind them came Wood and Chase paddling a bark canoe, and close in their wake appeared Drid, also paddling a bark canoe. His rancorous emotions had not subsided, and with every dip of the paddle he growled his unflattering opinion of the enemy whom he believed had been left behind.

As the rowboat containing the four men rounded the bend of the stream near the boulder its occupants caught sight of the motionless figure on the point, partially concealed by the glowing drapery of early autumn foliage. Sensing the tragedy about to follow, they raised their hands in warning to the two men who followed. Drid, observing the signal and fearing an ambush, hastily pushed his canoe abreast that of Wood and Chase, thus effecting a human screen between himself and the point. His quick maneuver, artful though it was, proved futile strategy against the shrewd marksman with whom he had to deal. As he came alongside the bachelors' canoe he spied Nat standing in the thicket, rifle poised and steady for the kill. With a scream of terror he half arose to plunge into the water, but at that moment two shots echoed from the point and he slumped slowly backward—dead. The rifle that never told a lie had sent twin bullets directly through his heart, and the long feud was ended. The "last Indian" had been killed.

After the second shot, Nat turned into the woods and started for home, so certain of his marksmanship that he neither paused to re-load nor to scrutinize the plight of his victim. Drid lay sprawled on his back, his arm hanging over the side of the canoe which rocked gently from side to side as it drifted slowly downstream. Shocked at the bloody outcome of their innocent expedition, the six white men drew alongside the death craft to view its contents, but all were reluctant to take a hand in disposing of the body. In consequence, the canoe continued to drift for some time, the lifeless arm hanging over the side trailing the water, and the six men, discussing the affair in awed tones, continued to drift behind it, the three craft forming an aimless slow moving cortege of unusual solemnity. The bachelors in particular suffered a noticeable case of nerves. The two balls from Nat's rifle had reached their moving target by passing between and unpleasantly close to them as they were seated in their small bark canoe. The superb quality of the old woodsman's marksmanship, however, should have dispelled their aftermath of nervous excitement at the thought of their exposure to his fire. Both bullets had pierced Drid's heart, but had made only a single small hole in his shirt. The second bullet had followed the path of the first to within an infinitesimal fraction of an inch, and before entering the body had passed through the tiny perforation already made in the victim's garment without perceptibly enlarging it.

It was Nat's uncanny skill of this character which had placed Drid at a disadvantage in endeavoring to carry out his murder-ous design during their twenty months' feud. To have way-laid an ordinary woodsman and shot him down in the woods would h..e been a comparatively simple job for the Indian. To successfully attempt the same form of aggression against Nat would have required a precision of plan and execution which Drid, conceited though he was, did not feel thoroughly capable of effecting. If the first shot failed to reduce the white man to helplessness, the latter's incredible quickness and ac-curacy in handling his weapon could have easily turned the tables, and the ambusher instead of the ambushed would have fallen victim in the exchange of fire.

To escape the dilemma imposed by the floating corpse, the six men concluded to make their way to the Manor and fasten the responsibility for its disposal upon Nat. They found him at home, dressed in his best settlement clothes, reclining peace-fully on his bed. He expressed no surprise when informed that Drid was dead, but cooly inquired, "Did he die in a fit?" Willingly returning with them to the scene of the shooting, he towed the body down the river to the Mill Stream dam. At no time did he deny or admit having played a part in the tragedy, nor did his friends intimate that they were aware of his participation. His reticence as well as theirs concerning the subject enabled the company to avoid embarrassment in their subsequent relations.

Drid was buried near the dam. A few days later his brother-in-law arrived from Canada, exhumed the body, and re-interred it with full burial rites of his tribe. During this ceremony the comely widow stood beside the grave but ex-hibited no trace of emotion other than a gentle smile which occasionally relaxed the stoic beauty of her face. Whether she smiled in relief or in resignation none could discern. Just be-fore the conclusion of the burial rites she stooped to the outstretched form of her dead spouse and clipped from his shirt a scrap of cloth containing the single jagged bullet hole above his heart. With this humble memento of a life and death tucked in the folds of her garments, she returned to her tribal home with her children and brother, leaving Drid at rest in the solitude of the forest whose quiet was broken only by the low roar of the Mill Stream as it tumbled over the little log dam. Many years later the grave was opened again and Drid, seemingly restless in death as in life, was re-buried in another grave about one hundred and fifty feet from the dam to avoid the desecration that would result from the construction and operation of a mill near his original place of repose. There he lies today, in a grave that is marked by a boulder and a small wooden railing, but unmarked with any inscription to tell his name or the story of his turbulent career and violent death.

Nat, in the meantime, having shot it out with his enemy, started for the settlements to argue it out with the law. Justices Joshua Harris and Lyman R. Lyon, both of Lewis County, refused to issue warrants for his arrest; so he was forced to seek farther to effect his incarceration. Martinsburg authorities were more hospitable. They accommodated him with lodgings in the local jail. After he had spent three days there, a party of friends arrived and accompanied him to Herkimer where he was confined to await trial. His case was tried in Herkimer on September 3 and 4, 1834, after he had been imprisoned for nearly a year in the county jail at that place. Because of his fame, the case attracted widespread attention and the court room could not hold the vociferous crowd of Nat's friends that journeyed to the county seat to attend the trial. The jury deliberated two hours, then returned a verdict of "not guilty." The anxious prisoner was deeply moved by their decision, and rising to his feet he exclaimed "God bless the people," whereupon the crowd demonstrated its approval of both Nat and the verdict by prolonged cheering.

The year of confinement while awaiting trial had been a severe strain, and Nat's health began to fail soon after his release. He wandered restlessly from place to place for a time, and finally made his home with his daughter, Jemima Edgerton, near the little settlement of Ava, in Oneida County. He died there on the sixteenth of March, 1840, and was buried in the family plot atop a sloping expanse of pasture land a quarter of a mile west of Ava. His grave overlooks a quiet pastoral scene of comfortable farm houses, green meadows and grazing cattle —a strange resting place for the indomitable old ranger of the wilderness. A few years after his death the plot was invaded by a malicious group of persons bent on violating the sanctity of the graves because of a grudge they bore against certain members of the Foster family. They hacked away the inscrip' tions on the dozen or so unoffending little headstones which preserved the identities of the sleepers, and left only the mute stubs of rock protruding a few inches from the ground to mark the location of the graves. At this writing the markers have not been restored, and Nat, like Drid, his victim, sleeps in a nameless tomb, leaving a knowledge of the contents of both graves to hang from the fragile grasp of memory.

For many years following the bloody conclusion of the feud, travellers in the Fulton Chain region paused to inspect Drid's lonely grave beside the Mill Stream and to review the events leading to its existence. Men of letters carried the story back to their homes, and later wove the facts into narratives of Adirondack travel, thus bringing the affair into prominence as an historic feud. The most comprehensive account of Nat's life is contained in a three hundred page story, *Nat Foster*, by Reverend A. L. Byron-Curtiss. This work, which was pub' lished in 1897 after two years of studious research by its author, was accorded a generous reception throughout the Adirondacks. Mr. Curtiss, who from his youth has been a constant lover of the forest, now maintains a summer home on the shores of North Lake, near Atwell, in the Adirondacks. The earliest authentic account of Nat and his quarrel with Drid is to be found in *Trappers of New York*, published by Jeptha R. Simms about five years after the white hunter's death.

At this writing, Nat's nearest surviving descendent is Mrs.

Celestia Eleanor Adams, a granddaughter, who resides at Constableville, Lewis County, with her son-in-law and daughter, Doctor and Mrs. Frank Ringrose. At the age of eighty-six Mrs. Adams continues to evince an active interest in the facts of her noted grandsire's career.

VI

THE ARNOLD REGIME

BESIDE the state highway that approaches a sharp knoll overlooking Thendara there extends a border of sandy cliff from
whose summit a plot of level land reaches back to the base of a
wooded rock ridge. The level area is hidden from the view
of passing motorists and passengers of the New York Central
Railroad whose tracks parallel the highway at this point, but
a brief climb up the slope readily discloses the now partially
overgrown plot. With no peculiarities of vegetation or land
formation to mark it as a site apart, the explorer may assume
it to be typical of numerous Adirondack clearings abandoned
by discouraged settlers. An inconspicuous depression (the
cellar of the once conspicuous Herreshoff Manor) is the sole
indication of the unusual which still remains to tempt the interest of observers. In the subtle manner of man's abandoned
haunts it hints of the dead past, and of the force of human lives
whose tragedies and triumphs of long ago are the glamorous
happenings of the region's history. Here it was that Herreshoff toiled, dreamed and died; and here Nat Foster muttered
a somber farewell to his beloved wilderness. Their stories have
been told in previous chapters, but there remains a third pioneer figure of the forest who came to know the humble cellar
depression more intimately than either of his predecessors. A
stolid, unimaginative type of woodsman, he held the attention
of Adirondack travellers for more than a quarter of a century.
During that time his home was the Fulton Chain's only temple
of hospitality available to mountain wayfarers, and he was the
central figure of the region's meager business and social life.
Because many significant events came to pass during his regime
(though few were traceable to his initiative) his story and that
of his family are included here at greater length than has been
accorded previous chapter topics.

In the late spring of the year 1837, Otis Arnold, a sturdy

young Boonville farmer, tramped his solitary way along the Brown's Tract Road that linked the settled country of the Black River Valley with the wilderness of the Fulton Chain and the quiet waterways extending eastward through the forest. The road, opened to vehicular traffic nearly twenty-five years before, had barely survived a long period of disuse, and a creeping growth of woods had narrowed its surface to little more than the width of a bridle path. Birch and cherry were rooted in tangled confusion within its borders, and lumpy obstructions of rock conspired with depressions in mud and sand to make the tramping difficult. At sundown Otis emerged upon the wide clearing that is now Thendara, within view of the Manor that had been vacated by Nat Foster four years before. He was a weary traveller and glad to be at his journey's end, for he had left home the day before to seek a new home site, and the rough lonely road had added to the difficulties of his quest. On the porch of the Manor he deposited his rifle, his pack and himself; and in a contemplative mood engendered by weariness and solitude he scanned the varying landscape which surrounded him.

Within view of the porch a stretch of clearing sloped upward to a crown of virgin timber that hid the sunset. From the rear of the Manor acres of cleared land reached out levelly toward the banks of the Moose River that curved and gleamed in the distance. Except for an occasional patch of briars and a fringe of wild cherry the flat land was easily tillable. A few cabins could be seen peeking from the surrounding rim of forest, but no welcoming curl of smoke rose from their stone chimneys, for the cabins, like the clearings on which they stood, had been abandoned years before. Beyond the river great wooded ridges rolled away, merging, one with another, until the gray haze of the farthest was lost in the twilight blend of the Adirondack sky. Wary eyed creatures of the brute world prowled the valleys that lay between. Food and sheltering thickets abounded for their comfort in every section of the region. So did the clear, cold water that rippled down an endless succession of slopes as it sought union with pretentious streams and lakes that enlivened the valleys.

From his vantage place on the porch Otis considered his environment with satisfaction, deciding that he had reached the goal of his pilgrimage. He had reached that, and more, for his toilsome journey over the Brown's Tract Road had brought him to the portals of fame in Adirondack history. His name would soon become a symbol of the great wilderness that now encircled him. The story of his family and himself would be carried far and wide through the channels of literature. He was destined to become the first inn keeper within the foot-hills of the mountains, the first resident guide and supplier of guides in the region, as well as the first farmer to successfully cultivate the thin soil of the Brown's Tract.

Otis was born in New England in 1804. In 1828 he married Amy Barber, the daughter of a neighboring farmer, and accompanied by the groom's brother, Erastus, the young couple set out for New York to begin life anew in the Black River Valley. They settled on a sandy hillside farm several miles southwest of Boonville which had been abandoned by a previous tenant. The three-room farmhouse, built several years before, was a loose, frail structure of boards that leaned judiciously with the wind to escape being toppled out of existence altogether. The few out-buildings were similarly lacking in the architectural properties of strength and roominess, and the place as a whole offered no advantages which were not excelled by the New England home which they had forsaken.

Prosperity never crossed the threshold of their little dwelling, but six healthy, hungry children did—and in rapid succession. Edwin, eldest of the six, was born in 1829, and Ophelia, the youngest, in 1836. Both became well known residents of the Fulton Chain region in later life. Enriched only by the family increase, and burdened with growing responsibilities, Otis fell to scrutinizing the harrassing problem of life with closer attention than his previous circumstances had demanded. The farm was not producing the abundance needed to match the family appetite, and neither brother relished the tedious rounds of labor which an increased yield would require. Otis, however, possessed a more daring spirit than his brother. Harboring a gnawing resentment against the fate that held him to the dull routine of tilling a sand blown hillside, he determined to improve his lot, or at least to change it, at the earliest opportunity. Thus it came to pass that he considered his chance of success in new fields as he rested on the porch of the old Herreshoff home. Although in need of repairs, the Manor seemed to him a palatial residence compared with his Boonville home. The rent-free clearings awaited the plow, and in the surrounding wilderness of lakes and forest, fish, game and furs could be taken at will. To a man in badly straitened circumstances the place extended an irresistible invitation, and Otis accepted promptly and heartily.

A short time later he again left Boonville and trudged the Brown's Tract Road, headed for the land of promise with his family and possessions. Erastus remained behind. It required nearly three days to make the short trip, but the little troop arrived safely, well pleased with the adventure in spite of the jolting they received on the way. Ignoring the customary details of ownership, leases and terms of rental, Otis settled his family in the Manor and his few head of livestock in the barn; then he proceeded to carve for himself a mountain empire over which he would hold dominion for the next thirty years.

A few small crops were produced the first year, and hunting and trapping added something to the family income. Joanna, the seventh child, appeared the next year, and five more children were born during the eight years which followed. At the birth of the last child, Elizebeth, in 1846, the Arnold offspring numbered an even dozen. In the order of their appearance, and including the first six who were born on the Boonville farm, the twelve children were Edwin, Elmira, Almeda, Amy, Eunice, Ophelia, Joanna, Dolly and Julia (twins), Esther, Otis and Elizebeth—ten girls and two boys. Until Elizebeth made her debut as a Central Adirondack resident in 1846, no physician had ever been summoned to attend the family. On that occasion Edwin saddled a pack-horse and started for Boonville in the early morning, but when he returned with the doctor the following day both mother and daughter were doing very well.

With nearly twenty miles of barely passable road stretching between them and their nearest neighbor, all the children grew to healthy maturity under conditions which were unusual even in a pioneering era. No school was established on the tract, and no course of study maintained for the childrens' instruction at home. The parents were hardly able to read and write, and they appraised book learning very low in the list of important accomplishments. The Bible was unknown in the home: so was religious training. Even the words of those simple, time honored prayers which are always dear to impressionable childhood were excluded from the early experiences of the dozen isolated children. This lack of religious influence in youth did not stifle the spiritual instincts of the daughters in after life. All became affiliated with various church organizations and were known as zealous adherents to their chosen faiths.

For amusements the children played simple games, such as they could improvise among themselves. Excursions farther along the Brown's Tract Road to the old forge were adventures of exceptional fascination, although the small adventurers were admonished daily by their parents not to stray from the road. Swimming and fishing in the Moose River near the Manor were diversions which brought seasonal delight, and bounteous platters of trout yielded by the stream were commonly served at the family table. Reconnoitering the scattered growths of wild berries, exploring deserted cabins and speculating in hushed voices about the former occupants, horseback riding, care of livestock, and general work in the house and fields were necessary and interesting employments. The boys wore rough homespun, while the girls were clad in blue jean, their hair dressed in the approved pigtail mode of the day, their

ESTHER AND JOANNA ARNOLD
Joanna, born in 1838, was the first white child of record born in the
Fulton Chain Region.

THE TWINS—DOLLY AND JULIA ARNOLD

THE ARNOLD HOUSE IN 1869

ED. ARNOLD

feet bare except in cold weather.

Sheep pastured on the clearings furnished an ample supply of wool which the daughters carded and the mother spun into sundry garments for the family wardrobe. From the goose pen and hennery came luxurious stuffing for man and mattress; several milch cows supplied an abundance of dairy foods, and the rifle procured a variety of meats. As his family grew, Otis increased his acreage under cultivation, and often harvested a surplus which he sledded to market twenty-five miles away. His chief crops were hay, oats, potatoes, peas and beans. These helped to diversify the family menu and provided stock feed for winter use. All in all, a surprising degree of prosperity and domestic contentment greeted the advent of the Arnolds on the clearings, and it soon appeared likely that a permanent settlement had at last been established on the Brown's Tract.

A few months after the family had moved into the Manor a fisherman knocked at the door in search of food and lodging. He was received hospitably and accommodated with pancakes, venison and a bed. In the morning he paid the modest reckoning, complimented the hostess on her cookery, and departed— a satisfied patron. That was the beginning of the hotel business in the Adirondacks. Other hungry wayfarers were housed and fed at intervals, hunters, trappers and fishermen, and occasionally a sight-seeing tourist. They were all received with hearty informality and at low rates, and in time the Manor became known as an inn. It was also a tavern, for Otis kept a stock of liquors on hand to be dispensed to thirsty travellers who had no appetite for spring water. Otis did not consider himself to be an innkeeper or taverner in 1837, yet the entertainment which he furnished to the public and for which he received compensation that year heralded the approach of the modern resort hotels which now dot the shores of the principal Adirondack lakes, and his Manor home is properly regarded as the first hotel to have opened its doors within the foothills of the mountains.

In a few years, the increase of patronage and the addition

of little Arnolds to the home circle caused serious congestion in the Manor, and Otis feared that members of the family would be forced to sleep in the barn if guests continued to multiply. To avoid that contingency he built a one-story addition extending the entire length of the house at the rear. Many interesting photographs of this historic building are in existence, but most of them convey a false impression of its situation with reference to the highway. The veranda, and front of the house, did not command a view of the present bounds of Thendara. It faced directly opposite—toward the Brown's Tract Road that passed between the Manor and the wooded rock cliff. After passing the Manor, the road sloped downward toward the Moose River and intersected the plot on which the New York Central Station now stands. No section of the old road is visible today from the state highway.

Otis and Edwin trapped, hunted and guided, while mother and daughters attended to the details of housekeeping and to the bulk of the farm work. Venison and furs were transported to the Boonville market by sleds in winter and pack horses in snowless seasons. The pack horse gradually became the saddle horse which carried visitors into the region after they had left the stage coach at Boonville or Port Leyden. As early as 1850, Otis maintained a stable of a dozen or more horses broken to saddle for the convenience of his guests and himself. The majority of travellers entering the woods at that time walked in along the Brown's Tract Road. Sportsmen of means who could afford the luxury of a saddle horse usually sent word to Otis to meet them at Boonville with horses, but sometimes they wondered painfully at the journey's end whether the noble animals were really a luxury after all. The rough road could not be used for vehicular traffic except when blanketed with snow, and the harrowing up and down motion of the horses in picking a course between rocks and ruts was the inspiration of numerous profanely disparaging remarks concerning the standard of Adirondack travel.

As advertising mediums, Amy Arnold and her ten daughters

directed more attention to the Fulton Chain and Central Adirondack region than did the sturdy Otis and his robust son, Ed. They did the house and farm work, cared for the horses and other livestock, and ministered to the comfort of the Manor's guests. It was no unusual experience for them to be aroused at midnight or later by a clamorous pounding at the door by travellers who desired food and lodging. On such occasions, Amy and one of the daughters hastily stirred a pancake batter, kindled the kitchen fire, and attended the hungry arrival until he had gorged himself to a state of drowsy contentment.

The daughters seldom mingled with the guests. Although comely and intelligent, they possessed an inherent modesty. In the presence of strangers they were painfully diffident. Travellers described them as "shy," but their aversion to social contacts was a natural result of isolation. Only on an average of once in five years during adolescence did they visit an outside settlement, and their knowledge of the world and its ways was limited to the earthy lore available within the boundaries of their clearing. To their unsophisticated eyes the crude little Boonville of the forties and fifties was a vertible fairyland of marvels with its dimly lighted shops and their contents, its stage coach, canal boats, churches, wooden sidewalks and rows of painted houses. The hilarious, loud voiced sportsmen who patronized the Manor were strange beings from another world who filled them with fear and embarrassment.

In the fields they performed the work of men. Barefooted and clad in blue jeans, they bent their slim, sinewy backs to the routine tasks of planting and harvesting. They formed a versatile combination of farm hands, "stable boys," dairy maids and juvenile housekeepers. Their love of animals and marked aptitude for managing them enabled them to achieve remarkable results in training domestic creatures. Travellers, lingering on the clearing at milking time, were astonished and amused by the spectacle of dairy cows, upon being called by the girls, walking to the seated maids and halting in convenient positions for the milking. If a plodding bovine failed to attain the required precision of stance she was gently slapped and chided, whereupon she obediently circled maid and pail and returned to position—this time with her mind on her work.

The girls' greatest fame resulted from their prowess as equestriennes. Their feats of daring were matters of admiring comment among all who passed through the region. The men of the family seem to have had little or no fondness for horses, for their care and training were left entirely to the girls. This suited the pigtailed lassies to perfection and they lavished the same depth of affection on them that girls usually reserve for household pets. At the same time they developed a skill in handling their mounts akin to that of the celebrated riders of the Arabian desert. Not only did they ride their horses bare-back over the flat land of the clearings at reckless speed, but they broke the untamed colts to saddle and harness and trained them to come at their call. There is scarcely a square foot of soil on the present site of Thendara that has not been bumped by an Arnold girl flung from the back of a plunging colt. Their courage and persistence were unlimited, and if a spirited animal won an occasional tilt with its rider its triumph was short-lived. Eventually the girl became mistress and the colt the devoted slave. The girls rode saddle-less and bridle-less with the mere touch of the hand for guidance, swam their mounts through the swollen waters of the Moose River and walked them across the ice.

Interesting comments are at hand from men of letters who visited the clearing during the middle of the century. Invariably they contain laudatory references to the daughters and their feats of horsemanship. A number of inaccuracies appear in several of these accounts, but on the whole they present an authentic picture of early days on the clearing. Thomas Bangs Thorpe, the humorist, records the following impression gleaned on a trip through the mountains a few years before the Civil War.

"Twenty years ago 'Old Arnold,' as he is now generally

termed, with a young wife and one child, took possession of the only dwelling left of all the original settlement, and without being overparticular about repairs he has lived in it ever since. It was a bold venture thus to turn with contempt from the clearings, and evinced a great deal of self reliance to choose such a solitary home. The move was, however, apparently a good one for Arnold, for he has prospered after his fashion—his wife has carefully raised a large family of children, and as he has never seen a sheriff or a tax gatherer since he resided in the old castle, he is not altogether destitute of this world's goods.

"Mrs. Arnold received us cordially, and with the dignity becoming her station as the lady of an old feudal castle. Engaged in the active duties of her household, she never ceased them for a moment, but continued her work, merely interlining her remarks, acting on the good sense rule that the most complimentary thing in her power was to hasten dinner, for our appetites and those of our fellow travellers were sharp set, and the steaming coffee and fragrant venison which was by the fire, and a large wheaten loaf on the table, and the busy attention of three blooming daughters, promised that we should soon be gratified with a most substantial meal. A little rest, some unimportant changes in our toilet, and we sallied out to enjoy the few moments which still remained of sunshine. While I was gazing about, Mrs. Arnold's twin daughters, now seventeen, and who had never been out of the woods, passed near me on horseback. They used no saddles or bridles, but the confidant equestriennes held such firm seat that I involuntarily expressed my admiration aloud. When they came to the bars that enclosed the yard about the house they beckoned to their mother and a few words passed, and the girls continued down the hill and were soon lost in the woods. While I was still gazing the old lady remarked that if I would keep my place I would soon see a fine race on the bottom land. And sure enough a moment afterwards the girls came rushing along at a speed that seemed almost dangerous, yet they displayed the most perfect skill, and sat so gallantly, and enjoyed the excitement so much, that it filled me with positive 'enthusiasm. The mother was justly proud of her children—twelve she had reared in her solitary home. Not a physician had ever crossed her threshold, yet they were pictures of health. The elder daughters had married and were excellent wives and mothers, and the three now grown to woman's estate, who had never seen a house except the humble one in which they were born, would compare favorably in address with those who possessed every possible advantage of city education. All this was the result of a mother's care. Truly Mrs. Arnold is a model of her sex."

Reverend James T. Headley, historian, biographer and lecturer, wandered through the Adirondacks during the summers of 1847 and 1848—ten years or more before the Thorpe expedition. Entering the Brown's Tract from the east, he paddled to the foot of the Fulton Chain, and his tribute to that waterway, which he terms "the eight Moose lakes," is worthy of reprinting here:

"A ride through these eight lakes is an episode in a man's life he can never forget. It furnishes a new experience —gives rise to a new train of thoughts and feelings, and opens to the dweller of our cities an entirely new world."

From the shore of First Lake he carried through the woods to Little Moose Lake, which he refers to as "Moose Lake." On this side trip he sighted two moose and six deer, and incidentally gathered information which may help to identify the first woman vacationist known to have penetrated the Adirondacks.

"A certain judge and his lady are accustomed to come in summer from the western settlements, and camp out two or three weeks at a time on its shores (Little Moose Lakes) and fish. The lady, accomplished and elegant,

enjoys the recreation amazingly, and once caught herself
a trout weighing nineteen pounds."

Proceeding toward the Arnold home, Mr. Headley paused
at the grave of Drid, and he subsequently described the feeling
of horror which overcame him upon beholding a murder victim's grave, forlorn and lonely, in the depth of the forest.
After relating somewhat erratically the history of the Brown's
Tract he tells of the Arnolds.

"Three thousand acres have been cleared up, which now
lies a vast common, with only one inhabitant to cultivate
it. He occupies it without being owner, yet pays no
rent, and no taxes; the Robinson Crusoe of this little
territory, he has what he can raise, and no one to dispute
his domain. The log dwellings of the settlers have all
rotted away, the mills fallen in upon the mill stones, and
the forge upon the hammers. One house alone, which
formerly belonged to the agent, remains standing, and
in this Arnold and his family reside. Boonville, twenty
miles away, is the nearest settlement yet here he lives
contented, year after year, with his family of thirteen
children—twelve girls and one boy—by turns trapping
and shooting and cultivating his fields. The agricultural
part, however, is performed mostly by the females who
plow, sow, rake, and bind equal to any farmer. Two of
the girls threshed alone with a common flail five hundred
bushels of oats in one winter, while their father and
brother were away trapping for marten. Occupying
such a large tract of land, and cultivating as much as he
chooses, he is able to keep a great many cattle, and has
some excellent horses which these girls of his ride with
a wildness and recklessness that makes one tremble for
their safety. You will often see five or six of them, each
on her own horse, some astraddle and some sideways,
yet all bareback, racing it like mad over the huge common. They sit their horses beautifully; and with their
hair streaming in the wind, and dresses flying about their

white limbs and bare feet, careering across the plains, they look wild and spirited enough for Amazons. Yet they are modest and retiring in their manners, and mild and timid as fawns among strangers. The mother, however, is the queen of all woodsmen's wives—but you must see her and hear her talk to appreciate her character. If she will not stump the coolest, most hackneyed man of the world that ever faced a woman, I will acknowledge myself to have committed a very grave error of judgment. Her husband's "saple line," as she terms it—sable line—is thirty miles long and he is often absent on it several days at a time."

A third impression of the Arnolds comes from the pen of Lady Amelia Murray, maid of honor to Queen Victoria, and seemingly a woman of marked refinement for whom the wilderness held no terrors. In 1855 she journeyed through the Adirondacks with a small party conducted by Governor Horatio Seymour of Utica. Governor Seymour had recently completed his first term as the state's chief executive and apparently had taken to the woods at the earliest opportunity after vacating the executive office. Between the years 1850 and 1862 he sought the governorship five times as nominee of the Democratic party, but succeeded only twice, being elected in 1852 and 1862. In 1868 General Grant, Republican nominee, defeated him in a stirring campaign for the Presidency of the United States, after which the ex-governor retired from politics. His lifelong interest in the Adirondacks led to his being appointed President of the State Park Commission, which was formed in 1872 to determine the practicability of converting the Adirondacks into a state preserve. Lady Amelia observes the best traditions of English writers who make hurried trips through America, for her account which follows contains several factual errors.

"Mr. Seymour remained to make arrangements with the guides while his niece and I walked on to Arnold's farm. There we found Mrs. Arnold and six daughters. These girls, aged from twelve to twenty, were placed in a row against one wall of the shanty (the Manor), with looks so expressive of astonishment that I felt puzzled to account for their manner till their mother informed me they had never before seen any other woman than herself. I could not elicit a word from them; but at last, when I begged for a glass of milk, the eldest went and fetched me a glass. I then remembered we had met a single hunter rowing himself in a skiff on the Moose River, who called out, "Where on 'arth do they women come from?" And our after experience fully explained why women are rare birds in that locality. At this point we expected to find horses, but owing to our twenty-four hour detention at Raquette Lake they had been sent off to bring up some gentlemen to Brown's Tract; pedestrianism was therefore our only recourse. Jamie M'Cleland came up from the river and explained that unless we made some progress this evening, we should not be able to get through the forest during daylight tomorrow, and delay was of importance, so we decided upon trudging on as far as possible. Jamie took the tent on his back, and Mr. Seymour and the guides were to follow as soon as they could select positive necessaries from our baggage. Mrs. Arnold was furious—she did all but try to detain us by force—declared that we could not go on—that she should soon see us back again; but necessity has no law; we felt the importance of determination, and we had become too experienced gipsies to fear camping out. For one mile we had a pleasant path, then commenced the series of bog holes which, with few and short intervals, were to be scrambled through for sixteen miles."

Lady Amelia's concluding sentence is one more addition to that bulky volume of literature which has made obeisance to the Brown's Tract Road. Her statement that Mrs. Arnold's twenty year old daughter had never seen a woman other than her own mother is faulty. Records of the family indicate that none of the Arnold daughters reached the state of young womanhood without having made at least one trip to Boonville. But her account tells a true story of feminine aversion to even a brief sojourn in the mountains at that time. The lack of travel and housing facilities and the presence of wolves and panthers robbed the Adirondacks of much of their endearing charm; moreover, feminine decorum and mountain climbing were incompatible in the mind of American womanhood of the mid-nineteenth century.

Years later, Esther Arnold recalled Lady Amelia's visit to her home, and volunteered the amusing information that the twins, red haired Dolly and brown haired Julia, had fled in terror from the strange presence to conceal themselves in the cellar, but had been marshalled forth for inspection by their alert mother. About the same time, an incident occurred involving another feminine visitor to the Fulton Chain which left a vivid imprint on Esther's memory. A New York journalist, accompanied by his wife, arrived at the Arnold home in search of rest and inspiration which they hoped the forest could provide. The thirteen year old Esther was induced to accompany them—in the role of "milady's maid"—to an open shanty at the foot of Fourth Lake where they planned to spend several days. Their daylight trip up the lakes was an enjoyable adventure, the camp was cozy, and its location a place of rare charm; and all went well until the setting sun faded beyond the timbered sweep of ridges that rise from the northerly shore of the Chain. Dusk was rather lonely and unpleasant, and darkness more so. The moon rose in consolation, but so did an impenetrable mist, and the wide expanse of lake and forest was soon hidden in the ghastly arms of a fog. The woman grew uneasy, and openly expressed fear for her safety. A confusion of sounds ensued—sharp, disquieting little noises at first, made by tiny creatures scurrying about in performance of their evening duties. They added to the mystery of the night, and to the camp's perplexity. Bigger and more ominous sounds followed which indicated the proximity of animals whose ferocity and size the terrified lady's imagination grossly magnified. Then came moments of silence which served to intensify the sense of impending danger. Finally a blood curdling crash shattered the morale of the three beyond repair as a too inquisitive beast lost its footing on an adjacent ledge. The combined efforts of the nervous Esther and the distracted husband could not quell the hysteria which beset the unfortunate lady throughout the remaining hours of night. They broke camp in the morning at the first rift in the fog and returned to the Manor. As fast as pack horse, stage coach and steam train could convey them, the couple hurried back to the less inspiring but far less terrifying environment of the metropolis.

Although the wilderness held scant attraction for women, men continued to visit it in increasing numbers. Trappers, sportsmen and nature lovers (the latter class becoming more and more in evidence) made their way to the Brown's Tract and usually stopped at "Arnolds" for food or lodging, for boats, horses, guides, dogs, information, sometimes for plain sociability. Otis had become famous. His name appeared on maps of the region to designate the one-family settlement that awaited travellers at the road's end. Sturdy, adventure loving young men lingered about his home during the busy fishing and hunting seasons to accept employment as guides. The name "Brown's Tract" was known far and wide due to the publicity which followed the John Brown and Herreshoff undertakings, and as late as Otis Arnold's time it was still in popular use to denote the entire Adirondack forest.

Otis was getting on very well with his public. He thoroughly enjoyed life in the woods, and thereby helped others to enjoy it. Honest, unpretentious and dependable, he enjoyed the confidence and respect of travellers. He guided them, hunted, ate and drank with them, and they liked his straightforward manner of speech and conduct. Occasionally he drank to excess, not often; but so did many of his guests, and as all quaffed the stimulating beverage in company nothing derogatory to his reputation as a host resulted. During his later years on the tract, two hundred people or more patron- ized the Manor annually to satisfy needs of one sort or another.

Many visitors to the Brown's Tract during the Arnold regime became identified with the region's development in after years. Following are some of the names familiar on the tract in the third quarter of the nineteenth century: Lyman R. Lyon, General Richard U. Sherman, H. Dwight Grant and his brother, Charles, Verplanck Colvin, John Brinkerhoff, Cap- tain Jonathan Meeker, Abner Lawrence, Sanford Sperry and his son, William, James Higby, Benjamin Stickney, Alonzo Wood, Ed Arnold, Sam Dunakin and Jack Sheppard.

The last named trio formed a triumvirate of hunters whose marksmanship hurried the extinction of Adirondack wolves and panthers; and Ed Arnold, with his father, figured in the killing of the last moose native to the Fulton Chain region in early December, 1857, near the Joy Lot spring. (The Joy Lot, or Joy Tract, borders Old Forge on the south. For many years the spring was known as the "Joy Spring" but is now generally referred to as the "Pullman Spring" because of the Hon. E. Bert Pullman having dammed its basin to provide a gravity water supply for his Joy Tract home.)

Otis Arnold and his son, Ed, were returning from a trapping expedition in the vicinity of Nick's Lake when they suddenly encountered a moose standing motionless in the snow a rod or so below the spring. Both men and beast were startled at the unexpected meeting, but the elder Arnold instinctively raised his rifle and fired. Though sent in haste on its errand, the shot proved effective, and the badly wounded moose wheeled and floundered in a snow filled depression a few feet away. Hoping to take the helpless creature alive, Ed hurried home for as- sistance while his father stood guard. When he returned with ropes, accompanied by two of his sisters, the animal was so evidently near death that Otis sent a finishing charge into its head. The kill gave rise to much speculation as to why the lonely moose had sought the neighborhood of the clearings, and for several months thereafter the Arnolds and visiting hunters were on the lookout for others of its kind, but none were seen. At that time the species were considered practically extinct in the Adirondacks. The last previous killing in the Fulton Chain country had occurred in 1855 when Sanford Sperry and Ed Arnold had slain a bull moose after tracking it several miles upstream along the North Branch of the Moose River. Alfred L. Donaldson reports the apparently truthful claim of Alvah Dunning, Raquette Lake's famous hermit guide, to having killed a moose near his camp in the spring of 1862. No native moose were seen in the Adirondacks after that time, but several attempts were made later to propagate the species with animals imported from Maine and Canada.

Ed Arnold, Sam Dunakin and Jack Sheppard were perma' nent residents of the Fulton Chain and Big Moose region for half a century or more. Their distinct, contrasting person' alities are still recalled by a few old time woodsmen although twenty-five years have elapsed since the last of the three de' parted.

Ed, a rosy cheeked lad of eight, wide eyed with wonder and enthusiasm, arrived on the Brown's Tract clearing with his parents in 1837. He left in 1906, a grizzled veteran of the for' est, to die in a Utica hospital. Nearly seventy years of con' tinuous residence in the region had tucked a fund of practical woodlore in his shaggy old head such as few have acquired. It was not lore acquired by seeking, for Ed was no seeker after knowledge or one to analyze and catalogue his experiences. His wisdom was rubbed in at the pores, so to speak. In the course of his long residence in the woods he had stumbled against every conceivable wilderness experience often enough to become wise in a casual, subconscious way that amounted to instinct. Easy going like his father, he usually felt pretty well satisfied with circumstances as he found them. He relished the slow drift upon the pleasant waters of life and the Fulton Chain, but he could pull lustily against the wind when pulling became imperative. Living agreed with him thoroughly, and he mellowed and fattened with age until his rotund, well fed figure and jovial bewhiskered face became a pleasant feature of the mountain landscape. He never clamored against Nature, and in return, Nature never clamored against him.

Ed had two conspicuous traits which inspired both humor- ous and caustic comments among his fellows—an insatiable appetite for fish and abnormal snoring power. Exaggeration, of course, plays its part in the reports at hand dealing with these traits. A former guide once declared that Ed had de- voured enough trout during his life in the woods to re-stock the entire Adirondacks with mature fish. This statement may be considered with logical skepticism. Whether that many could be dispatched by one man in a single lifetime is specula- tive; but the fact remains Ed liked fish, and plenty of them: he liked to catch them and he liked to eat them. He knew the locales where catches were certain better than any woodsman of his time, and his larder rarely lacked a store of freshly caught trout ready for the frying pan. Whether they were products of his own angling or of another's made no difference. He en- joyed the eating just the same. He was known on many occasions to rise almost unconsciously from a deep sleep upon the arrival of a late returning fishing party, wander in drowsy uncertainty to the camp fire, munch half a dozen fat specimens, smack his lips in compliment to the fishermen, and return dozing to his blanket, immensely pleased with life, and with the quality of its trout.

Ed's snoring was the famous noise of the Fulton Chain. A rollicking devil-may-care blast, it tore to shreds the sacred silence of the night, leaving his sleepless companions inarticu- late with consternation and amazement. It appeared with the suddenness of a typhoon, boomed its way upward to an ear splitting, nerve racking crescendo, then vanished abruptly, sometimes creating the impression of mortality ended. Many a novice in the woods has crept in alarm to Ed's side fearing the genial guide had died in his sleep, only to be greeted with a devastating revival of the uproar. Ed paid considerably less attention to the phenomenon than did his campmates. When tartly reminded of his nocturnal thunderings he waved the subject aside as a matter of no great importance and of comparatively trivial interest to him. His snoring didn't keep *him* awake. Anyway, it was a natural accomplishment, and, as he often remarked with becoming modesty, too much credit should not be taken.

Sam Dunakin, precocious, alert and interested, entered the woods with a hop, skip and jump. In 1849 he skipped school in his home village in New Jersey, jumped aboard a succession of vehicles headed northward, and hopped into the bosom of the Arnold family with the casual complacency of a long expected friend. His debut as a woodsman was a complete success. He made himself useful and entertaining; he hunted, fished and trapped, roamed the forest with the Arnolds, rowed the lakes, bore his share of the burden on the carries, and more than his share of the conversation at all times. At the Manor he became the life of the household. He played school with the younger girls, lining them against the wall in spelling bee formation, correcting, encouraging them, and nodding his sophisticated young head in approval of their cumbersome efforts toward literacy. It was a profitable pastime for the girls, and, incidentally, the only schooling they received during their life on the tract.

Sam's forte in entertainment lay in his artful mimicry. He amused the household with a repertoire of imitations of conspicuous characters then emerging from the straggly human stream that made its way into the woods; the novice huntsmen, gruff veterans, the occasional drunkard, scholarly wanderers with scientific or literary aims, and all whose distinctive traits came within range of his observation. With the passing of the years the inquisitive, keenly observant boy gained a comprehensive working knowledge of the wilderness that placed his name in the directory of famous Adirondack guides. Before his death in 1907 he was pictured on souvenir postcards as "Sam, the oldest guide on the Fulton Chain." White bearded, grim and disdainful, he scowled in color from these cards, best sellers in the early years of the present century.

The mellowing hand of Time failed to mellow Sam. His lovable vivacity gradually vanished to be replaced with an acrid disposition that earned for him the reputation of being wilfully and disagreeably unsocial. Unlike most pleasantly disposed guides of his day, he scorned the agreeable pastime of swapping yarns, relating experiences, or dispensing information from his great store gathered through the years. The thrill of many personal adventures lurked in his memory, but he never knew the thrill of turning them loose upon a group of listeners. Only to a few intimates did he occasionally reminisce regarding the high spots of his life.

Sam waged ruthless warfare against the wolf packs whose recurring invasions worked havoc among Adirondack moose and deer, and his accurate marksmanship was a factor in eliminating panthers from the woods. Wolves and panthers were deer killers of the first order, outlaws of the forest whose ravaging instincts branded them as the common prey of men. Of the two species, wolves were the deadlier menace to animal life. Panthers killed only to eat, and invariably devoured the whole of their kill before hunting again, but wolves often pursued their quarry for the sheer zest of the killing without the incentive of appetite.

In 1862, Sam enlisted with the 220th N. Y. Volunteers, served three years as a sharpshooter, then returned to the Fulton Chain. But the urge to roam dominated him and he spent three years more wandering through the forests of Michigan and Wisconsin before settling again in the Adirondacks. He never commented at length on his war experience, but company comrades carried the information into the woods that he had refused a commission offered him as a reward for conspicuous service.

In 1872 he built his camp on the North Shore of Fourth Lake beside the rippling little brook that carries the water of Carry Pond down a leafy hillside to the lake. He named the

SAM DUNAKIN

JACK SHEPPARD

THE MOOSE RIVER INN

THE MOOSE RIVER STABLE AND DANCE HALL

A Daughter of the Fulton Chain returns. Esther Arnold Jones, in 1930, visits the scenes of her birth and childhood at Thendara.

stream "Minnow Brook," and above the door of his camp he inscribed the name with letters of birch twigs. The camp burned to the ground several years later and he re-built on the opposite side of the brook, and again blazoned the name above the door. This doorplate of silvery woodwork was his sole indulgence of a taste for ostentation.

Sam was the last of the Fulton Chain squatters to cling to a homestead in successful defiance of legally recorded private ownership. During the Mohawk and Malone railroad building days Dr. William Seward Webb acquired title to the bulk of Fourth Lake's waterfront, including the plot on which Sam had built his camp. Upon being asked by Dr. Webb's agents to pay for the land or to vacate, Sam curtly refused to do either. Instead, he countered with the assertion that Dr. Thomas C. Durant, a former owner had deeded the property to him as an honorarium for special services rendered; that he (Sam) had neglected to record the deed, but had tucked it in a cupboard of his old camp; the camp had burned, and with it the deed; never-the-less, the place was his and he proposed to keep it, and with a significant nod toward his gun rack he intimated the wisdom of civil or judicial evictors coming well armed and ready to fight. Sam's claim rang true, and confirmatory evidence was not lacking. In support of his contention he referred to Ed Arnold. Blinking in the controversial limelight, Ed nodded a solemn affirmative and declared that he had seen the deed and was aware of the integrity of his old friend's claim. Public sentiment, what little there was of it at the time, favored Sam. Notoriously uncivil though he was, he was also notably honorable and guileless. No deceptive or fraudulent practice had ever been laid at his door. Dr. Durant's interest in the Adirondacks was varied and material, and Sam, a rare woods-man, had often been called by him for expert assistance. Unfortunately, Dr. Durant had died in 1885 following a remarkably successful career of railroad building and land de-velopment, and his estate became involved in a series of conveyances and partition suits. In the course of these legal complications the memory of his unrecorded gift to Sam had faded to a shadowy intangibility in the minds of all except the donee and a few of his confidantes. Without question, Dr. Webb held the legal whip hand in the dispute, but when informed of the involved facts he ordered his agents to abandon further attempts at dispossession. In 1904, William J. Thistlethwaite, of Old Forge, acquired title to Dr. Webb's Fulton Chain realty holdings and gave Sam a life deed to the premises.

Sam's last days were tragic. The gay mimicry of his boyhood became ironic reality. He outgruffed the gruffest veteran he had ever depicted, and enough hard liquor found its way into his brimming cup of life to submerge and crush a normal woodsman of his age. From the year 1900 to his death seven years later he was sober only when adverse circumstances denied him the opportunity of being otherwise. To facilitate his home-comings when under the influence of alcohol, he submerged the outer edge of Minnow Brook dock several inches under water. With a final pull at the oars he could then guide his craft atop the dock's sloping surface, where, tipping to its side, its recumbent position enabled him to tumble out high and dry without subjecting his unstable legs to the delicate operation of climbing out.

In 1906 his health failed suddenly, and a younger sister, arriving from Cape May, N. J., persuaded him to accompany her home. Reluctantly but helplessly the enfeebled Sam took his departure in the autumn of that year, to return no more. An Adirondack frontiersman to the last, he wrote to a Fulton Chain friend a month later thanking him for "the liquor and tobacco you sent me from the mountains," adding the information that a like quality of these prime necessities was not to be found in the entire state of New Jersey. In a subsequent letter he expressed a longing to see his personal Adirondack physician, and condemned the medical fraternity of New Jersey with the tart comment "I wouldn't give a row of pins for all the doctors there is down here." The last word of Sam reached the friend in January, 1907. It came from his sister. Sam had died the month before, cooly ignoring the bedside watchers, and uncommunicative to the end except for uttering a verbal bequest. If the friend wanted his fishing rod it could be found where he had always kept it—under the cabin porch. If he wanted his boat, it could be found in a thicket at the rear of the camp, where Sam had dragged it and covered it with a blanket just before he left. There was no other property to be conveyed, as the friend well knew. At the time of his departure, after half a century in the woods, Sam's rod and boat were the total of his material possessions.

Jack Sheppard came to the Fulton Chain six years later than Sam and left several years earlier. A thin, white faced, quiet youth, he came in search of health, slowly walking the Brown's Tract Road on the last lap of his journey from Michigan. Sam described the new arrival as being "so thin he has to step twice to throw a shadow." Jack stepped many times twice in swift vigorous strides before he left the woods. When he stepped out of the Fulton Chain scene in 1893 his departure cast a vast shadow of regret across the Central Adirondacks. He had gained the health he sought and with it the unbounded affection of his mountain associates.

During his early years on the tract he trapped, hunted and fished, living in open bark shanties except during the coldest months of winter. Otis Arnold, Ed and Sam took more than a casual interest in his welfare, and the close friendship that developed among the four lasted a lifetime. In 1862, Jack enlisted with the 117th N. Y. Volunteers, served until the end of the war, and on being mustered out of service returned at once to the Fulton Chain. He soon made his mark as a crack shot and an expert oarsman, equalling Ed and Sam in these useful attainments. At the same time he acquired a more profound and more effectively classified knowledge of the Adirondacks than either of his two friends. A thoughtful observer and reader, he supplemented personal experience with studious application to books during hours of leisure, and to him goes the distinction of being the first permanent resident of the region to undertake the methodical accumulation of a private library. As far back as the sixties he presented the Adirondack novelty of a rough and ready woodsman who found absorbing companionship in books of travel, biography, natural history, botany, geology, engineering, and other works of technical and instructive character. In a comparatively few years after his arrival on the Brown's Tract he was known as the best informed guide in the Central Adirondacks.

Jack's real name was Edwin L. Sheppard. The prefix "Jack" sprung from a decidedly incongruous source, originating as it did with Jack Sheppard, the English bandit, who was hanged at Tyburn Prison, London, in 1724. Jack, the bandit, was a rascally young fellow who sported a brace of unscrupulous pistols to the consternation of the general public—himself included, eventually. The income derived from the high-handed tactics of his lawless pursuits was used to gratify his perverted inclinations until his banditry and debaucheries were jerked to a sudden halt by the hangman's rope. Some years after his death a maudlin literature came into existence which feasted and thrived on his memory, and he became heroic and glorified in fast selling thrillers of fiction. Harrison Ainsworth outdid all previous biographers in 1839 when he published his novel "Jack Sheppard," a red-blooded mingling of fact and fiction which invested the long dead bandit with the admirable virtues of chivalry, courage, generosity, intelligence, modesty and other kindred attributes. This work was widely read throughout the English speaking world, and its stimulus to hero worship lingered long in popular memory. It so happened the Fulton Chain Sheppard actually possessed many of the excellent qualities with which the fictional Sheppard had been verbally embellished, and his friends, fully appreciating this fact, hailed him as "Jack"; and as Jack he was known during his thirty-five years residence in the Adirondacks.

Jack figured in the building of many early camps on Big Moose and Fourth Lakes. He owned and operated the first locally built steamer to ply the Fulton Chain, and he served in the capacity of guide and adviser on several expeditions that penetrated the mountains in quest of scientific data. As a guide on purely sporting excursions through the mountains his services were in constant demand by discriminating patrons of the hunt. He rendered invaluable assistance to Verplank Colvin in connection with the latter's topographical survey of the Adirondacks begun in 1872 by authorization of the legislature. Colvin's voluminous though highly interesting reports of his survey are unfortunately brief in their references to the identities and accomplishments of his guides. Colvin was an enthusiastic and energetic woodsman, but an unskilled one, and his technical education and experience could not have solved the many peculiar problems arising in the progress of his work without the cooperation of the best minds of the forest. Among the latter, Jack Sheppard was an outstanding figure.

Jack left the Fulton Chain in 1893, declaring regretfully the woods could never be the same to him after the inauguration of railroad service in 1892. His innate love of an inviolate wilderness had not been blighted by his commercial astuteness. He disposed of his steamboat business although well aware of its increased possibilities for profit resulting from rail transportation into the mountains, bade a quiet goodbye to his friends, and started west. He lived a number of years in Oregon and then moved to Idaho, where he died in 1921.

His influence on Adirondack affairs was manifold, unpretentious but effective, finding expression for the greater part in achievements which are formally credited to other and more celebrated individuals of historic interest. He pioneered in behalf of the forest, being an early and staunch advocate of conservation; early and late his skillful marksmanship was pitted against depredating animal life, and properly enough, the last of the Fulton Chain panthers met its doom at his hands. Perhaps the most significant and comprehensive tribute to his character is expressed in the simple newspaper caption, "He elevated the position of guide," printed beneath his published photograph at the time of his death. Many references to him are found in literature of the Adirondacks. All are sincere in their complimentary reports of his ability, intelligence and moral qualities. A striking comment by an early Adirondack traveller draws the following enlightening comparison: "Sam Dunakin was provokingly uncommunicative, while his old friend, Jack Sheppard, was pleasantly quiet." Unforgetting old timers still chat of Jack as though he had left the woods but yesterday instead of forty years ago. From their occasional reminiscences there inevitably emerges the lovable figure of this departed Adirondacker whom a very small Fulton Chain girl in 1880 described as "the grandest man on the Fulton Chain."

Lyman R. Lyon of Lyons Falls, Lewis County, a dynamic go-getter of the mid-nineteenth century type, enters our story briefly at this point. He is identified with Fulton Chain history because of extensive land purchases he made from the heirs of John Brown of Providence. His connection with the affairs of the Arnolds, however, is limited to playing the role of an indulgent landlord who never called for the rent. Lyman was a pioneer in a big way. He loved the feel of title instruments proclaiming his ownership of new lands, and he loved the feel of the land itself. Rich in material possessions and in mental and physical vigor, he employed his resources in the ceaseless acquisition of greater estates. He delighted in vigorous tramping over his great tracts of field and forest, exploring their streams, rowing their lakes, climbing their hills to enjoy the panoramic view of vast properties, and best of all, he seems never to have begrudged a like delight to trespassers. Wealth never weaned him from the soil, nor from his love of arduous labor. But as he swung his axe with the gusto of a strong woodsman, one hundred other strong men were swinging another hundred axes in his behalf. His insatiable appetite for land furnished an always current topic of Black River Valley gossip in his day. He acquired whole townships at a time, and looked about for more. At the time of his death in 1869 he was the largest resident land owner in Lewis County in addition to holding extensive acreage overlapping the county's borders. His speculative interest in the Brown's Tract began about 1840 and continued until he had acquired title to all of Townships one, two and seven and parts of three, four and five. While his far-flung investments in Lewis County land caused more than a ripple of comment among his neighbors, his plunge into the uninhabited Brown's Tract with an open purse inspired several of his acquaintances to tap their knowing heads in the sad conclusion that he had suddenly gone land crazy. But Lyman was far from crazy. He was one of Lewis County's sanest citizens. The blood of pioneering ancestors coursed through his veins, and he knew by inherited instinct the potential mill power of swift running streams and the wealth of board-feet that lurked in standing timber. His father, Caleb, had grappled successfully with the raw materials of water, soil, and forest to develop three distinct, widely separated communities. Before the city of Rochester was a village he had built mills on the Genesee River and had laid the foundation for a flourishing settlement there.

Lyman's sudden death at the age of sixty-three halted his designs on the Brown's Tract which had matured with his years of ownership. The nearest approach his enterprise made to the region took form in the erection and operation of a large tannery on the southerly border of the tract, in the Town of Greig, Lewis County. The locality became known as Moose River Settlement, and for a number of years it provided a convenient half-way stopping place for vehicular traffic from Boonville and Port Leyden to the foot of the Fulton Chain. It can be reached today from the Fulton Chain by turning to the right after crossing the state highway bridge at McKeever and travelling five miles along a dirt road of intriguing beauty that borders the river. The tannery business once flourished as a celebrated industry of northern New York, but it has long since been buried in the discard of obsolete methods, and today

Moose River Settlement is no more than a fast fading memory of "the old tannery days."

Lyman R. Lyon and two associates, Henry and Agustus Snyder, built the first of three tanneries there in 1866. A two story structure of rough pine boards, three hundred feet long and sixty feet wide, it was strategically located near the Brown's Tract Road in the heart of an expansive hemlock growth. Trees were felled and peeled in the late spring and early summer months, and horse drawn sleds carried the bundled bark to the tannery in the winter over improvised paths which were known as "bark roads." Hemlock lumber being unsalable at that time, many of the denuded trees were left lying to rot in the woods. The tanning ingredient was made available by pulverizing the bark and steeping it in huge vats with scalding water, much in the manner of a housewife's small scale operation of steeping a pot of tea. In the resulting liquid (from the bark, not the tea) malodorous raw hides were immersed until sufficiently impregnated with tannic acid, and the finished products were hauled back to shipping points on the railroad in the same wagons and over the same road that brought the green hides in. Of course, the odor of the place was terrific. Incoming buckboard travellers began sniffing the air in pained surprise a full two or three miles before reaching the tannery, and the nearer they approached it the more of-fensive and ghastly became the atmospheric assault upon their unacclimated nostrils. Many of them had made long journeys to breathe the pure air of the mountains, but the suffocating infusions to which they were subjected pointedly suggested that every member of the Adirondack animal kingdom lay dead and decomposed in the surrounding forest. The tannery was Lyman's only property in which he didn't enjoy inspection tours.

All in all, a bustling industry developed, bad smelling though it was, and Moose River Settlement eventually boasted a more or less drifting population of nearly three hundred. In time the bark roads penetrated the woods several miles in all directions, and with tributary roads intersecting at regular intervals, the whole formed a sort of immense spider web with the tanneries crouching in the center. A second tannery was built a few years after the erection of the first, and new blood became infused into the business, the Hersey Brothers, Boston, George and Henry Botchford, the Kennedys, Scudder Todd and others becoming identified with the industry.

The site of Moose River Settlement first appears in history as the "Fording Place" in Herreshoff's time because of the newly opened Brown's Tract Road's halting at the unbridged river there. It received its first impetus as a community when Abner Lawrence settled there in 1859 with his wife and infant child. The three lived in an improvised shelter of two large packing cases nailed together, opening one into the other. When Abner progressed in the building of his house to the point of roofing it, the family moved to the new and more commodious dwelling. Abner was an ardent hunter and fisherman, and his new homesite was wisely chosen with regard to satisfying his outdoor hobbies. He guided small parties of sportsmen through the region, and his house became a popular tarrying place for hunters and trappers. Finally it became a full fledged inn, with a bar, taproom and public parlour added as necessary adjuncts to the entertainment of a growing patronage. His house became so well and favorably known that certain maps of the section designated the ford as "Lawrence's." With the growth of the tanning industry and the increase of buckboard travel to the Brown's Tract, Abner's bar and dinner trade earned a tidy profit. But prosperity also brought a certain measure of dissatisfaction. The tanneries were despoiling the forest. The primitive charm of his once isolated home had succumbed before the advances of battalions of axemen and bark peelers. Abner mourned the loss deeply, and in 1875 he disposed of his place and took up his residence in Boonville.

Considering the character of the tanning industry, its remote location and the indifference to social discipline manifested by its proprietors, Moose River Settlement is remembered as

a comparatively peaceful community. Quarrels raged occasionally, not often. Usually they were unpremeditated, sometimes the result of intemperate drinking, sometimes the fatuous
outburst of unrestrained natures that subsided after a brief,
satisfying exchange of fistic compliments. One spasm of ill
feeling lasted long enough, however, to assume historic proportions as a specimen of the rough and tumble fighting days.
It began with a falling out between two friends, a spudder
and a feller (a bark peeler and an axeman). Both men were
endowed with the personality and physique that make for
social leadership among woodsmen, and both were supported
in their contentions by factions of admiring followers. The
affair gained momentum and hot blooded adherents with the
passage of time, and finally terminated in a battle royal with
more than fifty embroiled woodsmen taking part. It was an
orgy of cracked heads and broken friendships lasting far into
the night, and with charges, counter-charges, retreats and
sundry tactics of bloody scrimmage, it raged over a square mile
of timbered battlefield. But with the dawn, physical exhaustion and mutual admiration for the rivals' prowess supplanted
the old hatreds, and after drinks all around for those who
could stand up and take them, tranquillity reigned again. A
band of St. Regis Indians, employed by the tannery, enlivened
the woods with occasional noisy reactions to the stimulus of
fire-water which could be purchased in a neighboring settlement on pay days. Their chief, Bill Bero, an Indian of commanding presence, sober habits and adamant discipline, rarely
experienced difficulty in herding them back to a state of
penitent sobriety.

Several proprietors succeeded Abner Lawrence in the Moose
River Inn. Tom Nightingale, a sprightly mixer and promoter
of good fellowship, contributed to the social gaiety of tannery
life by remodelling the tavern stable loft into a dance hall. This
improvement inaugurated an era of Saturday night sociability
in which the squeaking notes of the fiddle pierced the dark
silence of the neighboring woods. In 1887, Charles M. Barrett

of Old Forge purchased the inn and effected several improvements in its service and conveniences. At that time it was
generally known as the "Dinner House" because of the timely
mid-day arrival of buckboards travelling to and from the
Fulton Chain.

In the early nineties, the inn, the tannery, and the settlement
surrounding both, dwindled to economic insignificance with
the coincident depletion of hemlock growth within a radius of
eight miles and the beginning of railroad transportation across
the Adirondacks. The cumbersome buckboard went to the
discard immediately, as a vehicle of Brown's Tract travel, in
favor of the fast, luxurious service of the rails, and the tavern
was shunted out of the entertainment picture by an equally
immediate loss of patronage. Today, the abandoned inn and
its auxiliary structure, the stable, together with a few scattered
ruins which are now overgrown, are all that remain of the once
busy settlement. Nature, forgiving and patient, is hard at
work hiding the scars of a ravaging industry with growths of
poplar, birch and cherry—and the inevitable briars.

A double tragedy, enacted on the Brown's Tract in 1868,
ended Otis Arnold's career of thirty-one years as a mountain
host. It sprung from a misunderstanding over a trivial matter
between Otis and a visiting guide, James Short. Short, whose
home was in the Town of Minerva, Essex County, arrived at
the Arnold home September 19th with a party of sportsmen
he had guided from the eastern section of the mountains.
After seeing the party safely on its way along the Brown's
Tract Road, he had tarried a few days at the Manor. During
this time he purchased a hunting dog from Otis, and a collar
and chain from another member of the household. For some
reason the latter transaction was not made known to Otis.

When ready to take his departure on the morning of the
21st, Short produced the collar and chain, intending to fasten
them on his dog. Otis appeared at the moment, and observing
Short in the act of harnessing the dog with what he believed
to be his (Otis') property, he curtly ordered him to desist.

Irritated by the peremptory tone of the old man's voice, Short continued his operation without deigning an explanation of how he had come into possession of the articles. Otis then threatened to cut the collar from the dog's neck if Short attached it, whereat the guide replied, "If you do, I'll cut your throat." It was an ominous sounding threat, delivered in a hard, even voice, but very likely an idle one. Short was a muscular young fellow, physically superior to his elderly host, and it is improbable that he seriously considered enforcing the terms of his ultimatum. His own brawny arms were weapons enough, if weapons should be needed.

Alarmed at Short's menacing words, Otis stepped quickly to a corner of the kitchen and snatched up a double barrelled fowling piece. But the younger, stronger man wrestled him against the wall, deprived him of the gun, and released him. A moment later, Otis again secured the gun, and with powder flask in hand attempted to charge it, but the wary Short forestalled him by striking the flask from his hand. Then a totally unexpected bit of action brought the quarrel to an abrupt and tragic end.

Stepping back a few quick paces, Otis raised the fowling piece to his shoulder and pulled the trigger. A charge of buckshot ripped its way into Short's body. Mortally wounded, the young guide sank to the floor, moaning "You've killed me." None but Otis, perhaps not even he, had known the second barrel was loaded.

No sooner had Short fallen to the floor, where he lay writhing in pain, than his vanquisher's hostility gave way to instant remorse. Dropping to his knees, Otis begged forgiveness, and pleaded with the stricken man to shake his hand. The magnanimous Short, unresentful in the shadow of approaching death, yielded to both entreaties. He murmured absolution and feebly pressed the proffered hand, and the two men parted friends.

Beckoning his daughter, Julia, to follow him, Otis walked from the house. In the yard he handed her the keys to his

trunk, whispered a few brief directions regarding the disposition of his personal property, and avowed his intention to
end his life. Vainly the tearful girl implored him to abandon
his purpose. He shook his head, grimly determined; embraced
her and kissed her with fatherly tenderness. "No," he muttered. "It's done, and I'm sorry; but it can't be helped now.
They'll never take me alive."

He walked down the slope and over the flat land to the
river, his evenly paced stride carrying his sturdy figure along
steadily, unhurriedly. Crossing the log bridge, he climbed the
sharp, timbered ridge that rises between Thendara and Nick's
Lake. The lake was his favorite retreat, and much of the path
leading to its shores had been worn by his own feet. At the
top of the ridge the land lay level a short distance ahead of him
before dropping swiftly to the water's edge, but the trail, winding among the trees, followed a leisurely course downward,
and along this Otis made his descent to the foot of the slope
where his boat was moored. He paused on the beach to gather
stones and handfuls of wet sand which he crammed into his
pockets. Then he untied the boat, and pushed off from the
shore. Near the center of the lake he dropped the oars: he had
come to the end of the trail. It had been a trail of contentment, thirty years long, and it ended now in a beautiful world
of lake and forest and September sky. Too beautiful a world
to leave so abruptly, so tragically, but the desperate man knew
that the liberty he had prized for many years was now irre-
trievably at stake, and beyond that nothing mattered. When
his body was recovered months later it was taken to Boonville
for burial.

James Short died five hours after the shooting, after whis-
pering a last message of love and farewell for his wife and two
children who were then awaiting his return to their Essex
County home. The whole regrettable affair was the unpremeditated result of sudden irritability on the part of one man, and
a moment of stubborn resentment on the other's, but it cast an
awesome shadow over the Manor which never completely dis-

appeared until the building was razed by fire nearly thirty years later. The dead guide had been a man of good character and habits, although his momentary belligerence had given Otis— who had no previous acquaintance with him—reasonable prov- ocation for shooting. But whether he shot in uncontrollable anger or in a misconceived notion of the necessity of self- defense will never be known. Otis, though emphatically the master of his establishment at all times, had been a genial, obliging host, willing to accommodate his guests and friends even at the cost of considerable personal embarrassment. Among the natural hazards of the wilderness he had often risked his own life to save another's but had never before taken one.

Complying with his parting request to Julia, the Arnold survivors transported their father's trunk to the home of his daughter, Esther, who had married DeWitt Jones, a prosperous farmer living on the Alder Creek road near Boonville. It was opened there in the presence of the family, and to the aston- ishment of all, it contained a fortune. Beneath a quantity of odds-and-ends, the accumulation of years, there reposed ten thousand dollars in gold carefully secured in leather pouches. It represented the savings of a lifetime, but the children had never imagined their father's being the possessor of so much wealth. After the money was divided equally among the twelve children, and the story of its existence had become known, rumors spread through the Fulton Chain region that a like amount or more could be found by digging in the cellar of the Manor. But the shadow of tragedy hovering over the place apparently discouraged any would-be prospectors. Al- though the rumors persisted and the principal sum became magnified to a fabulous figure there is no evidence to this day of the grass-grown cellar floor ever having been disturbed by the probings of a treasure seeker.

Mrs. Arnold died in the spring of 1869, several weeks before her husband's body was found. Ed, declaring that he could never again dwell peacefully in the old home, left the Manor in charge of Sanford Sperry, a personable and competent woodsman whose twenty years' residence in the region had been punctuated by four years of military service during the Civil War. Three years later, Ed changed his mind, for the time being at least, and returned to live in the house until the spring of 1873, when he moved to the Forge House to become the proprietor of that infant hostelry.

In the meantime, nine of the ten Arnold daughters had left their Brown's Tract home, and one by one had found husbands and homes, some in far remote localities. Elmira, who became Mrs. Baldwin, settled with her husband on the treeless prairies of Kansas. Eunice became mistress of a happy home in western New York. Ophelia married Alonzo Wood, a prominent Central Adirondack guide who built and operated one of the Fulton Chain's earliest public camps. As "Grandma Wood," hostess of Wood's Camp on the North Shore of Fourth Lake, she won an enviable measure of love and admiration from the increasing number of vacationists who tarried on the Chain during the last twenty years of the nineteenth century. Julia never married. After the death of her mother she lived with her sister, Esther, until her own premature death which was soon followed by the death of her brother, Otis. At this writing, Esther, who became Mrs. Dewitt Jones, is the only survivor of the twelve children. A widow, at the age of ninety, she continues to maintain her cozy home in the village of Boonville. She is deeply interested in the occasional gleanings of Fulton Chain news which reach her, and although the infirmities of age have severely taxed her old time vigor, she still retains a glowing interest in the subjects of speckled trout and fast horses.

In mid-October, of the year 1930, responding to the alluring memory of her wilderness childhood, Esther motored to Thendara, accompanied by several friends, for a last look at the long abandoned Arnold homesite which she had not seen in many years. Railroad and highway had joined forces in the process of defacement, and the once gentle slope leading up to the

Manor was now a sandy cliff of discouraging abruptness. Assisted by her friends, Esther climbed bravely and eagerly upward and at last reached the uncovered cellar which she knew marked the site of her former home. There she paused, in silence, as though beside a vast, open grave. A frail, gentle little old lady, her black silken dress rumpling sedately to the ground, her thin hand upraised to blot the glaring sunshine, she quietly surveyed the old familiar scene that reached away in a panorama of flat lands, winding river, and high wooded ridges beyond. The dwellings and business structures of Thendara hardly gained her notice. Neither did the railroad locomotive that panted by, nor the swiftly gliding motor cars that appeared and vanished along the highway at her feet. Across the vista of departed years she seemed to stare back, three quarters of a century into the past, searching out the things her memory had long treasured. The steady, unswerving intentness of her gaze told that she had found them, that nothing had changed; life moved on the clearings as always. Blue jeans and pigtails streaked through the autumn air as the hoof beats of an untamed colt echoed from the rim of the forest. Blue jeans and pigtails arose from the weary tasks of the harvest to consider the invitation of the cool murmuring river, but bent again, dutifully, to the sun-warmed earth. Strange, bearded men tramped into view. Their voices were harsh and loud: their appearance frightening. On their backs they carried bundles of bloody hides and bad smelling furs. They were hungry trappers who must be fed, and the weary dogs, as well, that slouched at their heels. Other men came, cleaner, less bearded, less hungry, more jovial than the others, bringing late news from the settlements. They were headed eastward, up the lakes, and the fortunes of the trap line lay before them. But they, too, would be weary and unkempt and in need of food when they returned that way weeks later—if they should return. It was all as it had been. Nothing had changed.

It may be said that when Esther picked her slow way back down the slope to the waiting motor car that day her descending footsteps sounded the final echo of the Arnold regime, for it is unlikely she will ever come again. It is an honest, hospitable and useful regime, though not a brilliant or adventurous one, that the region's history must credit to the Arnolds. They deserve to be remembered, above all, as a sturdy family of Adirondack pioneers who kept the home fires of the Fulton Chain burning—when no one else would.

VII

THE NORTHWOODS WALTON CLUB

THE reader must begin this chapter by re-tracing his hitherto chronologically progressive course back to the year 1857. In the winter of that year several friends met at a pre-arranged dinner in Utica's best known hotel. They were amateur anglers and hunters, sportsmen of the best class, few of them deeply versed in the secrets of woodcraft, but all filled to the brim with enthusiasm for the delights of rod and gun so boun-teously to be had in the great rugged dominion of the North-woods. Much good natured bantering spiced the menu and the intermittent flow of toasts, together with some pardonable verbal swaggering regarding personal exploits in the Brown's Tract wilderness. After a few jovial hours spent in satiating appetites for food and braggadocio, the diners settled down to the important business of the evening. They organized them-selves into a recreational club whose chief objective was stated to be an annual group outing or sojourn on the Brown's Tract, with trout fishing the piece de resistance of a varied program of sports. As a means of designating by their club's name the locale of their proposed outings they christened themselves "The Brown's Tract Association." At a meeting held in Albany on February 10th of the following year they re-named themselves "The Northwoods Walton Club." The change was made to more clearly indicate the character of their annual recreations.

General Richard U. Sherman, New Hartford, was elected president of the club; Charles A. Meigs, Brooklyn, George Dawson, editor of the Albany Journal, and Henry B. Miller, Buffalo, vice-presidents; James H. Ledlie, Utica, recording sec-retary; Major Charles M. Scholefield, Whitesboro, treasurer; and Richard U. Owens, Utica, commissary.

General Sherman, president and guiding spirit in organizing the club, was born in Oneida County, N. Y., in 1819. He made his first trip to the Brown's Tract region about 1853. He was known at that time as an expert angler and a well informed pisciculturist. His ardent interest in the preservation of the state's wild life led to his appointment as State Fish and Game Protector in 1879. He held the office eleven years, during which time he substantially increased the number of state-owned hatcheries. Colton's map of the "New York Wilderness," published in the last quarter of the century designated Big Moose Lake as "Sherman or Big Moose Lake" partly in recognition of the General's piscatorial prestige, and partly because of his known preference for the shores of that handsome lake body. He is reputed to have been the first successful planter of land-locked salmon in any American fresh water outside the state of Maine, having stocked Bisby Lake with the species in 1879. In 1878, he organized the Bisby Club, the first association of sportsmen to own a private preserve in the Adirondacks.

At the time of his death in 1895, General Sherman was one of the best known and most popular men of the state. His acquaintanceship was broad and intimate, and included several Presidents and Govenors and a host of notables from many lands and many walks of life. His son, James S. Sherman, rose to national distinction as Vice President of the United States in the Taft administration (1909-1913).

Because of the prominence of the club's charter members and the wholesome, contagious character of its activities, it attracted immediate attention among men who were then identified with important political, business and professional affairs in and out of the state. Its membership included John A. King, Governor of New York; Thomas G. Alvord (later Lieutenant Governor); Ransom Balcom, Justice of the Supreme Court; Major J. P. Goodsell, William B. Taylor and Silas Seymour, all heads of state departments; Alfred B. Street, for thirty years State Librarian and a poet of current fame, and a number of business and professional men and legislators. During the club's sojourns in the woods, practically all the state's important business, legislative excepted, could have been transacted on the shores of the Fulton Chain.

In 1857, the Adirondacks were not valued highly by the state's population as a whole. Their resistance to agricultural aspirations had branded them as a sort of black sheep in the family of state geographical divisions. Benton's "History of Herkimer County," a comprehensive, portly volume, published in 1856, had disposed of the Fulton Chain region with devastating brevity by describing it as a region of waste land visited only by a few amateur fishermen, and infested with the "musquito and midge," against whose poisonous bite the author warned all and sundry. Private Adirondack preserves were unthought of at the time, and no organized group or club of sportsmen or vacationists had ever penetrated the mountains in a body prior to the advent of the now-historic Waltonians. (This club is not to be confused with the Izaac Walton League, an admirable organization dedicated to the preservation of forest, fish and game. The League came into existence much later, and though not historically identified with the Walton Club the inspiration for its name traces to the same source— Izaac Walton, author of the famed old rod and reel classic, "Compleat Angler.")

An interesting pamphlet is at hand, published by the Club in 1859, telling of its first three years' activity. After briefly reviewing the events leading to the organization in 1857, the prefatory concludes:

> "We are glad to welcome within our circle true spirits, who can share in our enthusiasm for nature's enjoyments; who can find in the breathing of God's pure air and in the contemplation of the beauties of primitive creation, a sufficient recompense for the toil and privation from luxury which these enjoyments cost. In short, we would have for our associates such only as are confirmed in the faith of that best of moral philosophers—Isaac Walton —whose teachings none—whatever be their rank or vocation—can follow without becoming happier, wiser

and better men.

For such our arms and shanties are always open. But to the pampered son of luxury, who prizes nothing except as it ministers to his animal enjoyment; to the conceited cockney, who has no appreciation of the beautiful world lying beyond the city, and who knows his fellow men only as the tailor made them; as well as the worse than wolf who shoots down deer in mere wantonness, and takes trout from spawning beds, our doors are forever closed."

Certainly a praiseworthy sentiment—the concluding expression—but in part it was a purely rhetorical phrase, for the Club had no doors. During their stays in the woods its members were sheltered in open bark shanties located along the shores of six or more lakes. The main camp and commissary were situated at the head of Third Lake of the Fulton Chain where a settlement of several open shanties housed thirty members and a month's supplies. Other shanties were placed as far away as Big Moose and Raquette Lakes. The pamphlet cautions the novice against the hazards of Big Moose as follows: (Parenthesized remarks are inserted by the author)

"The North Branch Lakes (Rondaxe, Dart's and Big Moose) are celebrated sporting grounds, but they are to be reached only by severe effort by land and water, and none should undertake to visit them except those inured to the hardships of the wilderness."

A general description of the Moose River Lakes, their beauties and sporting possibilities, leads to a justified laudation for neighboring localities.

"Besides these, there are a large number of smaller lakes hidden in ravines, nestled on hill tops, and lying around "loose" in the wilderness, none of them difficult of access, and all capable of amply rewarding the fisherman's toil. Only a short day's march and row from the site of the main camp lies Raquette Lake, renowned in geography and legend for its beauty and sporting facilities. It has a circuit of forty miles of coast, and is so indented with bays as to appear to the visitor like a labyrinth of lakes in which even a good navigator might get lost. Beyond this, to the east, north and south, lay lakes great and small, extending to the exterior border of the wilderness, and all connected either by navigable waters or good portages. Nowhere in the world lies such a system of inland waters, when are considered their own innate beauty, the variety and majesty of their surroundings, their primitive condition, and capacity to satisfy the greed of the hunter for game or wild adventure."

With the goal of their pilgrimages hidden away in the heart of the unmapped wilds, the pamphlet thoughtfully included directions for finding the region. (Parentheses again are author's).

"The route by which the Brown's Tract is usually reached from the settlements is by way of Boonville, the northern-most town of Oneida County, to which there is daily communication by railroad with most of the prominent cities of the state. (Black River Railroad service had been inaugurated a short time prior to the publication of the pamphlet.) To Boonville, therefore, the travellers' path is easy, and for eight miles by one route and fifteen by another it is not seriously difficult, communication being open by fair wagon roads. One route is from Boonville to Booth's Mill, in Greig, Lewis County, where the old Brown's Tract road, opened fifty years ago for the vain purpose of facilitating settlement in that rough region, emerges from the wilderness. (Booth's Mill, now Porter's Corners, was a settlement of one house and a mill on Four Mile Creek. It was owned by Harvey Booth who had lived there for several years before Abner Lawrence pushed on four miles deeper into the woods to make his home at the Fording Place.) There is little left of the road save a difficult bridle path, leading sometimes through deep quagmires, and sometimes over dangerous heaps of boulders, and once crossing an unbridged, raging river—the Moose— where raft craft often comes in good play. Fifteen miles from Booth's Mill by this route, at a clearing made during the first attempt at settling this wilderness fifty years ago, lives, nearly twenty miles remote from the nearest neighbor, an old farmer, hunter, trapper and guide, named Arnold. On this solitary spot he has maintained himself comfortably and reared a large family during the last twenty years. He makes it his business when not pressed with his farming operations, to transport parties over the "Jordon" just described, and to act as their guide and oarsman up the lakes and through the wilderness. He keeps a number of horses, used to packing burthens. Through their aid, the visitor with his effects, may reach Arnolds safely in generally seven to eight hours time from Booth's Mill."

Seven to eight hours was, admittedly, an impressive span of time to allot to a mere fifteen mile lap of the journey into the forest, but the pamphlet's editor had more than a passing acquaintance with that lap, and he knew whereof he spoke. The directions suggest two methods of travel, by pack horse or on foot, and informs that "the two modes are usually alternated every three miles which contributes to render the journey less wearying than by exclusive walking or riding." Then comes a word of cheer as the Club members are instructed to stop over night at Arnold's to rest, "a hostelry they will welcome as an oasis in the desert." The matter of personal equipment required for a comfortable stay in the wilderness had been given careful thought by the Club's officers, and from their combined experiences there emerged the following recommendations:

"Two woolen undershirts, either woven or sewed.

Two outer shirts of red or gray flannel, with pockets.

Two pairs of drawers of the same material as the shirts.

Two pairs of woolen pantaloons.

One woolen vest, either single or double breasted.

One roundabout jacket, or short hunting coat, button-
ing close to the throat, and having many pockets.

One gutta percha or India rubber overcoat.

A waist belt of leather.

Four pairs of woolen half hose.

One Kossuth hat."

Other articles of equipment, weapons, ammunition, and fishing, tackle, are included in the list of recommendations. A
minute, authoritative analysis of the successful angler's needs,
written by the president, and embracing several paragraphs,
leaves nothing to the imagination of the novice. It concludes:

"The best bait for speckled trout in this region is the common earth worm. Each party should take in a supply
of these from Boonville. They may be packed in oyster
kegs, with millinet covers so as to admit of ventilation.
Clean sand and damp moss are the best materials to pack
them in.

Of sporting arms, one rifle and one double barrelled
fowling piece will be found to be quite sufficient for a
party of six. Of ammunition, the best sporting powder
only should be provided, with lead, buckshot, balls for
rifles and waterproof caps. The wire cartridge will be
found very efficient in the discharge of shot. Pistols and
bowie knives are unnecessary, and form only a useless
incumbrance to the person and baggage."

The term "guide," descriptive of men professing a competent knowledge of the Adirondacks, its exactions and requirements, was applied with sharp discrimination by Club officers.
From the rank and file of men then identified in some role with
life in the wilderness, certain figures loomed as guides of exceptionally well attested qualifications. A single paragraph of
the pamphlet captioned "Guides," which sets forth the Waltonian reflections on this important subject, is well worth a
reprint here:

"No party making an expedition in the wilderness of

Northern New York for sporting or exploring purposes, can successfully accomplish its object without the aid of one or more experienced and faithful guides. The title of guide is generally applied without much discrimination to all the employees of such a party; and is arrogated to many who have not a single qualification for its proper duties. The office of guide—one who is worthy the title—is difficult and multifarious. He rows your boat over the waters, and packs your effects over portages; builds your shanty and cooks your meals; conducts you to good hunt-ing and fishing grounds; looks out for your comfort and enjoyment in the field and in the camp, and by a score of nameless forethoughts and timely attentions, makes your labors light and your pleasures extensive. Hence it will be seen that one of the most important requisites to the enjoyment of such a trip is the securing of the services of a capable and faithful guide. Those who have before visited this wilderness region, will have become acquainted, more or less, with this class of men, and will therefore be able without much difficulty to make such a selection as will conduce to their enjoyment. The novice will have more difficulty, as from his inexperience he will be liable to overlook his interest or be imposed on by pretenders. To such we would advise consultation with some experienced friend; or better still, an association with a party numbering one or more veterans. There should be to every two men of a party, one boat and one guide. The usual price for the hire of a boat is twenty-five cents per day for boats used in trolling the first four lakes, and fifty cents per day for what are called carry-ing boats, that is, boats that are transported over portages. The wages of the guide are generally one dollar per day exclusive of the use of the boats. The best hands sometime command more."

Printed advice in the wise little monitor, the pamphlet, comes to an end in an itemized estimate of expense. On a basis of two weeks spent in the woods, the member is advised that he may enter into the delights of the wilderness for exactly thirty dollars, expended as follows:

Transportation from Boonville to Arnolds, & return_ $7.00
Board at Arnolds, going in and returning_____ 1.25
Supplies in the wilderness_____ 7.00
Boat and guide_____ 10.50
Contingencies _____ 4.25

Thus informed, admonished and equipped, the gay Walton-ians, congenial votaries of green forest and clear cool waters, moved onward over devious routes to the Fulton Chain in eager anticipation of forthcoming joys.   Their invasion intro-duced a distinct outing innovation—organized group recrea-tion in the Adirondacks.   Usually the length of their stay ranged from two to four weeks, depending on individual in-clinations and the urgency of affairs demanding a return to civilization.   The Club pamphlet had announced:

"Our company is at liberty to hunt and fish where they will, or to omit hunting and fishing entirely if they choose; to roam the woods, row the lakes, or rest in camp, as may suit their needs or inclination; to sing, hallo, dance, swim or turn summersaults, as they may be in the mood."

They were in the mood for all these unrestrained antics and enjoyments, and they indulged their moods to their hearts con-tent.   When, reluctantly, they set out on the homeward trail, they carried back a treasure pack of glowing memories which were unloosed with verbal eloquence at the Club's annual sup-per.   The supper was usually arranged during February in one of the larger cities of the state.   Being attended by a score or more of celebrities and another score or more of near-celebrities, it was accorded wide newspaper publicity in several eastern states.   A substantial menu of good food and good wine, glad reunions and jolly exchanges of enthusiasms, and a program of toasts and responses were the principal features.   The toasts were poetic, sincere utterances which did ample justice to the

natural beauties of the Adirondacks. Many happy echoes
from the Fulton Chain's past are encountered in their perusal,
and several are reprinted here.   The first is a profound testimonial to the Club's choice of its vacation land:

> "John Brown's Tract: An excellent work by the Author
> of all good and perfect gifts.   We are made better men,
> and better Christians, by our annual study and examina-
> tion of its sublime and beautiful contents."

What utterance of like brevity could proclaim the glory of
the wilderness more eloquently than the following outbursts
of poesy:

> "Our Spring Excursion: The sunlight of June, the north-
> ward journey, the fatiguing tramp, the misty mountains,
> the rushing streams, the gleaming camp fires, the cozy
> cabin, the refreshing slumber, and the blissful dream.
> Welcome to the Walton heart."

> "The Moose River Chain of Lakes: Each separate in
> itself, yet fed from the same fountain and linked to-
> gether by crystal streams.   May the hearts of the Walton
> Club resemble them in their purity, and mingle together
> in fellowship, like their peaceful waters."

No less a genius and gallant than the poet-librarian, Alfred
B. Street, responded to the toast to the ladies, ever absent from
the wilderness, but every present in the hearts of the chival-
rous.

> "The Ladies: Barred out of the forest by vindictive crin-
> oline. We miss their presence there, but we see their
> bright glances in the glowing sky of morning.   We hear
> their voices in the music of the woodland bird, and inhale
> their sweet breath in the fragrant zephyrs of the silent
> woods."

The fervency of the foregoing sentiment clearly indicates
that its Waltonian author must have loved, not only a lake,
but also a lass.   The ladies are also the theme of the next toast.
This seems to have been composed by a gentleman of mature
years and somber experience, for a hint of retribution is

tinctured with only a moderate trace of adulation.

> "The Ladies: The only reason why they are kept out of our Northern Wilderness, the Eden of the New World, is that their old mother cheated us out of the Eden of the Old. May that millenium soon be inaugurated that shall return them to their primitive station in our newly discovered Eden."

The hope of the mature-minded member has been only partially fulfilled. The ladies have long since taken possession of the New Eden, but certainly no evidence of a primitive station can be discerned in their fair conceits as they merrily disport amid the beauties of the mountains. Prophecy fails utterly in the following toast, as innumerable squatters, ejected from their humble cabins nearly fifty years later, would have testified with some bitterness:

> "The Shanties of the Hunter and Fisherman: Though humble and lowly, they are the abodes of freedom and good will. The sun and rain may enter them, but the foot of the oppressor, never."

A thought of conservation finds its way into the next several toasts. The moose and eagle mentioned in the first vanished many years ago, but trout and deer continue to thrive abundantly.

> "The Mountains and Lakes of the Empire State: The habitations of the moose, the eagle, the red deer, and the trout; the uncontaminated temples of God. May they never be desecrated by the feet of the "money changers and those who sell doves."

> "Our Deer Friends in the Mountains: May they never receive visits from any but gentlemen, and may the visits made them be at seasonable times, and under proper circumstances."

> "The Northwoods: The Central Park of the Empire State. May it always remain to be the center of our enjoyments."

> "The Red Deer of the Mountains: The creatures of pure

airs, bright sunshine, sweet herbage, and untainted breath: may no murderous band ever drive them from their mountain home."

"The Great Hunting Park of the Empire State: With the members of our Club for its Park Commissioners, it shall forever outshine all the parks in the world in its unrivaled beauty."

"Our Northern Wilderness: The Trout's Paradise, an unrivaled Deer Park: may the choice game of its woods and waters find protection against all who wantonly kill trout and deer out of season, in the judicious laws of our legislators; may no screeching locomotive ever startle its Fauns and Water Sprites; the people of the Empire State need just such a vast and noble preserve—may no present or future attempt to clear and settle it meet with success."

Grim shadows of civil war were lengthening across the nation's horizon as the merry Waltonians hunted, fished and banqueted. They were not unmindful, however, of their country's perplexities, nor of the ominous question "free or slave." Several Southerners were included in the membership of the Club. A single reference to national difficulties, forbearing and fraternal in its treatment of a delicate subject, appears in the program toasts:

"The Fishing Line: Though in these troublous times Mason and Dixon's line may keep our countrymen apart, yet the fishing line shall bring them together again in love when the sunlight of spring unlocks the streams of the North, and our Southern brethren come among us once more."

Seventh Lake takes a bow as a poetic admirer responds with a laudation, more fervent than tactful. It may have started a spirited argument among the members, each of whom professed loyalty to a favorite lake:

"Seventh Lake: Brightest gem of that chain of jewels that sparkle on the breast of John Brown's Tract."

It is as unfailing a practice of good sportsmen to toast good guides as it is to roast bad ones, and the Waltonians were not exceptional in the matter:

"Our Guides: Their willing endurance and toil in the Northwoods, in contributing to our comfort and hap- piness, entitle them to our gratitude, and our best wishes for their health and prosperity through life."

General Sherman was nothing if not a thoroughly versatile and efficient executive. Not only did he organize the Club, counsel it wisely, and serve as its first president, but he wrote its gathering song as well, "We are a Band of Brothers," a composition of fourteen verses set to the buoyant strain of an old hunting ballad. The Waltonian presence was unmistak- able when members young and old, vocally gifted and other- wise, joined its rollicking chorus that swelled the enthusiasm of every Club gathering. It was sung by clergymen, physi- cians, lawyers, authors, editors, financiers; by half a hundred notables, Honorables, Governors, and members of both Houses of the National Congress. They were all of the same band, brothers of a rare cult whose temple was the forest.

In camp, each squad or subdivision of membership sang with valiant harmony around the nightly camp fire that blazed at the water's edge. Before the outbreak of the Civil War, "We Are a Band of Brothers" echoed over the quiet waters of the Fulton Chain when not a semblance of a permanent human habitation stood on its shores. Its melody broke the evening calm of Big Moose Lake when no listeners were at hand except the singers themselves. On a score of lakes, large and small, Northerner and Southerner alike joined its chorus before the controversial institution of slavery weakened the bond of Club brotherhood.

The fourteen verses of the song are reprinted here because of their Central Adirondack origin, and consequent interest to that locality.

"WE ARE A BAND OF BROTHERS."
We flee from the care and striving,

Of the crowds in cities hiving,
From their bicker and conniving,
    To our happy wild wood's home.

        We are a band of brothers,
        We are a band of brothers,
        We are a band of brothers,
        Of the Isaac Walton Clan.

With gladsome laugh and shouting,
We hie to lake and mountain,
And by pleasant grove and fountain,
    Make our happy wild wood's home.
        We are a band of brothers, etc.

Here we spend our time of leisure,
In the sunny summer weather,
Finding daily some new pleasure,
    In our happy wild wood's home.
        We are a band of brothers, etc.

Of bark we build our shantee,
We make it trim and jaunty,
But we aim at nothing flaunty,
    In our happy wild wood's home.
        We are a band of brothers, etc.

Though we've no beds of feather,
We fear not wind nor weather,
Resting on the fragrant heather,
    In our happy wild wood's home.
        We are a band of brothers, etc.

Our sleep is sound and freshing,
Our stomach's crave good messing,

We pay small heed to dressing,
    In our happy wild wood's home.
        We are a band of brothers, etc.

We fear not flies nor punkies,
They frighten only flunkies,
Cocknies, fops, and other monkies,
    In our happy wild wood's home.
        We are a band of brothers, etc.

We fish with rod and angle,
And though oft our lines may tangle,
We never fight nor wrangle,
    In our happy wild wood's home.
        We are a band of brothers, etc.

Great skill we do not boast of,
Yet trout we take a host of,
And these we eat the most of,
    In our happy wild wood's home.
        We are a band of brothers, etc.

Our Nimrods, true and stable,
With venison too, are able,
To heap our rustic table,
    In our happy wild wood's home.
        We are a band of brothers, etc.

No rankling care or sorrow,
Nor thoughts of duns tomorrow,
Nor troubles aught we borrow,
    In our happy wild wood's home.
        We are a band of brothers, etc.

Exempt from strife and railing,
With spirits never failing,
We fear no ill nor ailing,
    In our happy wild wood's home.
        We are a band of brothers, etc.

Now three cheers altogether,
Shout the Walton Club forever,
Our true hearts none can sever,
    From the Isaac Walton Clan,
        Huzza! Huzza! Huzza!

Like our comrades gone before us,
We will shout and sing the chorus,
Till through the heavens o'er us,
    Resounds the loud huzza!
        Huzza! Huzza! Huzza!

With citizens so influential and widely scattered turning to the wilderness for relaxation, public curiosity turned with them. The activities of the Club became matters of state wide speculation and served to direct attention to the scenic charm and native recreational facilities of the Brown's Tract, which its pamphlet had described as "lying in the heart of the wilderness, studded with majestic mountains, gemmed throughout by crystal lakes, and swarming with game peculiar to the wilds of Northern New York." The members were no less enthusiastic than the pamphlet, and the lavish, though deserving praise they bestowed upon the scene of their rough and ready outings was given conspicuous space in the news columns of the daily press. Their annual egressions from the woods were viewed somewhat in the nature of an exploring party returning to civilization with graphic accounts of a beautiful, newly discovered continent.

The activities of the Walton Club first directed favorable at-tion to the region through the publication of a series of letters enumerating the members' experiences in the woods. These were originally published in the fall of 1857 under the title "Wild Wood Notes, by Scope" and were reprinted later in a number of journals. Of course, no influx of visitors to the woods resulted from all this publicity. The way was still too long and rough for any except confirmed sportsmen, but the publicity exerted a noticeable influence on public opinion. Slowly the picture of the Adirondacks underwent transformation, and a number of citizens began revising their conceptions of the Northwoods even though refusing to visit them. In time the barren, "musquito and midge" infested wilderness of the Brown's Tract became known for what it was, "studded with majestic mountains and gemmed throughout with crystal lakes," beckoning the stout hearted adventurer to a new world of beauty and joy.

To the Northwoods Walton Club must be credited the inspiration for another novelty in Adirondack affairs—the development of the privately owned sporting preserve. Following his several years' association with the Club, and several years more of active interest in the woods after the organization ceased to exist, General Sherman organized the Bisby Club in 1878. It was a natural outgrowth of the Waltonians, and most of its twenty-five charter members had belonged to that now defunct association. Changed conditions, more people coming into the woods, and even more likely to come each year, influenced the twenty-five to insure their reasonable privacy in the future by purchasing a tract of heavily wooded land. The tract lay in Township One of the Moose River Tract, about ten miles south of the site of Old Forge, and bordered First Bisby Lake. At the lower end of the lake the members erected a clubhouse. The transaction was the first purchase of Adirondack realty for the purpose of establishing a private club preserve. Several similar preserves have been established since, some much larger than Bisby, such as the Lake Placid Club and the Adirondack League Club. Henry J. Cookinham, the longest surviving member of the original Bisby incorpo-rators, died in Utica in 1931.

In selecting a name for their new Club the members deferred to the lake on which their land fronted. Bisby Lake derives its name from an Oneida County farmer who, like old Rip Van Winkle, preferred trout streams to corn fields. Farmer Bisby was a zealous angler but an unskilled woodsman. His only claim to woodsmanship was a bulging squirrel cap which he wore summer and winter, deeming it the proper article of headwear for discriminating sportsmen such as he considered himself to be. Early in the nineteenth century he made fre-quent trips into the woods, always accompanied by Nelson Grant, a guide, as he could never find his way out of the forest alone. The then unnamed Bisby Lake was his favorite resort, and there he tarried weeks at a time to the irreparable ruin of his crops and fences. Although his acquaintances did not adopt his style of headdress, they did apply his name to the lake of his avowed preference. In 1893, Bisby Club was merged with the Adirondack League Club, and is now one of the three club communities within the League's extensive preserve.

A single interesting fact remains which is worthy of men-tion before bidding adieu to the Waltonians. None of the members ever employed the name "Adirondacks" to des-ignate the mountains to which their annual pilgrimages were directed. They used only the terms "Brown's Tract," "North-ern Wilderness," "Wilderness" and "Northwoods." Adiron-dacks, as a generic name applicable to the series of ranges which form the topographical features of New York's vast contiguous tract of forest, had not yet come into common usage. Headley's story of travel in the wilderness, published in 1849, included the word "Adirondac" to designate the region, but Sylvester, twenty-eight years later, decried its use. When so well informed a group as the Waltonians had no familiarity with the now internationally known name "Adirondacks," it is readily apparent how slow was the process by which the term came into popular usage.

VIII

EARLY CAMPS

To place the finger of discovery upon facts pertaining to the building and the builder of the first camp in the region under discussion is, obviously, an utterly impossible task. For nearly two hundred years, white men, beaver-like in their habit of building shelters, have erected habitations ranging the architectural scale from brush or bark shanties to spacious lodges. The term "camp," as hereafter employed in this chapter, will refer, therefore, only to so-called permanent structures, enclosed on all sides, roofed, designed and equipped for many years' occupancy, and of substantial construction. The improvised brush or bark open shanty, as well as the more sturdily built lean-to of logs will not be considered in this classification. Structures erected during the John Brown and Herreshoff developments will be excluded also, primarily because of their lack of association with, and influence upon, the now more clearly perceived destiny of the region, and secondly, for the cogent reason that what little is known of them has already been told.

With few exceptions the earliest camps, both public and private, were built and occupied by squatters, woodsmen who knowingly entered upon others' lands without authority to effect improvements that would work to their personal profit. A good deal of the region's early growth as a resort section can be traced to this class of pioneer builders. Land owners tacitly sanctioned these trespasses, reasoning that the least expensive approach to the problem of enhancing the value of wilderness tracts lay in awaiting their development by squatters before enforcing their own rights to ownership. Their logic was sound enough, but most of them spent a long time waiting. Not until the nineteenth century was drawing to a close did it become expedient to make the fact known to camp owners that, after all, the land owner really owned the land, and that the squatter was only a squatter.

Early camps in the region came into existence slowly, over a period of years. The first was built just before the outbreak of the Civil War. It stood on a small clearing on the north shore of Third Lake, in front and a few rods to the east, of the present Bald Mountain House site. A one and one-half story log structure, containing three small rooms, it was the show place of the Fulton Chain. Its tiny water-front gable loomed palatially in contrast to any former architectural effort in the locality. Furnished throughout by a masculine Northwoods housekeeper of bark shanty experience, its equipment included essential paraphernalia for cooking, eating and sleeping—but nothing more. An ample guest room was made available by laying flat boards on the overhead cross beams. Women who were bold enough to accompany their husbands on fishing trips to the place occupied the upper chamber as sleeping quarters, while their husbands stretched themselves on wall bunks below, or on the floor.

Charles Grant, of Boonville, the builder and owner of the camp, was a surveyor by profession and a carefree sort of woodsman by inclination. Lyman R. Lyon employed him to establish lines in Township Seven, and after completing the job Charlie spent more time in the woods hunting and fishing than he did in following his calling. The result was that he and his profession eventually parted. After building his camp, he renounced the measurements and calculations of surveyorship to set himself up as a guide and purveyor to sportsmen. The camp proved to be a snug little haven to Fulton Chain visitors. Although Charlie made no pretense of conducting it as an inn, letters still in existence tell of happy times spent in the Grant camp, or in the "old Grant camp," thus indicating its popularity among visitors of former years.

Charlie, unfortunately, did not live many years to enjoy the luxury his handiwork had created. A cold, untimely death brought his career to a sudden close. Early in the morning of April 8th, 1868, he left Boonville, intending to walk to the

Fulton Chain by way of Moose River Settlement and the Brown's Tract Road. The day was bitter with unseasonable cold, and deep crusted snow still lingered in the woods and on the road. He stopped at the Settlement for mid-day dinner, and though wearied by his morning's tramp, he shouldered his pack to begin the twelve rough miles that would bring him to the Arnold home. Along the way he paused to rest from time to time. Never for long at first, however, for he was eager to push on, anxious to reach the clearing before dark. But the rest periods became more frequent and of longer duration as he proceeded; he grew steadily wearier, the pack more burdensome. Within two miles of the Manor he met Ed Arnold. Ed's mother had been stricken with a sudden critical illness, and he had left home on a hurried twenty-five mile night march to summon a Boonville doctor. The two friends halted for a moment's chat, Ed explaining his errand in a few brief sentences. Charlie inquired if he carried food. He was hungry and tired, he said, and would welcome something to eat or drink. Ed had neither. He was travelling light, but he heartily urged his hungry friend to fill up well when he reached the Manor. Then they parted, Ed heading swiftly toward Boonville, and Charlie staggering slowly the other way. A mile from the clearing he stopped for the last time, to rest beside a giant spruce that loomed invitingly above its fellows. The wind had died, and the dark green foliage of the spruce boughs formed a motionless, protecting arch across the road. In the meantime, dusk had settled on the forest, a glittering, starry twilight, deadly cold, but infinitely soothing to the tired man who dozed at the base of the great tree. A traveller found him there in the morning, seated in restful posture against the tree—frozen rigid. Awed by the discovery, the traveller hurried to Moose River with the news, and John Brinkerhoff with several friends returned to the scene with a handsled to bring the dead woodsman back to his last resting place in Boonville.

The unfortunate happening caused more than the usual stir

attending similar tragedies. A coroner's jury reviewed the facts following a post-mortem examination and an inspection of the Brown's Tract Road and death scene. Then it announced its finding, "death from natural cause." Public opinion demurred. Was it "natural" for one man to leave another helplessly exhausted to die by the roadside. The public eye stared meaningly at Ed Arnold. He had encountered and abruptly parted from the deceased shortly before his death. Why had he failed to succor his desperately spent friend. A few newspapers looked into the matter and one inquired editorially if there had not been a deliberate violation of a fundamental, unwritten law of the wilderness for which the violator could be called to account.

Thunderstruck at this turn of affairs, Ed hastened to his own defense. He explained that the deceased had in no manner intimated the degree of fatigue which had overcome him beyond the simple and comparatively unimportant admission of hunger and weariness—twin discomforts which commonly afflict woodsmen on the march. Within two miles of their meeting place stood the Arnold house, a modest distance which any normally tired or hungry woodsman could travel with ease. Ed's own mission, a race in the night against the threat of death to his mother, had distracted his faculties from the observation of any symptoms of exhaustion which Charlie might have shown.

Ed's version, frankly told, transformed the public's attitude from condemnation to approval. Even the most vehement, though least enlightened, of his accusers readily absolved him of culpability when the facts were made known.

Poor, honest, hospitable Ed! That long remembered, much discussed trip to Boonville proved to be as fruitless as it was vexatious. As he stood beside the open grave of his mother a few weeks later he pondered the matter in grieving self-reproach. Perhaps if he had tarried companionably with Charlie a little longer he might have detected the weakness his friend had tried so bravely to conceal. Perhaps, too, if he had hurried just a little faster on his long errand through the night he might have saved his stricken mother., His was a painful cross fire of regrets.

Several years after Charlie's death, Albert Buell, of Roches-ter, purchased the Grant place, and in 1881 leased it to Robert Perrie, of Utica. "Bob," as the new tenant became known, built a two story hotel adjoining the cabin. He installed a bar in the cabin, well stocked with liquid merchandise, which won quick popularity among the non-abstemious. In 1888 he pur-chased the place from Albert Buell, and continued in the hotel business until he sold out to Charles M. Barrett in 1893.

Although several men preceded Bob in building and operat-ing public camps in the region, his venture is of peculiar his-torical interest for a number of reasons. He was the first hotel proprietor whose association with the business was not the out-growth of a prolonged local residence, and whose previous occupation was other than guiding. Bob had been employed by a Utica department store for a number of years, and his business interests were limited to the fineries of feminine attire. In 1880 he spent his first extended mountain vacation in a log lean-to on Little Moose Lake in the interest of his wife's health. After one summer spent on the lake, the improvement in Mrs. Perrie's condition convinced Bob of the wisdom of remaining in the Adirondacks.

Bob was by no means a babe in the woods. He possessed considerably more than average skill as an angler, and had spent several annual vacations fishing the waters of the Fulton Chain. He was a skilful maker of artificial bait; his products were used extensively by visiting fishermen, and in time ac-quired a reputation beyond the borders of the Adirondacks. An excellent class of sportsmen and their ladies patronized the place. They enjoyed his companionship on fishing excursions and around the evening fire, and he enjoyed theirs. All in all, the abrupt transition from fashions to fishing and inn keeping was a congenial as well as historical change for the new host.

Bob gained another distinction by becoming identified with

The Grant Camp in 1869. Ed. Arnold and John Brinckerhoff at left.

MR. AND MRS. BENJAMIN STICKNEY

early Fulton Chain affairs. He was the first local managing-owner of a hotel with a legal right to occupy the premises of his business. Other camps offering entertainment to the public under the personal management of their builders antedated Perrie's, of course. But they were operated by squatters who enjoyed but a precarious tenure of their camp sites. (The Forge House was built in 1871 on legally acquired land. During the early years of its existence it was operated under lease by a succession of proprietors, but not by its owners). After selling his hotel, Bob made his home in a small private camp on the lower North Shore of Fourth Lake. There he continued to manufacture bait, never becoming so absorbed in his craft that he overlooked an opportunity of personally testing its product whenever a congenial fishing party hove into view.

Charles Barrett utilized the old Grant cabin and the two story Perrie addition for the accommodation of guests until he had built his new and more elaborate hotel, the Bald Mountain House. The two unoccupied buildings were then moved to the rear of the new hotel where they filled a variety of needs until demolished several years later.

Dull days in the Adirondacks followed the building of the Grant camp before a second log cabin made its appearance on the Fulton Chain shore. The Civil War had worked havoc with the recently awakened popular interest in the wilderness, for national attention became centered on the pressing business of feeding armies and winning battles. In 1866, interest revived, and in the spring of that year Benjamin Stickney, of St. Louis, built a camp on a point of land extending from the North Shore into the head of First Lake of the Fulton Chain.

More pretentious than the Grant Camp which preceded it, the Stickney cabin was designed to comfortably house its owner and a group of friends who usually vacationed with him. Stationary bunks fastened to the walls accommodated six sleepers, and a second cabin, erected at the rear of the main camp, sheltered the several guides who served the party each summer. The construction work was done by John Brinckerhoff, Clinton

Grant, Josiah Helmer and Chauncey Noble, all of Boonville.

The new camp owner, like Charlie Grant, entered into the annual enjoyment of his summer home with no more than a squatter's claim to the premises. But the cost factor played no part in determining his choice of a camp site, for he was one of St. Louis' wealthiest citizens and could have bought and paid for the entire acreage of Township Seven without taxing his resources in the least.

Benjamin was born in Newburyport, Mass., in 1808, one of ten children. In 1820 his parents moved to Boonville and the twelve year old boy trudged the entire distance beside the lumbering ox cart that carried the family possessions. He re- turned to Massachusetts a few years later in search of favor- able opportunities to begin business life, and found employment in the Bromfield House, Boston. During the next ten years he established the fact of his genius in hotel management to his own and his employer's satisfaction. In 1836, St. Louis claimed his attention and he moved there, eager to cast his lot with the fortunes of that growing river metropolis. Five years later, assisted financially by a friend whose interest he subsequently purchased, he built the Planters Hotel, a magnificent hostelry for its day, four stories high and extending the length of a city block. Under his personal management the place became na- tionally known for the modish, cheerful character of its hos- pitality, and St. Louis was quick to appraise and proclaim the civic usefulness of its progressive inn-keeping citizen. Other branches of commerce and industry attracted him through the years until he became prominently identified with business ven- tures in railroad, banking and utility fields. His natural graci- ousness of manner, unwavering integrity and sound business acumen, and his practical, generous philanthropies won for him many life-long friends from the nation-wide ranks of his acquaintances.

In 1846, Benjamin returned for his first vacation on the Ful- ton Chain. As Ben Stickney, the Boonville boy, he had once tramped with his father deep into the Adirondacks, exploring many miles of Moose River country in quest of moose and other game which tempted sober-minded farmers such as his father to occasional tests of marksmanship in the forest. The picture of cool waters and refreshing woods, encountered on that expedition, lingered to haunt his memory during the hard, vacationless years in which he toiled steadily upward to the heights of success. When he considered his material position established securely enough to permit of relaxation, he placed the management of his affairs in the hands of an assistant, and started northward.

For twenty consecutive years he summered in open bark shanties along the Fulton Chain before building his First Lake camp. Each succeeding year found the humble little shack at the water's edge a more welcome refuge from life in a broiling city than it had been the year before, for St. Louis was becoming far hotter than a mere thermometer reading could indicate. A border-line trade center between North and South, its citizens torn in their attitude toward slavery, it became a city beset by incessant partisan haranguings. From the North came statesmen, business and social personages, crusaders, all enemies of slavery; from the South came gentlemen of landed estates, courteous, lovable, influential Southerners whose fortunes depended on the continued legality of negro bondage. They all gathered at the Planters, all argued the question, all lost their hair-trigger tempers, and invariably brought the sweat of anguish to the brow of their distracted host.

When the stage coach from Rome or Utica, after traversing the dusty road to Boonville, drew up at the Hulbert House to discharge its cargo of annually returning vacationists, Benjamin Stickney alighted with a deep sigh of relief—the anguish gone from his brow. St. Louis was far away, and he would soon be at peace beside the calm, untroubled waters of the Adirondacks.

While temporarily forgetting his troubles, he didn't forget the country whom they concerned so vitally. Each year his vacation baggage included a new American flag of gleaming silk. Proudly bearing this banner on his own shoulders, accompanied by his guests and guides, he climbed Bald Mountain after the first night in camp.   There he solemnly affixed it to a pole atop the highest crag of "Mount St. Louis," the name he applied to the mountain during his 1846 vacation.   The new flag raised, the uncovered company faced its streaming colors to sing "The Star Spangled Banner."   Sometimes vocal harmony prevailed, and sometimes it didn't, depending upon the current gathering's musical gifts, but no matter—the occasions never lacked ringing sincerity.   This ceremonial continued annually without interruption for twenty-five years.   It was the only formality of camp life except religious worship. Mount St. Louis clung in designation of the bold cliff as long and as firmly as the silken banners clung to their staffs.   As late as 1876, Verplanck Colvin referred to Bald Mountain as "Mount St. Louis" on his maps and in his topographical survey reports which he submitted to the legislature.

Benjamin Stickney was by no means a too exacting employer of guides, but he was fortunate in having several of the best to serve him each summer.   John Brinckerhoff, described by A. Judd Northrup as "a guide with the face of a general," was born at Turin, Lewis County, in 1827.   His father, Gilbert, had roamed the Adirondacks early in the century, and as a youth, John eagerly followed in his father's footsteps.   He became a masterful though exceptionally modest woodsman, thorough in every undertaking on behalf of sportsmen whose safety and convenience were entrusted to his care.   His companionable personality found its way to the hearts of his charges by easy strides.   Inevitably, the name and fame of "General John" were carried back to civilization to become inseparably associated with pleasant reveries of Adirondack camp life.   John never uttered extravagant promises, never boasted of his prowess, never talked himself into a job, and never failed to give the fullest possible measure of service to his employers.

Jonathan Meeker, born the same year on a small farm on the outskirts of Boonville, made one too many expeditions into the woods in early youth. The result was that his boyish affections were weaned from his inherited vocation of agriculture, and concentrated on the practice of woodcraft. With the yearly hayingtime arrival of the Stickney party in Boonville, Jonathan discarded the pitchfork in quick contempt for this ageold symbol of agriculture, and hastened to join the forestbound cavalcade of vacationists. The Hanna members of the party, distinguished Ohioans, were especially fond of Jonathan. They gladly paid his salary in the woods in addition to several weeks' compensation for a hired man to take his place on the farm. This twice paid woodsman was well worth his wage. He was strong and skilful, eager to serve well, and thoroughly dependable.

Alonzo Wood hailed from the shores of Lake George, where he was born in 1839. At the age of seven he moved with his parents to Raquette Lake. It was a family migration which brought the father, Josiah, into historical prominence as the first white pioneer to settle there. In 1848, Alonzo's brother, Jerome, also became historically interesting by being the first white child born on Raquette Lake's shores. The Wood family grew rapidly with the arrival of six other children—Martha, Samantha, Amy, Cynthia, Harriet and William.

Alonzo took to the woods as a duck takes to water. He lost no time familiarizing himself with the waterways and ridges in the vicinity of his home, and each year he wandered farther afield. While still a very young man he was known as a well informed guide, equally acquainted with the topography of eastern and western sections of the mountains. His trips down the Fulton Chain, guiding travellers to the Arnold clearing, brought him in contact with his future bride, Ophelia Arnold, who, as a babe in arms, had been brought to the clearing by her parents in 1837. Having conducted a party to the Arnold's in the fall of 1857, Alonzo undertook the weightier responsibility of conducting Ophelia along the Brown's Tract Road to a Boonville parsonage. It was a rough trip to the altar, but the result fully justified the effort. The union lasted fifty-five years. It was severed by the death of Ophelia, on Fourth Lake, in 1912.

Paul Jones, for many years the Stickney camp cook, knew the acclaim due a bewhiskered, horny-handed woodsman who could evolve incomparable delicacies from the combination of skillet, brook trout and biscuit dough. His skill at the camp fire added much savory relish to the summers' enjoyments, and his appreciative employer overlooked no opportunity of boasting of the fact to his St. Louis acquaintances.

In 1868, Samuel J. Niccolls, a young clergyman, accompanied Benjamin Stickney to his Fulton Chain camp on his first trip to the Adirondacks. Three years before he had been called to the pastorate of the influential Second Presbyterian Church, of St. Louis, whose congregation included a large number of the city's prominent residents. The summer of 1868 which he spent on First Lake was the beginning of a long series of yearly visits to the lake which ended only with his death in 1915. (1915 was a memorable anniversary for Dr. Niccolls. At that time he had completed fifty consecutive years as pastor of the St. Louis church, and forty-seven years' association with the Adirondacks as a Fulton Chain vacationist).

Dr. Niccolls was born in Westmoreland County, Pa., in 1838. He was graduated from Washington and Jefferson College in 1857, from Western Theological Seminary in 1860, and ordained at the age of twenty-two. His first parish was in a small community near his Pennsylvania birthplace. In 1861, he joined the Union Army as a chaplain, and served four years. During the war he maintained a sort of long distance spiritual supervision over the parish he had deserted at the time of his enlistment. In 1865 he answered the call from St. Louis to become pastor of the Second Presbyterian Church with which Benjamin Stickney was affiliated. Mutual admiration, which lasted a lifetime, took form between the two men. Despite the disparity in their ages they became inseparable cronies in both St. Louis and the Adirondacks.

Dr. Niccolls' spiritual fervor was as much a part of his life in the woods as it was in the city. Each Sunday he conducted a simple out-door service in front of the Stickney camp. Often the congregation included only the camp members and their guides, but in later years, neighboring campers frequently landed at the point to attend the service. For a number of years Mrs. Stickney joined her husband on his summer pilgrimages to the woods. She contributed to the cause of religious expression by playing a small portable organ which had been brought to the camp from St. Louis at the time of her first visit. The organ remained in use long after the Stickneys had passed away. Dr. Niccolls, who survived his two friends nearly forty years, continued to conduct services on the point or in neighboring resort hotels until religious groups in the region were formally organized into church congregations. At times the Sunday morning gatherings on the point assumed the numerical proportions of a village congregation which warranted the pitching of a large tent in front of the camp on days of inclement weather. Two little wood-burning steamers, the Hunter and Fulton, sometimes skirted the shores of the Fulton Chain to transport worshippers from remote camps to the Stickney Point. After the services, members of the congregation lingered under the trees to exchange gossip of the week's happenings much in the manner of after-gatherings of country parishes where agricultural and country-side social affairs are discussed. On the Stickney Point, however, gossip usually pertained to such matters as the big fish that got away and the deer that walked right up to the camp door.

Benjamin Stickney died in November, 1875, and regretfully the Fulton Chain knew his benign figure no more. His passing was widely mourned, but no one, perhaps, mourned his loss more deeply than Dr. Niccolls, to whom fell the grievous lot of officiating at his beloved friend's burial service. From the St. Louis Republican, dated November 20th of that year, comes a hint of the pathos that must have marked the ministerial function on that occasion:

"The funeral of the late Benjamin Stickney took place yesterday afternoon and was largely attended. Mr. Stickney was a member of the Second Presbyterian Church, and a warm personal friend of its revered pastor. It was therefore no ordinary duty of his high calling which Dr. Niccolls was yesterday required to perform, and the emotion which frequently choked his utterance in the course of the service, and the remarks which followed, revealed to an impressive degree the close ties of friendship binding the two men together."

Dr. Niccolls continued to vacation at Stickney Point, which in time became known as "Niccolls Point."   After Lyman R. Lyon's death in 1869, his three daughters, Julia, Mary and Florence, had deeded the point to Benjamin Stickney, and after the latter's death, the Stickney heirs deeded it to Dr. Niccolls. It is now owned by Mrs. May Geyer, the daughter of Julia Lyon and William Scott de Camp, who maintains her summer home there.

The well known Stickney fondness for the Adirondacks stimulated vacation traffic between St. Louis and the Fulton Chain. Shortly after Benjamin's death, Samuel Dodd, another prominent resident of that city visited First Lake. He shared temporarily with James and A. W. Soper, of Chicago, a camp which had been built on the lower shore of the lake by Thomas Griffin several years before. Following the organization of the Adirondack League Club in 1890, he built a camp on Little Moose Lake. From time to time other residents of St. Louis visited the locality, and a pretentious colony of Missourians soon established itself on the Fulton Chain.

John Brinckerhoff remained with Dr. Niccolls until failing health forced his retirement from active life in the woods. He was succeeded by several able woodsmen in turn, Oscar Wood, William Weedmark, Ben Sperry and George Villiere. George remained with him until the summer of 1915, when the venerable clergyman died suddenly while participating in a day's outing on the League Club preserve. He was seventy-seven

Perrie's Hotel in the Eighties. Bewhiskered proprietor is seated at lower right.

The Stickney Camp, First Lake of the Fulton Chain.

DR. NICCOLLS AND SAMUEL DODD

A. W. Soper (left) and Samuel Dodd (right) with a party of First Lake Campers. Guides standing: Gus Syphert, Merrill White, Phil Christy. Photo by Mary Linden Dodd.

The Cold Spring Camp, Fourth Lake.

at the time of his death. To perpetuate his memory locally, the Old Forge Community Church, in dedicating its new church structure in 1918, applied the name "Niccolls Memorial Church." Dr. Niccolls preached his last sermon in Old Forge, having occupied the pulpit of the Community Church the Sunday before he died.

The Snyder camp, the third to be built on the Fulton Chain and the first on Fourth Lake, was built in 1869 by Jack Sheppard and Sam Dunakin for H. D. Snyder, of Port Leyden, a member of the Snyder Brothers tanning firm. It was located on the lower North Shore of the lake near a spring that bubbled from the ground in a stream of crystal-clear water a few rods from the shore. The spring, famous among guides for the satisfying quality of its water, had long been known as "Cold Spring," and the Snyder Camp, borrowing the good name of its bubbling little neighbor, became known as "Cold Spring Camp." The Snyders occupied the camp for several seasons after which it passed to other owners. George May, a Boonville and Herkimer hotel man and a jovial, straight-shooting sportsman, owned it for a number of years. He sold it in 1912 to Otto M. Eidlitz, a New York business man who re-built it into a commodious summer home.

Cold Spring—the water, not the building—takes precedence over the camp in historical interest, due to its having furnished the site for the first structure in the region designed for artificial fish culture. In 1885, a building 20 x 36 feet, scientifically equipped for pisciculture, was erected on a plot one hundred feet from the spring. A supply of water was conveyed to it through a three inch wrought iron pipe. The building and equipment were designed by General Richard U. Sherman, State Fish Commissioner, and Seth Green, dean of American fish culturists, who was at that time the Superintendent of the Caledonia State Hatchery. When completed, the hatchery became known as the "Fulton Chain Hatching House." It was not a State project, but owed its origin and maintenance to the Boonville Sportsmen's Club and to local guides and visiting sportsmen who were eager to preserve the piscatory fame of the region's waters.

In spite of its eminent parentage, and a host of friends deeply concerned with its welfare, the infant hatchery proved to be a weakling. It functioned for two years, but with less than moderate success, due chiefly to the water entering the troughs without having undergone a sufficiently animating process of aeration. In 1887, the building and its contents were rafted down the Fulton Chain, skidded around the dam at Old Forge, and set up as a gift to the state, on the site of the present hatchery. A section of it still remains incorporated in the hatchery building which the state now maintains. It is well to mention here that the propagation of fish by artificial methods in the Adirondacks did not originate in the Cold Spring Hatchery. Local pioneering in this highly useful science was done by Emmett Marks, one of Seth Green's Caledonia proteges, who, at this writing (1931) resides in Old Forge. In 1878, Emmett improvised a small hatchery under the sawmill adjoining the Old Forge dam, and in the spring of that year successfully hatched several thousand trout from eggs which he had transported from Caledonia. Like the Cold Spring Hatchery, his operations were financed by the Boon-ville Sportsmen's Club.

The Pratt Camp, built in 1870 for Charles Pratt of New York, was the fourth of the region's permanent structures. It stood on the upper South Shore of Fourth Lake, between the sites of the present New Neodak and Ara-ho hotels. A hewn log structure of rustic design, it was built by the old reliable firm of Jack and Sam who, it seems, achieved a temporary monopoly on the erection of camps.

At the time of its construction, Charles Pratt was making history in the petroleum industry—perfecting his "Astral Oil," a medium of illumination which became known in all the principal markets of the world. He had pioneered in oil when the great fields of Pennsylvania were just beginning to hint of their vast, unprobed stores, and before his death in 1891 he had witnessed the rise of this commodity to a dominant position in international trade. After the merger of his interests with Rockefeller's (which became the Standard Oil Company), he devoted a substantial part of his huge fortune to philanthropic enterprises. The most noted institution of his benevolent founding, the Pratt Institute, has furnished vocational training and other educational advantages to thousands of impecunious students.

Charles Pratt and members of his family made use of the camp for more than thirty-five years, after which it was utilized as a vacation place for certain persons connected with the Pratt institute. After serving this purpose for several years, the building was demolished, and the land passed from the family ownership.

IX

THE FORGE HOUSE

THE Forge House, built within a stone's throw of the old forge, and named for it, came into existence as a product of the first deliberately conceived plan of providing hotel entertainment for Fulton Chain travellers and vacationists. Coupled with the hospitality plan was the development scheme, a contem' plated program of land subdivision designed to evoke profits through the sale of mountain camp sites. The hotel won its way to financial success, and even to fame, but with few excep' tions the profits derived from the development idea proved almost as negligible for all concerned as they had on several previous efforts to wrest a fortune from Adirondack land.

The will of Lyman R. Lyon, who died in 1869, bequeathed his estate of land, moneys and securities to his wife, Mary, and to their five children, Chester, Lyman H., Mary, Florence and Julia. He designated his wife as executrix, and his son Chester, together with his "good and trusty friends," Ela N. Merriam and Stephen Miller, as executors with authority to administer the estate in their discretion.

At about the time of Lyman's death, Dr. George Desbrough of Port Leyden, and J. Milton Buell, both optimistic in their esti' mate of the future of the region, decided that the erection of a hotel at the foot of the Fulton Chain would be a paying prop' osition. The steadily increasing number of travellers to the locality seemed to warrant the introduction of more modern and commodious accommodations than the Arnold house, then conducted by Sanford Sperry, could offer.

Proceeding in harmony with their convictions, the two men purchased from the administrators of the Lyon estate a tract of land embracing 1358 acres (plus a fractional part of an acre), roughly, two square miles, for the published considera' tion of ten thousand dollars, an average price of $7.36 an acre. This tract included all land adjacent to the Forge Pond and the lower extremity of the Moose River flowing into the Pond from First Lake, together with the present lengthy area of Old Forge village and a contiguous plot adjoining on the south. The instrument of title also conveyed to the purchasers the right to raise the dam at the Pond's outlet, but not in excess of three feet additional. The entire plot became known as the "Forge Tract" due to Herreshoff's forging operations having been centrally located on it.

With the initial financial and legal phases of their under-taking settled, the partners began the job of converting the tract into a resort center—a novel enterprise for both men. Dr. Desbrough, in particular, found himself embarking upon a venture which differed sharply in character from his usual occupations. He had begun his professional career as a veter-inarian, and for several years had applied the medical and surgical principles of his cult to the cure of Lewis County live-stock with gratifying results. Being an ambitious man, ever eager for more worlds to conquer, he applied himself to a course of study from which he emerged as a Medical Doctor, an academical achievement which enabled him to at once re-duce the size of his patients, though, it is hoped, not their num-ber. No relationship existed between the Doctor's commercial interest in the Brown's Tract and the mountain rest cures which he occasionally recommended to convalescing patients. For the skeptic's sake it is well to add that he was a man of known integrity, and that he observed the time-honored ethics of his latest and noblest profession as conscientiously as he ap-plied its healing formulas.

After repairing the dam and building a sawmill adjoining it, Buell and Desbrough erected a dwelling house a few hundred feet from the dam to house the workers needed for the con-struction of the hotel. This was the first house to be erected in the old forge area since the time of Herreshoff fifty years before. The site chosen for the hotel lay on a knoll overlooking the Pond. It commanded a vista of river that sparkled invit-ingly between walls of trees before it disappeared eastward through a billowing growth of forest.

At the time these preparations were under way, the Forge Tract was included in the Town of Wilmurt, Herkimer County. The Herkimer County Directory (1869-1870) described Wilmurt as being fifty miles long and sixteen miles wide, the largest Town in the state, but one of the least populous. It contained no industries except a modicum of lumbering and agriculture, which, with its meager population, were limited almost entirely to its southern extremity. A census of 1865 recorded its population as 148, average school attendance 39, and the annual expenditure for school purposes, $761.00.

The first wing of the Forge House was completed and opened to the public in the spring of 1871, and a wing of nearly equal size added the following summer. Its two wing, two and one-half story presence effected a conspicuous change in the landscape, and no sign board was needed to inform travellers that they had reached the shelter of an hostelry. Built of rough sawed, perpendicularly arranged spruce boards, battened at the crevices, it contained thirteen guest rooms, attic accommodations for guides, a parlor, office, servants' quarters, and a bar. Dining room appointments included two long tables, one for the use of guides, the other for the more profitable and consequently more distinguished clientele—sportsmen, tourists and a miscellany of other full-rate visitors. A barn at the rear stabled horses and dairy cattle, and provided storage for vehicles and kennel space for hunting dogs. A rail fence surrounding the hotel grounds permitted the restricted grazing of a few milk cows. Incoming travellers on the Brown's Tract Road encountered the fence near the present busy corner of Old Forge. By letting down a single slim spruce log which formed the gate, they were enabled to drive into the enclosure along the noose-like road that circled the hotel before returning to the gate.

Completed, the Forge House faced an interesting career as the first structure to be erected in the region for hotel purposes. During its fifty-three years' operation—terminated by a July afternoon conflagration in 1924—it sheltered visitors from many different lands. On its registers the signatures of distinguished world figures sandwiched themselves between the names of guides, humble travellers, and a host of ordinary happy-go-lucky vacationists. In time the hotel grew famous and a multitude of guests carried reports of its hospitality and the beauty of the region to distant, widely separated localities.

It became famous for reasons other than its hospitality, too, for it could probably boast of more owners, more proprietors, more conveyances, warranty deeds, mortgages, assignments and foreclosures than any hotel of like size and age in the Adirondacks. In fact, for so unsophisticated and rustic a little inn it appears to have attained unique legal eminence by its early familiarity with the nomenclature of jurisprudence. Many of its perplexities were not of its own making, however. They came as the outgrowth of speculative activity in the Forge Tract, the two square miles of land to which the hotel remained legally as well as physically attached for a number of years.

Before completing the first wing of the hotel, Buell and Desbrough leased the place to Sanford Sperry, proprietor of the Arnold house, who welcomed the opportunity of conducting a more pretentious and desirably located establishment. Sanford, whose full name was Cyrus Sanford Sperry, had come to the Brown's Tract as a very young man twenty years before. He was born on the banks of the St. Lawrence in 1833, the son of Eneas and Thankful Sperry, and in 1840 he moved with his parents to the Black River Valley. When seventeen years old he definitely adopted woodsmanship as a vocation, and though he failed to reach a fortieth birthday he left a highly respected name for good woodsmanship and good comradeship among the members of his craft. In 1860 he married Jane Noble, a personable school mistress, the orphaned daughter of a Central Square, Oswego County, inn keeper. The following year he joined the 117th N. Y. Volunteers and marched away to war. Five months after his enlistment his son,

William, was born, but father and son never met until the war ended and Sanford returned to his family, an honorably discharged Sergeant. In 1863 his wife moved to the Brown's Tract to assist in the management of the Arnold house. With her she brought her fifteen months old son on his first trip into the wilderness—peeping over the rim of a pack basket.

With the moving of the Sperry family to the new hotel the social and commercial center of the Brown's Tract shifted from the Arnold clearing to the Forge Tract. Sanford announced the change by mailing attractively printed bills to prospective patrons, the first ever used to attract visitors to the region. In the main, these bills told a straightforward, unembellished story of conveniences to be found on the Tract. Their reference to the fact of the Brown's Tract Road being repaired to a state of feminine accessibility may be considered a bit of optimism on Sanford's part, although repairs were actually under way at the time. Women did travel over the road, on horseback or strapped in buckboards, but none of them were ever heard complimenting their host for its smooth riding qualities. Nevertheless, Sanford had done his best, and accomplished much, rough road to the contrary. In assuming the new proprietorship he had clearly perceived three requisites for peopling an attractive resort region, namely, adequate hotel conveniences, transportation facilities, and advertising.

The first wing of the Forge House opened its doors about the first of May, 1871, and its expectant host cheerfully awaited the public's arrival. He waited two long weeks before it finally arrived in the person of a solitary traveller. In the twilight of a mid-May day, E. M. Marshall of Ithaca climbed painfully down from a buckboard, limped into the office, and wrote the first name on the hotel register. Jack Sheppard, his guide, had come down the Fulton Chain to convey him up the lakes for a week's fishing. The two men planned to spend the night at the hotel, so Jack also signed the register, his name with the title "guide" added being the second registration. That was a start, at least, and the proprietor waxed cheerful.

The First Proprietors of the Forge
House

SANFORD AND JANE SPERRY

June 1st 1871

ARE YOU GOING INTO THE WOODS?

The Undersigned, having rented the new Hotel at the "Old Forge," (John Brown's Tract,) for a term of years and furnished it in Good Style, is now prepared to accommodate

Fishing, Hunting & Pleasure Parties,

With all the Comforts of a first=class COUNTRY HOTEL Good Rooms for persons and their families who wish to stay at the house any length of time.

SUPPLIES OF ALL KINDS

And of the Best Quality will be Furnished at Reasonable Rates.

GOOD GUIDES AND BOATS
Always in Readiness.

The house is at the foot of the pond—12 miles Boating in either direction and no carry--2½ miles from the 1st Lake Fulton Chain—12 miles to the head of 4th, all good rowing.

Parties stopping at the House would require no Guide if able to manage a Boat.

The road from Boonville is being repaired so as to be accessible to Ladies as well as Gentlemen.

GOOD CONVEYANCES

will be in readiness at Boonville or Port Leyden, to convey parties to the Wilderness, by addressing

C. S. SPERRY,
BOONVILLE, ONEIDA CO., N. Y.

Facsimile of the Fulton Chain Region's first Resort Advertisement. The name "Adirondack" is not used.

On May 17th business picked up briskly, and Sanford's cheer increased in proportion as fourteen guests in a single party signed the register—eight sportsmen and six guides. The sportsmen were General Sherman, R. U. Owens, S. Sherwood, A. J. Canfield, B. A. Son and W. J. Martin, all of Utica and vicinity, and L. D. G. Brookes and Theodore Gray, of New York. They came on pleasure bent, completely equipped for a tilt with the Brown's Tract lake trout. The half dozen guides accompanying them were Dwight Grant, Jerome Wood, Josiah Helmer, George Ballard, John Van Valkenburg and James Higby. All were first class woodsmen.

During the twelve months immediately following the arrival of the Ithaca guest, three hundred and forty-eight names were inscribed on the register. These included thirty-two women and girls and seventy-nine guides, and were coupled with residence addresses in eleven states and one foreign country. The more distant states were Illinois, Kentucky and Missouri. Far less than three hundred and forty-eight distinct identities were revealed by the year's registrations, however, as many of the guests—especially the guides—registered several times during the twelve month period. This number furnishes a reasonably accurate quantitative picture of Adirondack travel in 1871. Very few visitors arriving from the west failed to sign the register either for lodging or meals, and most of the outgoing travellers from the east stopped for similar reasons.

The hotel's first register is a fascinating old tome, massively bound in leather, and of sufficient thickness to have served its purpose for forty years provided the passage of time brought no increase over the first year's partonage. "FORGE HOUSE— BROWN'S TRACT" appears in blocky type across the top of each page. To the left of this caption a deer is pictured bounding away in fright, and to the right, an indolent trout lazies its way to the edge of the sheet. The pages are perpendicularly lined into four columns marked Names, Residence, Destination and Remarks. This classification, popular at the time, invited guests to record information concerning themselves if they cared to do so. Vivid personalities flash in inky succession across the pages, and a perusal of this old book is a glimpse of the Fulton Chain's quickening surge of life and colorful figures of sixty years ago.

The first woman guest, Mrs. Frank Armes, of New London, Conn., arrived June 5th, 1871, and the next woman to be registered was Mrs. Richard H. Moore, New York, whose July 27th arrival brought the total of feminine guests to two for the first three months of the hotel's operation. Ladies were beginning to surmount the barriers of crinoline and furbelows, apparently, for they continued to make their way into the region during the rest of the summer.

James Constable, of Constableville, stopped for a night's rest in late July before proceeding to his registered destination, "Big Moose, North Branch." His famous relative, William Constable, had purchased nearly two million acres of Adirondack land in 1798, from the sale of which he realized a quick fortune. James was accompanied by James H. Peabody, of Philadelphia, on his Big Moose trip. Asa and Charles Puffer were their guides.

The venal hand of industry left its mark among August registrations with the laborious little signature, "Scudder Todd, Moose River Tannery." Scudder was a guest whose glance may well have set a forest trembling. He was outside man for the tannery, and the task of selecting suitable areas of hemlock trees to be felled and stripped of their bark devolved upon him. An expert in his calling, he could read the very vitals of a tree, and the fate of huge timber tracts often hung in the balance under his appraising scrutiny.

George Perkins, an irrepressible vacationist from Salem, Mass., signed the register on September 8th. He was headed for "Salem Camp," an open bark shanty on Fourth Lake. George had made the trip on horseback from Moose River Settlement, thirteen miles away, and his aching bones prompted the information which he recorded after his name. In the Destination column he wrote "Bound in, Salem Camp, Fourth Lake." In the same column he sketched himself astride a five-legged horse whose peculiar gait suggested an unpleasant thirteen miles for its rider. In the Remarks column he wrote "Three hours, fifty minutes from Lawrence's. - SORE! - The last of the flock."

George was a versatile traveller. He could ride or walk. Two weeks later he signed the register again and after writing "Bound out" in the Destination column, he drew a tiny picture of a traveller waving a lusty farewell as he set out on foot along the Brown's Tract Road. He displayed good judgment in resorting to pedestrianism, but his recorded riding time of three hours, fifty minutes was exceeded by Jacob Van Woert, of Greig, who wrote after his name "Six hours from Lawrence's."

Alvah Dunning, of Raquette Lake, and Orlando Gregory, of Medway, stopped at the hotel in September. They were bound for Alvah's isolated camp on Raquette's westerly shore. Orlando revealed their mission by sketching a bushy tailed creature endeavoring to extricate a forepaw from the jaws of a steel trap.

Then appears the signature, "A. Augustus Low, 31 Burling Slip, N. Y." He was a wealthy tea importer at the time, who, with his partner and relative, Abiel Abbot, operated a fleet of tea and spice carrying clipper ships between America and the Orient. With the growing use of steam vessels as cargo carriers, and the innovation of trans-oceanic cables, the clipper fleet gradually faded from the seas, but the owner's interest in the Adirondacks survived until his death. His son of the same name, A. Augustus Low, who now maintains a home estate near Sabattis in the Adirondacks, recently discovered the following notation scribbled in a book which his father had carried on one of his numerous journeys into the wilderness:

> "1867—camping on Big Moose Lake; not a building on the entire shore; a solitary trapper shantying at the other end of the lake; wolves howling in the wilderness."

The year 1871 came to a close, and January of the new year found the frozen lakes and tree covered ridges surrounding the lonely hotel at the foot of the Fulton Chain blanketed under deep snow. Almost ignored by the outside world, the little inn remained open to welcome any wayfarer who might brave the wintry trail leading to its doors. Its loyalty to the travel- ling public did not pass unnoticed, nor entirely unrewarded. Twenty-four names were written on the pages of its register during the first three months of the year, although during the previous December only one guest had enjoyed its hospitality.

The solitary December gentleman was M. L. Breese, destina- tion "Panther Hunting"; guides, Jack Sheppard and Sam Dunakin. The register discloses the facts that he arrived De- cember 22nd, killed two panthers, and departed January 28th in high satisfaction, taking along the skins of his tawny colored victims.

Seth Green and his assistant, Johnathan Mason, both from Rochester, registered January 18th. They were accompanied by John Brinckerhoff and Charley Phelps who had sledded Seth's baggage—several cans of live fish—from the Boonville railroad station. Seth, an outstanding American pioneer in fish culture, was busily engaged at that time teaching the coun- try how to conduct this delicate operation successfully. No locality seemed too remote for the personal exemplification of his methods, and his January trip to the Forge House was made for the purpose of planting fish of his own culture in Little Moose and Raquette Lakes. Their object accomplished, the party returned to the hotel where Johnathan recorded the event with the following notation scrawled in the register's Destina- tion column after his employer's and his own name:

"Put 31 Black Bass in Rackitt Lake and 2000 White fish in Little Moos Lake, any one should take any of thes fish will pleas put them back."

Johnathan was neither a skilled penman nor orthographer, but he was a fish man who took a genuine interest in his work, and the scrawled notation resulted from his forethought for the well being and propagation of Raquette's and Little Moose's new inhabitants. Six years later, while guiding a party on Raquette, John Brinckerhoff remarked that he considered himself a sort of ancestor to the lake's family of bass because of his connection with the first planting of the species in its water.

Seth Green remembered the Raquette Lake expedition for a number of reasons, one of which he greatly enjoyed telling in after years. During the party's return march from the lake he became exhausted to a degree that prohibited his further progress until his physical vigor should be restored by a period of rest. As night was approaching, Sam Dunakin, who had joined the party at the Forge House, urged Seth to seat himself on the handsled and permit others of the party to alternate in dragging the sled to their temporary destination, which was Sam's partially completed camp on Fourth Lake. The noted pisciculturist swallowed his pride (somewhat gleefully) and during the remainder of the journey enjoyed the snow-covered landscape as he rested his weary legs on the sled. Arrived safely at camp, he inquired for food.

"What would you like?" asked Sam.

"Panther meat," replied the revived and jocular Seth, assuming, of course, that the obnoxious panther's flesh would be the least accessible of the region's game meats at that particular moment. Sam nodded a humoring acquiescence and left the room. It so happened he had killed a panther a few days before, and after removing the skin, had cached the carcass in a snow drift at the rear of his camp. It required but a few minutes to recover the creature from its snowy wrappings, carve off a few thick steaks, and return to the kitchen. In a short time the hungry guests were smacking their lips over a hot supper. At the conclusion of the meal their host listened in silence to a voluble round of compliments anent his cookery. Then he inquired, "You liked it?"

"Delicious," exclaimed Seth. "What was it?"

"What you asked for, of course; panther meat," replied Sam.

Seth and Johnathan gasped, dismayed and speechless. Either

would have dined on carrion almost as readily as on the flesh of the unpopular beast that had just supplied their supper. Experienced, discriminating John Brinckerhoff looked on with unconcern. He had been aware of the character of the menu, and had enjoyed it. Like Sam, he was one of a limited group of woodsmen who were actually fond of panther steaks, but Seth and John distinctly were not.

There is no accounting for taste or prejudice in their respective relations to food. A hungry diner, served with an appetizingly browned portion of roast which he assumes to be commestible and in common use, will feast in satisfaction until his appetite is appeased. When the last morsel has disappeared, if he be informed that he has devoured a creature rated shockingly low in the brute kingdom's social register he will sit aghast, his relish transmuted to revulsion. He may even turn a sickly green and hurry with all speed to the reviving influence of the great outdoors. The panther meat repast was a favorite prank among former woodsmen, but the Adirondack novice is immune today, for the last panther was shot out of the mountains many years ago.

The green and white landscape of the Fulton Chain coaxed only one party to the hotel in February, but it was a jolly, roistering, picnic-bound party of twenty-two members, sixteen men (five of them accompanied by their wives) and one child. They arrived in a cavalcade of steaming horses and warm, straw-buffered sleds, muffled to the ears in a profusion of fur caps, woolen blankets, mittens and bearskin robes. William Kennedy of Port Leyden and Moose River Settlement signed the register for the group. He wrote an artistically flowing hand, but exuberance overcame chirography on one signature and the broken pen left a splatter of ink on the page resembling an attempted portrayal of sunrise.

Two musically gifted brothers in the party, Ed and Riley Parsons, of Leyden, had brought their violins, and the artistic William recorded the fact by writing the word "fiddles" after their names. Each day's outing in the woods and on the lakes came to a nightly climax in the hotel parlor with the Parsons brothers tuning their instruments and swinging into lively accompaniments for the Schottische, Money Musk and Virginia Reel as the entire company joined in rhythmic execution of the steps.

After three days of merrymaking, indoors and out, they bundled themselves into their sleds and departed, leaving their official scribe's final flourish, "A tip top time," written in the register as a testimonial to the Sperry brand of hospitality. Eighteen years later one of the musicians, Riley Parsons, returned to make his home on the Fulton Chain. But "fiddles" could no longer be written in just appreciation of his talents, for the name of Parsons became synonymous for a high order of craftsmanship in guide boat construction.

March brought the frolicsome Byron P. Graves, Boonville sportsman, merchant, fur trader and confirmed panther hunter, on a snowshoe trek to the Forge House. He came in quest of his favorite game and found Jack Sheppard with rifles, provisions and a dog waiting at the hotel to accompany him. Success in panther hunting required patience and endurance rather than skill. An expedition of this sort, resulting in a kill, sometimes demanded several days' steady tramping on snowshoes. With a dog held in leash, the hunter followed the panther's clearly defined trail that wandered aimlessly over immense areas of forest. Sooner or later, he came upon a partly devoured deer carcass which served warning that the object of his search lurked in the vicinity. Panthers usually remained in the neighborhood until they had consumed the entire edible portion of their kills. The dog, unleashed, quickly took up the scent near the carcass and the hunted game was soon brought to bay. An Adirondack panther, weighing nearly one hundred pounds, cat-like in instinct and habit, would seek the safety of a tree top upon being confronted with even the smallest and least formidable species of Adirondack deer hound. With his prey snarling down from its supposedly safe retreat, the hunter, being a sporting gentleman, aimed at the under side of the creature's head to bring it tumbling to the earth. A shot in the body lessened the degree of triumph and detracted from the victim's value as a trophy.

Byron and Jack enjoyed their usual success on their March expedition although they suffered an inconvenience which was not uncommon to the sport. Byron's brisk notation on the register tells the story:

"Through to Long Lake and back on snow shoes. Fodder played out. So did I. Dined mostly on oatmeal and panther meat. It's good!. Try it! Directions: first kill your panther."

The previous year Byron, Jack and Sam had killed three panthers on a single expedition. One of them, killed near Little Moose Lake, is pictured in this chapter.

The first twelve months of the hotel's operation came to a successful close, and during the next twelve a larger number of guests availed themselves of its conveniences. In the meantime, the register continued its function of collecting and disseminating information of a personal nature. Such remarks as "A good time," "Bully time," "Excellent guides," "Lots of fish," "Good sport," "Going home," "Will return," etc., are sprinkled among the registrations. John C. Lowny, of Philadelphia, suffered an injury while at the hotel, and in explanation of his prolonged stay some one wrote, "He cut his foot and did not leave until it got better." George Perkins returned from Massachusetts for another vacation, this time astride a unique animal, which, according to his pen and ink sketch on the register, seems to have been a six-legged horse. With this dexterous mount he was enabled to reduce his travelling time of the previous year by thirty minutes, and he so recorded the fact by writing "Three hours, twenty minutes from Lawrences's."

An unsolicited testimonial comes from the pen of George H. Albro, Westchester County, who registered with his guide, James Christian. After writing "Splendid" in designation of the quality of service rendered by his guide, he continued:

The Forge House in the Early Eighties

Buckboard leaving the Forge House in the summer of 1888. William Scott de Camp bids adieu to departing friends as local guides look on. Included in the group are Agnes Dodd, Anna Champion, Mary Soper, Mrs. Arthur Soper, Mrs. Andrews, Sam Dunakin, Will Sperry, Chris Goodsell, Jonathan Meeker, Josiah Helmer, Len Ingersoll, Arthur Harvey, Pete Rogers, Bob Roberts, Francis Helmer and William Weedmark.

Adirondack panther killed by Byron P. Graves on the shore of Little Moose Lake in 1871. Guides—Sheppard and Dunakin.

"Spent a very pleasant month in this section—plenty of
sport—and a deer every time Jim went for it. Couldn't
wish for a more attentive and kind host than Sperry has
proved to be. Success to him! Off for home."

Big Bill Bero, St. Regis Indian Chief, put in a belated September appearance. His signature appears on the register, first
in abbreviated English script, then in a painstakingly inscribed
Algonquin version of the name. It is a big name, worthy of a
big Chief, and its twelve syllables, scratched across the entire
width of the page, obliterate the Destination and Remarks columns, leaving no space to record the motive which prompted
the dusky tribesman to pay the region an autumn call. He
wrote as follows: "Na-San-Ni-Ka-Wa-Na-Wa-Na-A-Na-Ko-
Wa-Ne."

Big Bill was a peaceful, welcome guest in spite of his awe-
inspiring name, but even Sanford Sperry's plump register could
not have long withstood the onslaughts of such space-filling
signatures.

Charles A. Willets, of Flushing, L. I., homeward bound in
October, embellishes the register with a report of his season's
success in figures the modern sportsman would discreetly hesi-
tate to publish.

"Have been here since the 27th of July. Caught 350
speckled trout, five salmon. Shot seventeen woodcock,
twenty-two partridges, two deer, etc."

The next notation is a brief, penciled announcement of
tragedy:

"Mr. C. S. Sperry was drowned in Limekiln Lake on Saturday, November 9th, 1872, at about one o'clock P. M."

By a harsh thrust of fate, Sanford's promising career as a
mountain host was cut short with tragic abruptness. With his
ten year old boy, Will, he joined Jack Sheppard, Sam Dunakin
and Dan Sears on a frost fishing and deer hunting trip on the
morning of the ill-fated day to secure provisions for use at the
hotel. Leaving Sam and Dan near the head of Fourth Lake,
Jack (with the dogs) in one boat, and Sanford and his son in

another, rowed to Fifth where they landed and left their boats. Jack then struck out through the woods to release the dogs at a strategic point, while Sanford and the boy hurried southward along the three miles of dimly blazed trail to Limekiln Lake where a small boat had been left on a former expedition. The day was a cold, blustery display of November's ill humor, and a light snowfall of the previous night still powdered the ground. The normally placid surface of picturesque Limekiln was lashed to a choppy commotion that demanded extreme caution in navigating the small craft at Sanford's disposal.

Soon after their arrival at the lake, the resonant baying of a hound giving voice on the scent warned of the probable approach of a deer. When hounded, a deer usually takes to water, a piece of brute strategy calculated to throw the pursuer off the scent. Unfortunately for the deer, this self-preserving instinct fails to mitigate the dangerous human factor; in fact, it becomes a self-destructive instinct when man is the pursuer. While swimming a lake the creature may be easily dispatched by a waiting marksman stationed on either land or water. Sanford shot the first deer that entered the lake and secured it to the stern of his boat. Will, watching from the shore, lustily applauded his father's marksmanship.

Another warning bay echoed across the water, and Sanford turned in the expectation of sighting a second deer taking refuge in the lake. But as he partially arose to face the direction of the sound a quick conspiracy of wind and wave capsized the boat and plunged him headlong into the icy water. His prolonged struggle to right the overturned craft was fruitless. Strong swimmer though he was, the wind and waves were stronger and the floundering boat doggedly eluded his attempts to right its position. Heavily weighted with wet clothes, and weakened by his exertions in the cold water, he was fortunate in being able to climb up on the keel. With one oar, salvaged as it floated by, he began as best he could the tortuous labor of propelling the boat to shore, hoping to reach the safety of land before succumbing to the paralyzing effect of cold. His position on the keel was none too secure, and cold had already numbed him to the point of weakening his grip on the oar. With every ounce of his strength summoned to the task, he continued desperately to paddle, but the tossing boat moved landward at a barely perceptible pace.

When about two rods from shore the oar slipped from his grasp but he clung helplessly to the boat, making no effort to recover it. In the meantime, the little boy, having frantically scoured the vicinity for a branch of suitable length, discarded his jacket and waded shoulder high to meet his father, hoping to tow him ashore, but the branch failed to reach by several feet. Even if it had answered the purpose with respect to distance, it is unlikely that the distressed man could have gripped it firmly enough to aid the towing process. He had reached the limit of physical endurance. Slowly his position on the keel relaxed. The brave boy, completely submerged now except for his head, pleaded with him to hold on, but the father was powerless. He realized that he had waged a losing fight. With a last muster of strength he murmured, "I'm going. Don't cry, Willie." Then he slipped from the boat and disappeared beneath the waves.

Horrified at the tragic outcome of his father's struggle for life, the boy waded back to land and stood shivering on the lonely shore as he tearfully pondered his desolate situation. To the best of his childish knowledge there were, at the time, only three human beings ranging the vast area of forest that stretched between Limekiln Lake and his home at the foot of the Fulton Chain. His chance of encountering any one of the three was distinctly unfavorable, but his wet, cold condition demanded instant activity and he decided not to await the inevitable searching party that would arrive later in the afternoon to ascertain the cause for his father's and his own absence. If he could follow the trail to Fifth Lake, and there launch one of the beached rowboats, it might be possible to row the remaining distance to the Forge House and tell his mother what had happened. With this plan in mind, and no alternative presenting itself, he hurried off along the trail.

He had hardly vanished into the woods when Jack Sheppard emerged on the opposite shore. Seeing the overturned boat across the lake, and sensing a mishap to his friends, Jack hurried around the curved shore line to the locality the boy had recently quitted. A single quick scrutiny told the story: the father drowned, the son making his way to Fifth Lake—possibly with the intention of rowing the Fulton Chain in childish anxiety to reach his home. Will was a sturdy, courageous lad despite his tender age, but if he should attempt to brave the whistling November wind and white-capped waves of Fourth Lake he would undoubtedly meet the same fate that had overtaken his father. Fearing that a second fatality might result from the day's expedition, Jack started swiftly in pursuit.

The little footprints followed the course of Limekiln's vaguely marked trail with surprising accuracy considering the inexperience of the small boy who was leaving them behind. Occasionally they deviated from the way, for in less sheltered spaces the wind had effaced tracks in the sparse snow made by Will and his father earlier in the day. Then a confusion of footprints and marks of the boy's hasty scrambling over fallen timber and around thickets in his efforts to re-locate the trail encouraged the intent woodsman who followed in the hope of overtaking him before he reached Fifth Lake. The nearer he approached the trail's end, the higher rose his hopes: the tracks indicated increasing bewilderment and slower progress on the part of the frightened little fugitive. But Jack was doomed to disappointment. When he reached the lake only one boat lay on its shore. The boy had arrived ahead of him, and had already pushed off for Fourth Lake Inlet.

Will, having negotiated the three miles from Limekiln, arrived at Fifth Lake considerably the worse for wear, although still eager to push on toward his home. He lost no time shoving a boat into the water, and after rowing to the foot of the lake, entered the Inlet, a forest-walled stream that empties the water of the upper lakes into the head of Fourth. But at the mouth of the stream he abandoned his plan of reaching home by water. The surface of the lake was a rolling succession of great waves that prohibited further attempts at navigation. Turning, he rowed back upstream a few rods, dragged the boat ashore, and set out through the woods to continue his journey by land. He had proceeded but a short distance when Jack Sheppard's hailing shout brought him to a sudden, joyous halt, and a moment later, encircled by his big friend's comforting arms, the boy was sobbing out his bitter story.

At the Pratt camp, Jack kindled a fire and ministered to Will's urgent need of warmth and consolation. When the other members of the party arrived at camp all started at once for the Forge House. Joined there by Ed Arnold, Alonzo Wood, Gus Syphert and Tom Griffin, they returned the same evening to the Pratt camp, and at daybreak hurried to Lime-kiln to recover Sanford's body in the early morning calm. Successful in this gloomy task, the cortege returned by land and water to the Forge House, and thence by wagons to Boonville where Sanford was buried from the home of his brother, E. Menzo Sperry.

Jane Sperry and her son remained in the hotel until the following spring when they left to make their home in Boonville. Seven years later they returned to the Fulton Chain where mother and son in a business partnership built and conducted the Sperry Camp on the South Shore of Fourth Lake.

In 1887 Will married Elizabeth Klinck, of Forestport, who had spent her first season on the Fulton Chain the year before. This marriage united two young Adirondackers who could trace their mountain ancestry farther, perhaps, than any other married couple in the region. Elizabeth Klinck's great-grand-father, Caleb Sweet, had settled on the Brown's Tract in Herreshoff's time and had been one of its prominent residents for a number of years. Will's great-aunt, Emmiline Sperry, taught school on the Tract at the same time, and while living there married Caleb's son, David. Will and Elizabeth Sperry have lived in the Fulton Chain region continuously since their marriage, and at this writing (1931) reside in Old Forge.

After the Sperrys' departure a long line of proprietors, managers and managing owners occupied the Forge House. So numerous, in fact, were Sanford's successors that it appears to have been a sort of civic duty for all in the region to take a hand in the business at one time or another. Sam (Pop) Briggs took three hands. On three separate occasions he leased and operated the hotel. C. I. Thomson and his son, Dr. R. E. Thomson, purchased the place in 1915, after it had been enlarged and improved several times, and as managing owners operated it for a longer period than any of their predecessors. Their occupancy terminated with the destruction of the hotel by fire in 1924. Following is a chronologically arranged list of persons connected with the hotel in the role of host:

Sanford Sperry, Proprietor.
Jane Sperry, Proprietress.
Ed. Arnold, Prop.
Bart Holliday, Prop.
Joel Comstock, Prop.
Emmett Marks, Mgr. (Six weeks in 1879.)
James Barrett and his son, Charles, Props.
Charles M. Barrett, Prop.
Joseph Harvey, Prop.
Mort Alger and George Kitts, Props.   (Operating as the
    firm of Alger and Kitts in 1891.)
Samuel Garmon, managing owner.
Sam Briggs, Prop.
Edward Schenck, Prop.
J. G. Hoffman, Mgr.
Sam Briggs, Prop.
Philo Wood, Prop. (1903-1907.)
John and James Quinn, Props.
Joseph Lampkin, Mgr.
Lew Fuller, Mgr.
Lawrence Charbonneau, Mgr.
Sam Briggs, Prop.

C. I. and Dr. R. E. Thomson, Managing owners (1915-
    1924.)

Ed Arnold left the Arnold house to become the proprietor
of the hotel in 1873, succeeding Jane Sperry. From that time,
the once pretentious Herreshoff Manor never again opened
its doors to the travelling public. In 1875, Bart Holliday
joined Ed in the management of the hotel, but the following
year the pair relinquished their joint interest to Joel Comstock,
who remained until 1879. Joel left in February of that year,
the Barretts, meanwhile, having leased the place with the intention of taking possession in the spring.

Not wishing the hotel to stand untenanted during the several weeks of winter intervening between Joel's departure and
the Barrett's arrival, the owners persuaded Emmett Marks to
take charge until the new lessees should arrive. An obliging
youth, Emmett abandoned his plan of returning to Caledonia,
and remained at the hotel. At that time, the region still remained so unpopulous a frontier that the total of its permanent
residents could be counted on the fingers of one hand. They
were Ed. Arnold, Jack Sheppard, Sam Dunakin, Frank Johnson
and Slim Jim Phifield. By a singular concurrence of January
migrations on the part of these five, the population suddenly
dwindled to two temporary inhabitants, Emmett and Johnny
Van Valkenburg, the latter a guide who remained until mid-
February. Ed Arnold had left for an extended stay outside the
woods. Sam and Jack were engaged in a prolonged excursion through the eastern section of the mountains, while Frank
Johnson and Slim Jim were off and away on an unknown mission that detained them until spring. The nearest remaining
neighbor to the east was Alvah Dunning, snug in his hermitage
on the shore of Raquette Lake, twenty-five miles away. Thirteen miles to the west lay Moose River Settlement, its population industriously feeding huge tanning vats with hemlock
bark.

On February 15th the Forge House garrison suffered a fifty

per cent cut. Johnny packed his duffle and started west. Rue-fully, Emmett viewed his departing comrade as he snowshoed along the Brown's Tract Road to where it curved and vanished in the forest thirty rods from the hotel. Then he realized his awful prominence as a local resident. Except for his own solitary presence, human animation throughout the entire Fulton Chain and Big Moose region had collapsed to an absolute zero. The dead silence of an unpopulated wilderness howled in his ears. He was alone, and as he expressed it later, "homesick as hell."

For the next six weeks Emmett found lots of time to think things over. Not a single traveller arrived to disturb his medi-tations, and his former unbounded enthusiasm for life in the wilderness quickly gave way to the emotions of a castaway who finds himself cut off from the world by leagues of trackless sea. The painfulness of his situation contrasted vividly to the bliss-ful contentment of his distant neighbor, Alvah the hermit, illustrating the diverse patterns of human reaction to en-vironment. While Emmett was beset by an intense longing for the companionship of his fellows, Alvah was exulting in his own complete isolation from it.

The hotel's supply of literature included no more than one copy of a January newspaper and Radway's 1878 Almanac. When Charley Phelps and the Barretts plowed their way to the hotel the first day of April, Emmett had practically mem-orized the entire contents of both journals.

Early camp on Big Moose Lake. Guides, left to right, Richard Crego, Peter Rivett, Ned Ball and Jack Sheppard

Dutton Camp on Big Moose Lake. Billy Dutton is seated at extreme right.

X

CAMPS AND CAMPERS

HAVING completed the Pratt camp in 1870, Jack Sheppard and Sam Dunakin parted company so far as further construction work was concerned. Sam harbored an urge toward domestic independence, and in the fall of 1871 he began the erection of a camp on the North Shore of Fourth Lake, near the present Minnow Brook, which he finished the following year. A somewhat roomier structure than his personal needs required, it was designed to accommodate sportsmen whom he guided. Many visitors to the region were beginning to express a preference for enclosed shelters rather than for open bark or brush shanties.

On the lake shore in front of the camp Sam built a small ice house of notched logs for the safe keeping of fish and game during warm weather. In 1876 this little hut served a far more somber purpose than its builder had anticipated. Sam's niece arrived at the camp in the autumn of 1875, hoping to bolster her failing health by a few months of undisturbed rest in the mountains. Her condition failed to respond to the stimulus of her new environment, however, and she died four months after her arrival. A season of heavy snowfall and generally unfavorable weather had blocked the Brown's Tract Road to an impassable state except for snowshoe travel, and the bereaved Sam was prevented from returning with his niece to her New Jersey home. In this emergency he deposited the dead girl, carefully bundled in blankets, in the ice house to await the opening of the roads. Three weeks more of storm and drifting snow assailed the forest before a sled bearing the body could be dragged along the twenty-five mile road leading to the railroad at Boonville.

Jack Sheppard, sharing Sam's ambition to become a householder in his own right, built a camp on the South Shore of Fourth Lake near the present Cohasset Hotel in 1874. Here he entertained visitors whom he guided, and the place, like Sam's, became known as a semi-public camp. In the fall of 1877 Jack deserted the Fulton Chain for Big Moose Lake, and Ed Arnold moved into his camp. From that time it was known as "Ed's Place," and its rotund host found himself catering once more to the forest-loving public—this time in his third establishment. Ed's boyhood association with agriculture exerted a tempering influence on his woodsmanship. Wherever he located, even though but for a single season, he neglected the rod and gun long enough to clear and cultivate the nearest available plot of level ground whose fecundity promised to reward his labor. Like the mighty Iroquois of old, he perceived the wisdom of trusting to Autumn's harvest as well as to the fortunes of the chase for his winter's supply of food. His career, geographically, may be traced to this day by a trail of overgrown garden plots that wanders across the Central Adirondacks.

After occupying the camp several years, Ed disposed of it to a Lewis County family of Sopers who operated it as a hotel under the name of "Forest Home." They, in turn, sold it to Josiah Wood (Alonzo's son) who demolished the building and erected a larger one on the same plot which he operated as a public camp under the name of "Cohasset Hotel."

Jack Sheppard moved to Big Moose Lake in compliance with a request from several New York sportsmen that he build a camp on the lake for their private use. The New York group included Charles Arnold, Martin and Travers Van Buren and others who had spent several summers on the lake, and had wisely concluded to look no farther for a permanent camp site. The building was erected in 1878 on the site now occupied by the Kingsford Camp, and became known as the "Club Camp." Jack Sheppard, Richard Crego, Bart Holliday and Johnny Van Valkenburgh did the construction work, and later acted as guides for the Club members. This was the first permanent camp built on Big Moose Lake.

Three years before, in 1876, Jim Higby had built a pretentious bark shanty on the North Shore of the lake for the seasonal use of William H. Dutton, a Philadelphian. It was intended to serve as a permanent summer camp for its owner, but this type of construction proved inadequate for the purpose. It was fashioned of a framework of poles, roofed and sided with spruce bark. Above its open entrance was inscribed the name "Pancake Hall" in recognition of Jim's foremost culinary achievement. Another shanty of similar construction stood near the Hall, built by Jim for a party of Philadelphians. Above its entrance an arrangement of birch twigs fastened to the wall spelled the name "Camp Germantown."

William Dutton was a prosperous piano and organ builder, a plump, benign little man with a wealth of silken white beard. He first came to Big Moose Lake about 1870 or 1871, escorted by James (Jim) Higby. The rare scenic charm of Big Moose, plus Jim's supreme skill in manipulating a pancake griddle, lured him back each summer thereafter until he became the most prominent local vacationer. In 1880 he built a second and more commodious camp, a permanent, rustic structure of logs, on the island near the westerly shore of the lake. The building of this camp brought Henry Covey, a young blacksmith and wheelwright, of Glenfield, Lewis County, to Big Moose for the first time. He came in response to a letter from Jim Higby informing him that a construction job on the Dutton Camp awaited his arrival at the lake for which he would receive one dollar and twenty-five cents a day, and board. The camp was completed and its owner took squatter's possession in the late summer of 1880. The island, previously unnamed, then became known as "Dutton's Island," an appellation which eventually gave way to "Page's Island," and later to "Fiske's Island."

For ten happy summers "Billy" Dutton, as guides and other residents of the lake privately referred to the genial organ builder and woods lover, occupied his island camp, entertained guests from New York and Philadelphia, many of whom were well known vocal and instrumental artists, and enjoyed himself with a sense of contentment which few vacationists have surpassed. He ate Jim Higby's pancakes, drifted hours at a time in a small canoe (said to be the first ever brought to the lake by white men), or sprawled dreamily on the bald rocky crest of the ridge that towers high above the lake's western shore line. His fondness for this exalted perch was well known in the eighties, and the crest became known at that time as "Billy's Bald Spot." The name still clings to the crest although Billy died forty years ago; and sojourners on the lake still follow the old trail up the ridge to view the expanse of lake and forest that stretches away in three cardinal directions from the bald spot.

After Billy's death the island passed into the possession of Mr. and Mrs. Theodore Page, of Oswego. They replaced the old camp with a more spacious and modern structure built on the same site. One log, salvaged from the razed building, was carried up to Billy's Bald Spot and incorporated in a small cabin erected there as a temporary shelter—a sort of rustic monument to the departed occupant of Pancake Hall. At this writing (1931) the island is owned by Harrison Grey Fiske and his wife, Minnie Madern Fiske, the noted actress.

Early camp builders on Big Moose Lake were beset with greater difficulties than those which confronted Fulton Chain builders, principally because of the lake's inaccessibility. No road led to its shores from the Fulton Chain, and the foot trail was only a thinly worn path of limited width. From the North Shore of Fourth Lake it extended to Bub's, Moss and Dart's Lakes and thence to the South Shore of Big Moose Lake near its outlet. Boats left on the shores of the three intervening lakes afforded brief respites from the toil of packing materials and supplies along the trail, as part of the distance could be covered by water. Lengthy burdens such as finished lumber were usually carried by two men, each harnessed with a common boat yoke balanced across the shoulders, from which ropes were suspended and fastened to the ends of the loads.

Bub's Lake owes its name to Otis Arnold Jr., the younger son of Otis and Amy Arnold whose early settlement on the Brown's Tract has been recorded in a previous chapter. During the fifties, guides and sportsmen stopping at the Arnold home usually referred to the youngster as "Bub," a form of address then commonly employed by men when conversing with small boys. While on deer hounding expeditions Bub invariably watched from the shore of his favorite lake, rifle in hand, hoping to bring down a fat buck. His preference for that body of water led to its being called "Bub's Lake" by his older companions, and the name gradually grew into common usage.

Moss Lake bore the name "Whipple's Lake" as early as the Civil War period, the name, undoubtedly, being supplied by O. W. Whipple, of Utica, who was a charter member of the North Woods Walton Club. In the early seventies the name "Morse Lake" came into use because of Professor Morse's admiration and preference for its shores. Professor Morse, a New England educator and artist, spent several summers on the lake in a bark shanty, fishing, boating and painting. Some of his canvases are at hand which are really artistic products of brush and palette, the subjects being sectional views of the lake and its picturesque island. In time the name "Morse Lake" contracted to the more easily pronounced term "Moss Lake," and by this less historic but equally serviceable appellation the beautiful little lake is known today.

Dart's Lake, the second upstream widening of the North Branch of the Moose River, was known as Second Lake, North Branch, until 1901. During that year, William Dart, the owner of the land adjoining the lake, petitioned the Conservation Commission to employ the more distinctive name "Dart's" in designation of the lake. At the same time, Frank Cristman, having acquired title jointly with William Thistlethwaite and Charles E. Snyder to First Lake, North Branch, in 1899, requested the Commission to designate that lake as "Rondaxe." The Commission granted both petitions.

The Lawrence Camp on Fourth Lake, the most pretentious of earlier Fulton Chain private camps, had its beginning in the days of the North Woods Walton Club. Lewis H. Lawrence, of Utica, during the course of his wanderings through the region in the late sixties, became attracted to a point of land on the North Shore which the Waltonians had named "Fair View." (It is now known as "Lawrence Point.") The Club had erected an open log lean-to on this point which had sheltered its members for several seasons and still remained a substantial, weather-proof structure. Lewis camped there a few summers by way of trying out the neighborhood, then began a program of improvements which extended over a period of years and eventually transformed the little hut and its surroundings into a pretentious summer home. With its expansive level of well kept lawn, its main camp building of unique design, and the adjacent guides' quarters, stables, kennels and a miscellany of outbuildings, it loomed as a show place during the last quarter of the century.

Variety was emphatically the spice of camp life for Lewis H. Lawrence. He built and occupied three other camps on Limekiln, Moss and Seventh Lakes. These were suitably furnished miniature reproductions of his Fourth Lake camp, and offered him a complete change of environment whenever he felt the urge to roam. He roamed often, from one camp to another, always accompanied by a staff of guides, and carrying the necessary trappings for enjoyment and comfort in the woods. His Limekiln and Moss Lake camps, both built in 1886, were the first permanent structures erected on the shores of those lakes.

Lewis Lawrence, the father of Lewis H., was nearing the end of life's trail when he first tramped the trails leading to his son's several wilderness homes. Born in 1807, in comparative poverty and obscurity, he had risen to great wealth and social prestige during a conspicuously constructive and honorable career in Utica, the city of his adoption in boyhood. His business interests centered mainly in lumber, although railroading and other development projects also claimed his attention and added to his wealth. A man of fine ideals in all his spheres of activity, he became known politically and socially, as well as commercially, as an important citizen of the state.

Up to 1879, when he was seventy-two years old, he had never visited his son's Fourth Lake camp, nor, in fact, had he ever visited any section of the Central Adirondacks, although its proximity to Utica rendered the trip a relatively easy one. During that year he succumbed to his son's importuning, and journeyed to Fourth Lake for his first vacation in the Adirondacks. Considerably surprised and deeply impressed by the region's scenic charm, he endeavored to compensate for the lost years by tarrying as long and frequently at the Lawrence Camp as his devotion to affairs in the city permitted.

Afflicted with rapidly failing health in 1886 which his physicians were unable to relieve, he requested that he be taken to the Camp. He expressed supreme faith in the curative properties of the lake and forest environment which he had grown to love during the past seven years. His physicians demurred against the change, fearing that in his enfeebled condition he could not survive the hardships of the journey. But the patient insisted—and the trip was made. With a physician, two nurses and other attendants in his party, he left Utica in July on the Black River Railroad. At Boonville he was transferred to a cushioned buckboard which carried him in comfort to Moose River Settlement. There a specially designed arm chair supplanted the buckboard, and a group of stalwart guides were waiting to carry him over the thirteen rough miles of the Brown's Tract Road to the Forge Pond. At the Pond the party took to boats and arrived without mishap at the Lawrence Camp.

The aged patient voiced his satisfaction upon reaching camp and declared that he would soon be on the road to complete recovery. His expressions of confidence were unprophetic, for he died in September; but he enjoyed the satisfaction of spending his last days in an environment of his choice. Newspapers throughout the state published comprehensive accounts of his life, but none commented more significantly on his last trip to the Fulton Chain than did a small country weekly.

"He died," said the Boonville Herald, "where he wished to die."

Lewis H. Lawrence occupied Lawrence Point until 1905, the year of his death. After the death of his wife in 1914, the camp passed into the possession of her relative, Charles E. Barnard, of Utica, and at this writing it is owned and occupied by his widow, Mrs. Nellie C. Barnard, also of Utica.

Two more private camps were built on the South Shore of Fourth Lake in the late seventies before a hotel, publicly advertised as such, made its appearance on the lake. The private camps were Flat Rock, built by E. W. Buell and W. J. Bissell, of Watertown, and Turin Camp, built by Gates Emm and Moulten Riggs, of Turin, Lewis County.

Camp building on Seventh Lake began in 1879 when Artemus (Artie) M. Church, of Lyons Falls, erected a cozy log cabin on the upper North Shore. A few years later Artie built a second and larger camp on the same side of the lake, a short distance west of his cabin. This became known as the "Manhattan Club Camp" because it was utilized by a small group of sportsmen who had organized under the name "Manhattan Club," for recreational purposes. Eight travelling men hailing from as many eastern cities comprised the membership of the Club. Their objective resembled that of the North Woods Walton Club, and the scene of their annual outings was Seventh Lake. They were a vigorous, jovial group of huntsmen and anglers, good fellows all, who hied to the woods each summer for a month's respite from business, and the entire countryside was made instantly aware of their seasonal arrivals. The Club remained in existence twenty-five years but its membership never exceeded eight men. Upon the death or retirement of a member the name of another knight of the road known to all was proposed for membership. The candidate usually accompanied the expedition during the summer

The Lawrence Camp on the North Shore of Fourth Lake

Early Camp on Big Island (Alger's Island), Fourth Lake

Alonzo Wood Camp, Fourth Lake.   Built in 1880

ALONZO AND OPHELIA ARNOLD WOOD

following his proposal, and if he proved to be a good sportsman and a good comrade under the varying circumstances of wilderness life, his election to permanent membership resulted.

In 1879, camp builders invaded Big Island (Alger's Island) in Fourth Lake to erect a small camp for Fred Rivett, a guide. Fred and his younger brother, Peter, who now resides in Old Forge, became skilful, well known woodsmen in the seventies and eighties although they were mere youths at the time. Fred's camp came into being because of its owner's desire to provide convenient accommodations for hunters and fishermen whom he guided. Sam Dunakin and Fred were the builders, and the structure was located on the lower end of the island about two hundred feet from the point on the southerly shore. It was constructed mainly of hewn logs and hand-hewn shingles.

After occupying the camp for several years, Fred sold his squatter's rights to Sarah Clarke who, in turn disposed of them to Mort Alger, of Rome, N. Y. Mort was an early and enthusiastic devotee to Adirondack camp life, and his son, Ollie Alger, of Bay Side, L. I., having inherited his father's fondness for the woods, still makes use of the island as a summer home.

In 1905, the original building was demolished and re-built on its present site, each log being restored to its former position. In 1906, Sam Dunakin rowed to the island bringing the axe he had used while building the original camp in 1879. A premonition of approaching death undoubtedly prompted him to present the axe as a keepsake to Mort Alger, for the two men had been friends for many years.

"I thought you might like to keep this," muttered Sam, handing over the axe, "I'll never have any use for it again."

A month later he left for his sister's home in New Jersey where he died the following January.

Alonzo Wood's Camp, the first full-fledged public hostelry on Fourth Lake, was built in 1880, about two miles below Eagle Bay, near the present New Kenmore Hotel on the North Shore. Seven guest rooms, boat house facilities, guides' quarters and kennels were included in the establishment. In 1881, the year in which the hotel was formally opened to the public, several guest rooms were added to the main camp.

Lon Wood's Camp, as the place became known, immediately attracted a high class clientele of sportsmen and their ladies. Both Alonzo and his wife, Ophelia, were popular among visitors—Alonzo because of his expert knowledge of the woods and dependability as a guide, and Ophelia because of her naive mannerisms, the endearing simplicity of her character, and her motherly concern for the comfort and happiness of her guests. It was an era of quoits, bean-bags and nightly bonfires beneath the trees that bordered the shore, and guests en masse imploring their host and hostess to relate tales of personal adventure. Ophelia furnished the greater fund of story-telling entertainment, being more loquacious and sociable than her taciturn husband. But Alonzo, when pressed into service, delighted his listeners with solemnly voiced tales of long forgotten happenings in the mysterious depths of the woods.

Five children were born to Alonzo and Ophelia—Alfred, Oscar, Josiah, Cornelia and Millie. Oscar and Josiah became able woodsmen and their services as guides were available to Camp guests, while the daughters assisted their mother with house work. Only one of the five children retains a direct interest in the Adirondacks today. Millie, who married Milo Bull, still owns and occupies a summer camp on the North Shore of Fourth Lake.

The building of the Wood Camp brought a seventeen year old boy to the Fulton Chain who later became one of the region's well known guides. David Charbonneau, better known as "Dave," left Moose River Settlement in the first week of April, 1880, with a horse-drawn sled piled high with lumber. His destination was the site of Lon Wood's proposed building operations on Fourth Lake. At the Forge House, the Brown's Tract Road connected with a narrow winter road which skirted the South Shore of Old Forge Pond and continued in an easterly direction along the channel leading from First Lake. At the foot of First the road ended and teamsters desiring to proceed farther up the lakes were required to drive the remaining distance on ice. Dave was a good teamster and negotiated the distance to First Lake easily enough, where he stepped his horses onto the lake's frozen surface. Then his troubles began. An unseasonable March balminess had impregnated the ice with springtime wanderlust, and it plainly felt the urge to move. With every onward stride of the horses it exhibited a buoyancy which Dave could not share, for the pride and joy of his young life were centered in the hard pulling span of bays intrusted to his care, and he had sound cause to fear for their safety. It was a nerve racking trip, but he reached his destination and unloaded his cargo without mishap, and hurried with all speed back down the lakes. Not until he had regained the First Lake shore did he breathe a happy sigh of boyish relief.

Fred Hess, the progenitor of Inlet's architectural development, roamed the Central Adirondacks for more than forty years. Fred was a much loved, local prodigy of strength, the Iron Man of the forest. A big hearted, big muscled woodsman and an almost invincible grappler with the forces of the wilderness, he possessed, like Achilles, a vulnerable spot which proved to be his economic undoing. It was an irrepressible itch to be at work with hammer and nails.

Fred was born in Greig, Lewis County, in 1840. He explored the Moose River country in the sixties, and in the early seventies built a bark shanty on Cedar Island near the head of Fourth Lake to accommodate a convalescing friend. The friend recovered and returned to his home but Fred had been permanently won to the woods and he remained. From time to time he improved his camp until it became a substantial cabin. When Alonzo Wood built his hotel on the North Shore of the lake, Fred built one on the island which became popular among sportsmen and attracted an excellent class of patrons.

It was near this island inn in the winter of 1887 that Fred and three of his cronies, Artie Church, Jim Higby and Will Sperry dispatched the last native wolf known to have been killed in the region. The wolf appeared from the wooded shore, near the site now occupied by Rocky Point Inn, and trotted in a curving path toward the island. At intervals it dropped to its haunches and looked back leisurely as though expecting a mate to follow. The four woodsmen on the island marked its course, and arming themselves, started out across the ice. Favorable wind and steadily falling snow enabled them to approach within easy range of the animal, where they halted to take aim. Meanwhile, the wolf sat complacently awaiting the mate that failed to appear, blissfully unaware that the stage was set for the extinction of its kind in the Fulton Chain region. The explosions that followed came from the guns of expert marksmen, and when the smoke of the discharges drifted away the gray ravager of Adirondack deer lay quivering on the ice. Its skin was made into a rug that adorned the floor of Jim Higby's Big Moose Camp for a number of years. An investigation revealed the tracks of a second wolf leading from Rocky Point eastward. It had stood on the shore at the moment of the shooting, and its widely spaced foot prints indicated precipitous flight.

Fred conducted the Cedar Island Camp for several years, and disposed of it in 1892. He then began the erection of a hotel near the present *Arrowhead* in Inlet. The small cabin he built there at the time to house himself and his workers was the first building erected on the site of Inlet. The new hotel, which was soon completed, was known as the *Hess Inn* and later as the *Arrowhead*. It burned to the ground a number of years ago, but a larger and more handsome *Arrowhead* has since replaced it under the management of Charles O'Hara. The building and operation of the original hotel was a losing proposition for Fred. His talent for business management fell far short of his excellent woodsmanship, but he persisted in combining the two. In 1897 he built a third hotel (now operated by Philo Wood as "The Wood") near the site of the Arrow Head which he conducted under the name of "The Hess Camp." This enterprise also resulted in a financial loss, so Fred gave up camp building as a bad job. He left the Fulton Chain in 1899 and settled in Maine.

In the meantime, the years had dealt lightly with Fred's superb physique and capacity for endurance. At the age of seventy-five he set out with a companion upon an expedition into northern Canada. The pair had penetrated the wilderness several days' march beyond the outposts of civilization when the companion was laid low by a febrile ailment. Fred hurried back alone to the nearest settlement where medicine and supplies could be procured, and returned to his sick comrade in time to nurse him back to health. In 1923 he visited the Fulton Chain after an absence of nearly twenty-five years. He was then eighty-three years old. In March, 1924, he engaged in beaver trapping along the North and South Branches of the Moose River, following his trap lines on snowshoes, and packing supplies on his back. On one trip he snow-shoed from camp at the head of the Big Plains, eleven miles southwest of Inlet, along the South Branch to Silver Run Brook, thence to its headwater, Cellar Pond, after which he started back along the same route without pausing to rest. He and his companion were overtaken by darkness before they could reach camp. Fred had carried a forty pound pack, the snow was wet and the going laborious, and the eighty-four year old woodsman admitted to a tinge of weariness. He then prepared for the night as he had done many times before during his years in the forest. He built a fire, cooked supper, rolled himself in his blanket, and slept the night through as peacefully as a weary child. Arising at daybreak, cheerful and refreshed, he eagerly resumed his journey.

Later in the spring Fred announced his intention of returning to his Maine home by an all-water route which included the Erie Canal, the Hudson River and the Atlantic Ocean. He started from Inlet in a canoe, entered the Middle Branch of the Moose River at Old Forge, and paddled down that stream past its confluence with the North Branch. Before he reached Lyons Falls log jams interposed serious objections to his plan, and he resolved to walk home. Friends whom he encountered feared that age had impaired his mental faculties, and they persuaded him to return to Maine by rail. He died in Augusta in 1925.

William Dart, a lank, keen eyed woodsman, twenty-six years old, tramped into the Central Adirondack region in 1876, seeking employment as a guide. He found enough work to keep himself alive, and enough incentive later to embark upon a rather elaborate hotel enterprise. When he left the region fifty years later to make his home in Florida, he had earned a wide reputation as the proprietor of a distinctive resort, and to a clientele of half a century he had become known as "Bill" Dart, typical of the colorful, self-reliant woodsmen of the old Adirondack school.

Bill was born in Laurens, Otsego County, N. Y., in 1850. When still a very young man he began hunting and trapping in the Bisby Lake country, and after several years spent in that locality he came to the Fulton Chain. In 1879 he built a cabin on the shore of Second Lake, North Branch (now Dart's Lake). Here small parties of sportsmen were sheltered, and Bill, the host, did the cooking, guiding and a good deal of the story telling. His interesting personality and good woodsmanship kept business coming. In 1887 he built a second camp on the lake to accommodate a party of Bostonians who vacationed there each summer.

In 1888 Bill went hunting for a bride, and found a good one —Mary Krohnmiller of White Lake, a young lady of Adirondack experience whose charm as a hostess and skill at the kitchen range contributed a large measure of success to Dart's Camp. Bride and groom arrived at the Forge House in the summer of 1888, rowed to the North Shore of Fourth Lake, and from there followed the carries and water routes to Dart's. It was a honeymoon of woods and water with hard work awaiting at the end of the trail, but the couple were young, ambitious and in love, and they began their life companionship with a determination that never faltered this side of success.

In the fall of 1888 Bill erected a large rustic camp on the lake
which was filled the following summer with appreciative patrons.
As business increased he built other camps, all of rustic design,
and his place eventually grew to be one of the most picturesque
and outstanding of Adirondack public camps.   Like many of
the early camp builders, Bill began business as a squatter. After
the building of the railroad in 1892 he purchased the entire
lake shore from Dr. Webb on a contract calling for the payment of principal and interest over a period of years.

Early days of camp life at Dart's were times of novel hardship modified by the delights of contact with the primeval
forest and the enjoyment of its multiplicity of diversions.
Sportsmen who patronized the camp reached it by an arduous
route which included not only the notorious Brown's Tract
Road but a trek through the woods from Fourth Lake.   Visitors usually discarded their city clothes at the Forge House,
or at some camp farther up the lakes, in favor of rough toggery
better suited to the strenuous purpose of the wearers.   The
railroad later solved much of the problem of transportation,
but not all of it.   A road cut from the Big Moose Station to
the western shore of Big Moose Lake (near the site of the
present Glenmore Hotel) enabled travellers to reach Dart's by
horse-drawn vehicles and boats.   A second road was cut from
the South Shore of Big Moose Lake, near its outlet, which
led to Dart's.   The Big Moose Lake end of this road was
known as "Dart's Landing."   Guests embarking at the western
shore were rowed to the Landing and then conveyed by wagon
to the Camp.   The going was still rough in spite of these improvements, the Station road in particular, with its succession
of miniature precipices, being little better than a rocky travesty
on the ancient art of road building.

Bill Dart introduced a unique equipage into the transportation service between the Landing and his Camp.   He hitched
a gentle little red bull to a two-seated spring wagon and evolved
a turnout that commanded instant attention, and at the same
time performed excellent service.   The harnessed bovid was a

grade bull, considerably more native stock than high grade, its unassuming dull red splotched with mild gray. Driving reins fastened to the nose ring extended upward to smaller rings protruding from the tips of its horns, and thence back to the driver. Passengers and baggage were hauled to and from the camp for two years with this plodding outfit before Bill bowed to the march of progress and bought a horse. The patient animal caused a good deal of merriment among Camp guests and a certain amount of effective advertising for its owner. It was a general handy man about Camp, doing heavy chores as thoroughly if not as speedily as could have been accomplished by a horse.

Following the erection of the Wood and Hess Camps on Fourth Lake, the Sperry Camp opened its doors to the public. This Camp, a rustic structure of hewn logs and natural bark exterior with a capacity of twenty guests, was the third public place to be built on Fourth Lake. It was built by Will Sperry, on the South Shore just below Big Island (Alger's Island). Will and his widowed mother, Jane Sperry, managed it in partnership until 1884 when Jane married Andrew Alexander. Will, who was then twenty-two years old and a self reliant woodsman, struck out for himself. He built a semi-public camp on the lower North Shore of the lake which he christened "Camp Cuba." Here he entertained hunting and fishing parties whom he guided, or occasionally leased the camp outright to summer vacationists. After his mother's second marriage the Sperry Camp became known as "Camp Alexander."

Johnny Van Valkenburgh built the first camp erected on Second Lake in 1880, a roomy semi-public camp of unpeeled logs and rough-sawed boards. Johnny, a skilled and popular woodsman and guide, occupied it for several years, then drifted off to Michigan. An unfortunate mishap in the mid-western state brought his career to a close. While on a prolonged hunting trip his feet and legs were frozen so severely that a resulting gangrenous condition proved fatal.

"Slim" Jim Phifield, a homespun sort of character, slow

BILL AND MARY DART

Dart's bull, a genial handy man about camp.

going, quaint and eccentric, but an able young woodsman, wandered into the Fulton Chain region in the early seventies. He brought his dog, gun and boat, and proclaimed himself to be seeking a home-site, having wearied of his boyhood environ- ment in Essex County. There were unlimited home-sites avail- able—in fact, the entire region, unpeopled and architecturally unimproved as it was, offered an endless vista of free building plots for the mere choosing. But Slim Jim was conservative. He took his time, looked the country over carefully, and ten years later, in 1884, built a small log cabin on the lower South Shore of Fourth Lake, on the site now occupied by a Herkimer Y. M. C. A. organization. Here he set up bachelor housekeep- ing on a modest scale, evincing a degree of satisfaction with his lot that usually comes only to one who has realized the ambition of a lifetime. He guided sportsmen, sheltered some of them in his cabin at modest rates, took a hand in community affairs, and settled down in the security of his squatter proprietorship to an enjoyable existence in the locality of his choosing. Neighboring guides delighted in his companionship. In the leisurely winter months especially, they sought diversion in his company, for his mannerisms, philosophies, solemn ob- servances of outworn social amenities, and even his clothes were characteristic of a man fifty years behind the times.

Slim Jim had occupied his snug little cabin but a short time when a singular affair brought his bachelorhood and his local housekeeping to an abrupt end. A sick man, accompanied by his wife, arrived on Fourth Lake hoping to restore his impaired health by a stay in the mountains. Being in moderate financial circumstances, they stopped at the Phifield cabin because of its low priced accommodations. In spite of his avowed dislike of women, the eccentric proprietor took them in, as guests were not numerous and he always needed money. The frail husband stubbornly fought the disease that afflicted him, and his wife, devoted and attentive, bravely helped in the fight. But the hardships of the journey into the mountains proved too great a handicap, and the odds swung heavily against them.

He died within a month of his arrival, leaving Slim Jim face to face with a situation involving a newly bereaved widow and the care and transportation of her husband's remains. He rose to the occasion slowly and awkwardly, but as best he could, extending to the grief stricken woman such rude consolation as lay in his power to express. At the same time he arranged for the removal of her dead spouse to the railroad at Boonville. His honest sympathy and ready disposition to render assistance in her hour of sorrow affected the widow with a sense of high esteem for the character of this uncouth woodsman who had now become her sole protector and counselor in the wilderness. When the freight wagon and buckboard were ready to start on their melancholy mission to the railroad she requested him to accompany her as far as Boonville.

Meanwhile, Slim Jim had drastically revised his adverse estimate of women, frankly conceding that much of his life-long antipathy to the sex had been based on unwarranted prejudice rather than on experience and understanding. He was beginning to appreciate them, in fact to admire them, especially the lonely specimen in his charge, and he regretted her departure.

On the way to Moose River Settlement the two sat side by side in the buckboard as it followed the heavier vehicle which bore the rough box. Slim Jim's arms were constantly alert to shield his gentle companion from the shocks of travel engendered by the rutty surface of the road. In turn, she reciprocated, nestling trustfully. Their conversation, impersonal at first, graduated to subdued intensity. Slim Jim's platitudes in vernacular and her conventional responses gave way to an animated exchange of confidences. The strong arms slowly tightened their hold, and the two voices dropped to intimate whisperings as words almost inaudible passed between them, earnest, low-spoken utterances which the straining ears of the buckboard driver failed to catch. When they reached Moose River the pair were engaged, or so the driver reported when he returned to the Forge House the next day. At all events, Slim Jim followed the deceased not only to Boonville but to his home: he stayed for the funeral, made himself useful afterward, and some time later married the widow. He disposed of his cabin to Josiah Helmer and Sarah Clarke, moved with his bride to Iowa, and eventually settled in Idaho.

The Helmer-Clarke partnership, which became a marital one, built a larger structure adjoining the cabin which they conducted as "The Fourth Lake House." The construction work was done by George Goodsell who came into the woods about 1880, and who acquired an early and well deserved reputation as one of the region's most competent and prolific builders. Charles Holliday and his wife, Ella, purchased the place after a few years, and operated it under the same name. Charles died during his proprietorship, and Ella, with two relatives, Messrs. Niles and Crawford, built and operated Rocky Point Inn near the head of the lake which is now owned by Arch G. Delmarsh. Nick Powers managed the Fourth Lake House until 1902 when it was purchased by James H. Hill and its name changed to "The Manhassit."

After the building of the Club and Dutton Camps, private camp construction on Big Moose Lake continued with the building of the Moore Camp on the South Shore near the entrance to South Bay, and the Williams Camp near the inlet. Both were built by Jack Sheppard and Richard Crego, the first named structure for Mr. and Mrs. F. C. Moore of New York, and the other for Frank Williams, also a New Yorker.

The first public camps on the lake were erected by two lifelong friends, James Higby, better known as "Jim," and Henry Covey, both Lewis County men. Jim made his first trip into the Adirondacks in 1868. He was then twenty-five years old. By spending his first summer in the employ of Otis Arnold he earned a little money, improved his delicate health, and learned a good deal about local geography. During the next eighteen years he hunted, trapped and guided, and in 1886 launched his first building project on Big Moose Lake. He built a log cabin on the South Shore of East Bay, the forerunner of the present Higby Camp on the same site. By a process of architectural evolution and expansion of service it became one of the lake's well known resort hotels.   Jim, of course, occupied the land as a squatter during his log cabin days, but in 1892 he purchased the site from Dr. Webb.   In the meantime, he had erected a second building, a handsome rustic structure large enough to be classed as a full-fledged hotel.

Jim's early clientele included only sportsmen who made their way to his cabin on hunting and fishing expeditions.   The erection of the second building attracted another type of visitors, summer vacationists, men and women who tramped the trail from Fourth Lake to enjoy a month's outing in the picturesque environment of Big Moose.   The new hotel and the increased patronage accorded it gave rise to a new problem of transportation which Jim attempted to solve.   A winter road partly cut and partly worn from Fourth Lake enabled Big Moose residents to haul supplies by sled during seasons of favorable snowfall, but the road was impassable for vehicular traffic during snowless seasons.   Until the building of the railroad in 1892, pedestrianism offered the only means of reaching the lake in summer, and vacationists who were bound for Jim's camp underwent a good day's exercise in reaching it.   The Station Road, opened in the fall of 1892 from West Bay to the railroad provided better transportation facilities, for guests could then ride the entire distance to Higby's and engage in pedestrianism at their later inclination.

Necessity, the mother of invention, together with man's innate impulse to harness every conceivable form of potential energy, inspired Jim to harness a milch cow for the performance of routine work during his early years in the hotel business. The cow was an ordinary milker, more versatile than Dart's bull, for it could both work and give milk.   It made its way to Camp by a circuitous route.   Driven along the road from Watson to Stillwater, it was led through the woods from the latter place to the westerly shore of Big Moose Lake.   There it walked onto a waiting raft and spent an unemotional hour inspecting the beautiful scenery as two rowboats towed it to

Higby's. It thrived for some time in its new home, plowing, hauling, skidding logs, mindful also of its responsibility as a one-cow dairy. A day came, however, when the Camp ran short of venison. Reluctantly the members of the household turned their eyes toward the barn. Undisturbed by the situation the patient creature came forth to the slaughter, to make its last grand sacrifice on the altar of roast beef medium. Then Jim bought a horse.

Henry Covey, of Glenfield, Lewis County, arrived on Big Moose Lake in 1880 to ply his smithy and carpenter trades in the construction of Billy Dutton's island camp. He had already served his apprenticeship in the woods, having hunted the Beaver River country since boyhood, and Jim Higby helped him to perfect his woodsmanship by accompanying him on several expeditions through the Central Adirondacks. Henry liked the region well enough to build a camp for his own use. In 1882 he built a portable camp in his Glenfield shop which he sledded in sections into the woods and stored in the Forge House barn. In the spring of 1883 he set it up on the lower North Shore of Fourth Lake. Artful hook-and-eye appendages spaced along the edges of the several sections enabled him to fit it together as an habitable dwelling with less than a half day's work. After it had stood on the lower shore two years, Henry unhooked it, towed it farther up the lake, and hooked it up again near the site of Alonzo Wood's Camp.

In 1886 Henry went into the hotel business on Big Moose Lake. He chose a picturesque location, a rugged point of land extending into the lake between East and West Bays, and built a large rustic camp which he named "Camp Crag" because of the point's sharply pitched topography. Like Dart's and Higby's, the place became a noted rendevous for a good class of sportsmen and vacationists. Natural impediments similar to those affecting contemporary builders were encountered in the construction and operation of Camp Crag. Much of the finished lumber, millwork and furnishings, were transported by man power from Fourth Lake. Henry's establishment boasted no cattle-drawn vehicles such as Bill and Jim used, but a fast moving dog team helped to quicken the transportation pace and lifted innumerable burdens from the shoulders of Henry and his men. The dogs were strong, rangy deer hounds that hauled supplies and passengers over the snow-bound landscape at a rapid gait. They were also used as deer runners to supply the Camp with venison.

In 1889, Emil Meurer, a native of Alsace Lorraine, who had migrated to America as a boy and after considerable wandering had made his way to the Adirondacks, built a small hotel on the North Shore of Fourth Lake near the present Becker Camp. His place served as a way station for travellers to and from Dart's, Higby's and Covey's. Visitors bound for these places left Fourth Lake at that point to follow the combined land and water trail to their destinations. Articles of clothing and other baggage deemed non-essential during their stay up the North Branch were deposited in Emil's care to be claimed on the return trip.

Henry Covey's son, Earl, inherited his father's pioneering and building instincts—to the greater architectural glory of the Big Moose locality. As a very small boy he gave promise of being a fine grained chip of the old block. In February, 1897, he made his way to Twitchell Lake on snowshoes to begin the erection of the commodious Twitchell Lake Inn, the first public camp on that slender, scenic body of water. Earl and his helpers on the job set a nearly all time record for speed in resort hotel construction. Exactly ninety days after their arrival at the lake, the Inn opened its doors to a party of guests who had come for a week's fishing.

The design of Earl's new hostelry followed the best traditions of camp building established by early settlers on the lake, a rustic sort of architecture, shielded from the waterfront by dense thickets inconspicuously harmonizing with the surrounding forest. Happily, this method of locating and building camps has dominated construction work throughout Twitchell's entire history, and today the little lake presents a leafy shore line that is almost unmarred by man's architectural inconsistencies.

The lake derives its name from Charles Twitchell, an amateur sportsman of Lewis County, who frequented its shores in the mid-century period. Not until 1870, however, did the first permanent building appear on the lake, a humble log hut built on the upper north shore by Hiram Burke, a native of Lowville. Hiram was born in 1839 and roamed the Adirondacks as a youth, often being accompanied by Chauncey Smith, the celebrated guide and woodsman of the Number Four region. He married Chauncey's daughter, Ursula, and having resolved to make woodsmanship his life's career, he erected the Twitchell Lake camp to shelter himself and sportsmen whom he guided. He packed the products of his gun and trap lines through the woods to Lowville where he spent off-seasons manufacturing hand-made fur gloves. Prior to his death in 1903, his two sons, Fred and William had become well known guides in the Number Four and Fulton Chain-Big Moose regions.

Next in order on the Twitchell shore were the Young and Holmes camps, the former near the head of the lake and the other on the south-easterly shore. Francis Young, a well known guide, shared his camp for a number of years with a clientele of sportsmen who patronized the lake. The Holmes camp, owned by R. A. Holmes, of Winstead, Conn., was originally built by William Cullen, a guide, and Professor Emory L. Mead, an educator. Professor Mead's early comradeship with Twitchell's residents proved to be educational as well as interesting. He developed into a first class woodsman, and for the past fifty years has vacationed in the Adirondacks. At this writing he owns and occupies an artistically designed rustic camp, the product of his own labor, on the shore of Seventh Lake.

Little Moose Lake, long a favorite haunt of sportsmen and retreat of nature lovers, owes its beginning as a "residential section" to Frank Johnson, a self-exiled Englishman who entered the woods in the late sixties. Frank was, perhaps, the quaintest of all the region's contemporary woodsmen. Tall, rugged, taciturn to the point of eccentricity, he made his way into the forest in search of solitude, a condition which abounded to his heart's contentment. After two years' residence on the Fulton Chain, he built a sturdy log cabin at the foot of Little Moose Lake which he occupied for some time, mysteriously coming and going at his pleasure, coldly indifferent to the friendly overtures of his fellow woodsmen, and bluntly averse to taking part in discussions involving the facts of his past life. Admirably gifted with the instincts and physique requisite to good woodsmanship, he roamed the woods on solitary hunting and trapping excursions. Invitations to join other expeditions were usually refused, although he occasionally surprised a con' genial acquaintance by seeking his companionship. The ac' quaintance thus favored needed to be very congenial indeed for the Englishman's reserve acted as a depressant upon all but ultra-ardent devotees of silence.

Frank was an orderly housekeeper, meticulous in the care of his little camp which he kept ship-shape inside and out. Curiosity prompted passers-by who knew him to look in at the camp in the guise of neighborly visitors, hoping to engage him in informative discourse. Their visits never pro' duced a shred of evidence which might lead to a solution of the mystery. Frank, if at home, could usually be found rocking slowly in a rustic armchair, engrossed with his work—knitting socks or mittens—and cooly unconcerned with the identity or mission of his visitor. Somewhere he had learned to ply knit' ting needles in a skilful and practical manner and several articles of his personal apparel were of his own making. If the visitor experienced surprise upon discovering the brawny Englishman engaged in this dainty pursuit he later experienced a sense of chagrin when, after he had spent a half hour or more in the cabin, the host had barely deigned to acknowledge his presence. In distinct contrast to housekeepers of normally gracious and hospitable temperament, Frank uncivilly re' fused to lay aside his knitting for the trivial lure of a social

Sperry's Camp on Fourth Lake—later known as Camp Alexander

JIM HIGBY

HENRY COVEY

Burke Camp, Twitchell Lake

chat. If he uttered a conventional farewell at his guest's departure it was the utmost that could be expected in the way of verbal compensation for the visit. Needless to say, community interest in Frank and his conspicuous reticence remained at a high pitch during the pioneer days of Little Moose camp life.

After dwelling in his little hermitage a few years, Frank suddenly bowed to a bibulous urge and a longing for sociability. He laid in a stock of liquors and invited a few woodsmen in to help drink it. The woodsmen came willingly enough, anticipating an evening of unusual entertainment. They found the refreshments potent and mellowing, and all partook without stint—the host included. One by one the iron bonds of silence fell from Frank's uncommunicative tongue, and long before the black night had merged into the misty gray of dawn he had reminisced at eloquent length on the facts of his more than forty years' existence. A spirited, fascinating conversationalist, he commanded the rapt attention of his guests, and they listened in astonishment to the story of the transformed Briton who had never been known to utter more than ten consecutive words. When they left in the wee small hours they departed silent and somewhat awed, impressed by the volume of their host's conversation rather than by the significance of his revelations. As he extracted no pledge of secrecy the tale soon went the rounds.

Before coming to America, Frank had taken informal leave of the naval authorities of Her Britanic Majesty, Queen Victoria. He was a deserter. For twenty years he had sailed the seven seas on Her Majesty's ships of war, visiting far ports, penetrating strange lands, witnessing queer sights, and winning promotions for faithful discharge of duty. A loyal subject and a hardy seaman, danger and hardship thrilled him; so did the uncertainty of human life that could be soothed or annihilated on the mighty bosom of the sea. But on a certain voyage of the fleet to the South Atlantic a strange revulsion against the necessary discipline of the service overcame him with such force that he resolved to gain his liberty at the earliest opportunity. He still loved and courted adventure, but it must be adventure of his own choosing. He deserted ship at an African seaport, and after wandering over the dark continent sailed for America —a man without a country. The Adirondacks appealed as a secure haven from Britain's vengeance, and he made his way to the Fulton Chain, his natural reserve of manner and speech being intensified by a resolve to guard the secret of his deser-tion.

Frank's precarious status in the eyes of the British Admir-alty, now publicly known throughout the region, in no way affected his social standing in the sparsely peopled frontier of the Adirondacks. Local woodsmen were more or less accus-tomed to contact with men who had made their way into the forest for urgent reasons which they preferred keeping to them-selves. Frank continued to hunt, trap, fish and knit, and to keep a close mouth except when responding to alcoholic stimuli.

Until the building of the Lewis H. Taylor Camp in 1882, his cabin at the foot of the lake remained the sole habitation on the Little Moose shore. The Taylor camp was built by Will Sperry, Tom Griffin and Frank Johnson near the site now occupied by the Club House. It preceded by one year the erec-tion of the Burnham camp a short distance below it. Frank regarded this inflow of two camp builders within a single year with no little disfavor, but he accepted the job of guide and caretaker offered to him by Lewis Taylor and moved from his hut into the newer and larger building.

For several years things went well with Frank. He dwelt comfortably in the new quarters, enjoyed a year round salary with but a minimum of obligation due his employer, and found little to complain of except the straggling appearance of new camp builders whose industry desecrated the lake's virgin shores and disturbed its peaceful solitude. In the mid-eighties he joined Jack Sheppard on a panther hunt which accomplished the ex-tinction of the species in the Fulton Chain country. The two men tracked their victim to the summit of Pico Mountain and shot it out of a tree-top where it had snarlingly taken refuge. The kill gained considerable local attention as panthers were already considered a vanished division of the animal kingdom in the locality.

In the late eighties, disquieting rumors of a proposed rail-road-building project reached Frank's ears. The road, it was said, would penetrate the Central Adirondack region on its route across the mountains and would bring thousands of visi-tors swarming into the woods. Frank denounced the project in vehement terms, vowing he would leave the country when the first rail was spiked to its cross ties. But before the propo-sition could be shaped into tangible form an actual calamity confronted him. The Adirondack League Club came into being. In 1890, a wealthy group of forest lovers organized for the purpose of maintaining a vast private preserve in the Ad-irondacks. By lease and purchase they acquired a tract of two hundred thousand acres with scores of rivers and lakes lying within its boundaries—including Frank's dearly beloved Little Moose Lake. A spacious club house would be erected near his camp, and the entire shore line would be surveyed and mapped into building lots. Furious at the wholesale trespass, he packed his clothes, rifle and boat, and left. His destination, he said, was Florida, and he would make his way by water from Boonville to New York and thence southward along the Atlantic coast. He put his boat in the water at Boonville, rowed to the Erie Canal, then to the Hudson River and on to New York. In New York he reaffirmed his intention of row-ing to Florida, but if he carried out his plan he steered an amaz-ingly roundabout course for a veteran of twenty years' experi-ence in deep sea navigation. Six months after leaving New York he turned up at Slim Jim Phifield's home in Idaho. Some-where on the way he had abandoned his boat, but he still carried the rifle. He stayed one day with Slim Jim, then set out toward the Pacific—a gaunt, lonely figure, nearing three score and ten, without friends or country, and utterly power-less to acquire either. He never returned to the Adirondacks, and his mountain friends never heard of him again.

Camp de Camp, built in 1887 by William Scott de Camp and his wife, Julia, on de Camp Island near the head of First Lake, bore the distinction of being one of the very few early private camps not erected by squatters. The builders owned practically the entire acreage of Township Seven in which the camp was located.

William Scott de Camp was a native of Morris County, N. J. He descended from a family of industrialists whose prosperity had been wrested from the iron business. Unfortunately, the family fortune dwindled to insignificance during the life of William's father, Edward, and the nearly penniless son attempted to recoup by engaging actively in the ancestral industry which his father had neglected. He had made substantial progress toward realizing his objective when iron ore deposits, richer and more accessible, were discovered in the mid-west. Almost overnight the well laid foundation of William's New Jersey enterprise crumbled to ruin, and again he faced the world without immediate prospects. Temporarily dejected by this cataclysmic reverse, he accepted the invitation of a friend, a lumber man, to accompany him on a business errand into Lewis County, N. Y. The friend was interested in certain timber lands owned by the estate of Lyman R. Lyon who had died five years before.

During their stay in Lewis County the two men were entertained at the Lyon home in Lyons Falls, a handsome residence of gray stone which has since been destroyed by fire and replaced with a large frame dwelling. The house was then occupied by Lyman's three daughters, Mary, Julia and Florence. Their brothers, Chester and Lyman Howard, had taken their respective patrimonies in cash and negotiable securities and were engaged at the time in sundry business enterprises. The daughters still held their heritage in a common parcel— large tracts of agricultural and timber lands which lend themselves less readily to liquidation than securities, and with ordinary management are apt to survive other forms of wealth as a dependable source of income.

The meeting between William and Julia resulted in mutual admiration. The visitor from New Jersey was a man of impressive appearance, slow of speech, considerate, plainly a gentleman of excellent moral and intellectual substance. Julia was an attractive young woman, accomplished in the pretty feminine mode of her day, but possessed, also, of an instinctive practicality and mental energy inherited from a long line of utilitarian ancestors. The two had much in common. No courtship developed, however, during William's stay at the home. When he returned to New Jersey he considered his new acquaintance in perspective and decided that a more desirable life-mate than Julia was not to be found. He then penned a letter to her, a straightforward statement of his high regard for her and a proposal of marriage, and hopefully awaited an answer. After a proper lapse of time it arrived— in the affirmative. They were married the following year, in 1875.

At the time of the division of the Lyon estate among the three daughters Julia chose, among other items, the bulk of Township Seven of the Brown's Tract. The management of this inheritance fell to her husband who, though a newcomer to the Adirondacks, proved to be thoroughly capable of supervising the development of the tract. This consisted mainly of disposing of stumpage rights and the supervision of the activities of contracting lumbermen. William constructed several roads, one of which led from Thendara to Indian Rapids on the North Branch and another to Nick's Lake. He also inaugurated steamboat service on the Moose River to form a connecting link between the Fulton Chain and the narrow gauge railroad which operated between Moose River Settlement and a point on the river known as Minnehaha. With his son, Lyon, he conceived the feasibility of operating a saw mill at Carter, a junction of the Adirohdack division of the New York Central and the Raquette Lake Railways. William died in 1905, ten years after the death of Julia, but Lyon erected the proposed mill and operated it successfully for several years. Later, he dismantled and moved it to Thendara to replace the Brown's Tract Mill which had been destroyed by fire.

One daughter and two sons were born to the de Camps, Mary, Horace and Lyon, all of whom (at this writing) main' tain summer homes at the head of First Lake. Lyon, having been closely associated with his father in the various phases of development work, purchased the land equities of his sister and brother after the death of the parents and is still actively concerned with the managerial details involved in his large proprietary holdings.

XI

TRANSPORTATION

THIS chapter is devoted to the history of the regional develop-ment of transportation and communication, together with the personalities involved in the evolution of these facilities. An all important problem in the region's early growth as a recrea-tional area, the question of transportation has faded to one of casual significance due to the construction of highly perfected routes of travel and the employment locally of gasoline and steam as agencies of locomotion.

The 1881 edition of Stoddard's guide book, "The Adiron-dacks," contains a humorous though pithy reference to the riding qualities of the old Brown's Tract Road, then the only means of vehicular ingress to the Fulton Chain. According to this pert little volume, a certain traveller, having survived the harassing buckboard trip from Boonville to the Forge House, upon viewing the forest-bordered outlet of the Fulton Chain for the first time, exclaimed with tempered rapture "The Gates of Paradise—reached through Purgatory!" He voiced no metaphorical injustice either to the road or the region, but though his memories may have been painful at the moment, his hardships were ended. He had reached a land of many waterways, and pleasant trails that respond softly to man's tread. Quiet, smooth-riding boats awaited his pleasure—and sturdy guides to row them.

Lakes and rivers were the way, and boats the vehicles, of travel in the early days of Adirondack recreational life. Sturdi-ness of physique played an important part in the guide's career for heavy boats, easily handled in water, became cumbersome burdens on the carries. Countless members of the guiding profession were often heard muttering improprieties of speech as they staggered under the weight of such craft. Not until the Adirondack guide boat had been evolved from a rude be-ginning into a dainty skiff of great strength and capacity did

the emancipated guides face the carries with cheerful counten-
ance. The development of this boat to its present perfected
state effected something of an epochal change in the modeling
of Adirondack water craft. Several names, many of them
familiar to present residents of the Central Adirondacks, are
associated with the boat's history, notably H. Dwight Grant
and his two sons, Lewis and Floyd, Theodore Seeber, Riley
Parsons and his two sons, Ira and Ben. To this group of
craftsmen a large measure of credit is due for the forty years
or more of the boat's wide popularity.

The idea of a light weight, oar propelled boat had its inception at Long Lake in the forties. A diminutive craft of limited
capacity came into use among guides there and gradually
became adopted in other localities. From time to time, changes
effected in its lines improved its bearing and increased its capacity and general usefulness. William A. Martin, a Saranac
Lake boat builder, added further improvements until the model
gained recognition as being superior to any other type of
Adirondack water craft although it still weighed rather heavy
in proportion to its capacity.

In 1879, Dwight Grant, an experienced guide and all-round
woodsman, thoroughly familiar with the problems confronting
a wilderness oarsman, applied his talents to further enhancing
the guide boat's utility. Characteristic of his usual approach
to a new task, he studied the problem from the ground up—or,
in this case, from the keel up—and invited a Saranac Lake
boat building friend to his Boonville home for a consultation
regarding certain innovations which he proposed to embody
in an improved design of the old boat. The friend accepted
the invitation, and for several weeks the two men spent their
time hard at work in Dwight's little carpenter shop on Post
Street, Boonville.

Dwight was an outstanding woodsman, easily one of the
most versatile and accomplished of his time. Born on a farm
near Boonville, the son of Nelson Grant, a farmer-guide, he
made his first trip into the Adirondacks in 1850. Accom-

H. DWIGHT GRANT

"I esteem the good name of guide more than my title of Honorable."

panied by his father he tramped through the woods to Limekiln Falls on the South Branch of the Moose River, and there fash-ioned a small log raft. On this rude conveyance the pair floated leisurely downstream to Moose River Settlement, fishing and camping along the way. The experience converted young Dwight into an ardent lover of the forest. He returned often, and roamed across the region in an ever widening circle. At the age of twenty-one he was known as a trustworthy, well informed woodsman. He guided General Richard U. Sherman on the latter's first extensive excursion across the mountains, and, incidentally, introduced the General to the Adirondack mountain-ash cocktail, a mixture of spring water, spirituous liquor and juice extracted from the inner bark of the ash. It was a bracing refreshment with a tangy smack of the woods, eagerly welcomed after a hard day on the lakes and carries. In a letter to Dwight, written thirty years later, General Sherman recalled this drink as the tastiest concoction he had ever im-bibed.

In 1862 Dwight enlisted for Civil War duty in Company I, 117th Regiment of New York Volunteers, and served three years, rising to the rank of Lieutenant. His finely penned diary written during six months' confinement in Libby and Charles-town Prisons furnishes an enlightening word picture of the tribulations of a Northerner in a Confederate prison. Prior to the war he had followed the trades of millwright and car-penter in Boonville and had spent several months of each year guiding in the Adirondacks. He built many of the early camps along the Fulton Chain, including the Lawrence Camp where he served as head guide from 1873 to 1896. In 1879 he was elected to the State Legislature from Oneida County. He was then a man of scholarly and distinguished appear-ance, a thoughtful, effective speaker, profoundly versed in affairs of the forest which he loved. At Albany he gained the immediate confidence and respect of his associates as he had done in the woods. By exerting his influence in behalf of con-servation of the State's wild life he effected a notable revision

of the game laws. As "Honorable H. Dwight Grant" he continued to follow his multiple vocation of guide., builder and
business man, frankly declaring that he cherished his good name
as a guide more than his title of Honorable. In 1897 he assumed
the management of Mountain Lodge, the name then applied to
the Adirondack League Club's main club building on Little
Moose Lake. Three years later he became Superintendent of
the Club and served in this capacity until 1906 when failing
health forced his retirement. He was succeeded by his son
Lewis, who at this writing maintains a summer home on Fourth
Lake.

Dwight's 1879 experiments in his Boonville shop brought
forth two guide boats, the designs of both being distinct de-
partures from the Saranac models. He continued to build an
increasing number each year, altering the designs as his ingenious mind evolved added improvements. With no concession
of strength or capacity, these boats, which became known as
the Grant Model Adirondack Guide Boats, provided water
conveyances thirty to sixty pounds lighter than any former
models, and of greatly improved bearing. A design of ribbed
framework describing a gradual upward and outward curve
added bearing from keel to wale and enabled boatmen to transport heavy loads without endangering the stability of their
craft even in rough water. A fifteen foot boat of this type,
weighing less than seventy pounds (oars, seats and neck yokes
for carrying included) could safely carry three men, their
duffle, a hound or two, and a couple of deer carcasses. Needless to say, this innovation in transportation was hailed with
relief by members of the guiding fraternity. It literally lifted
a load from their shoulders. But Dwight did not rest on his
oars after his initial success. He incorporated other improvements from stem to stern as new boats went into service under
varying conditions. New models were designed; new materials
and methods employed to effect further reductions of weight.
The boat shop at Boonville underwent a process of enlarge-
ment to accommodate an increased staff of builders but the

supply rarely equalled the demand, for the boat rapidly became the most popular of all Adirondack watercraft.

In 1890, guide boat building became established as a local industry in Old Forge. Because of the wide demand for this type of craft, Riley Parsons and Theodore Seeber equipped a small shop on the third floor of the Garmon and Crosby mill that stood on the south shore of the Moose River beside the State dam. Both men were artizans of exceptional skill. Theodore had been associated with Dwight Grant for several years before coming to Old Forge and had familiarized himself with the fine points of boat building. He was an all-round mechanic, but an especially skilful worker in wood, and he chose his partner for the local enterprise as he did his tools—he selected the best.

Riley Parsons, whose violin had furnished the exhilarating music for a Forge House party in 1872, was born in Leyden, Lewis County, in 1839. He possessed the combined qualifications of a good carpenter and a good woodsman, an ideal equipment for the production of the buoyant craft which had so completely met the needs of Adirondack woodsmen. A good part of his early life had been spent in the woods, and later, while carrying on his trade in Bonnville, he had embraced every opportunity of returning to the Fulton Chain. In 1889 he helped to rebuild the Forge House, and from then until his death in 1904 he continued to make his home in Old Forge. Gifted with a high degree of intelligence and probity, his presence as a local resident contributed to the social and business life of the slowly growing community.

Seeber and Parsons conducted their business in the mill loft until 1892 when they built a two-story shop on the opposite side of the river adjoining the dam. In 1896, Riley purchased Theodore's interest in the business and continued the building of Parsons' model guide boats and the heavier St. Lawrence boats. In 1902, he moved the shop sectionally to its present location between the Eagle Bay Road and the North Shore of Old Forge Lake.

Riley's two sons, Ben and Ira Parsons, settled in the Fulton Chain region several years before their father's arrival as a permanent resident. As youngsters they had roamed the Adirondacks on frequent excursions, giving free rein to their youthful bent for adventure in the woods. They had also been trained from boyhood to ply the tools of their father's craft with precision. By a happy allotment of their vocations to the changing seasons they engaged harmoniously in the dual callings which training and inclination prompted. Fall and summer months found them tramping the forest, inducting sportsmen in their care into the mysteries of trout fishing and deer hunting. In the winter they built guide boats. After their father's death they carried on the construction of Parsons' model boats in a shop adjoining the Eagle Bay highway on the outskirts of Old Forge. In this shop they have maintained an annual output to date, but on a steadily diminishing scale. Changed conditions and new methods of travel have all but terminated the demand for their product, and at this writing the prestige of the famous Adirondack guide boat is sadly on the wane.

The technical variations between the Grant and Parsons' models were comparatively negligible. Both embodied the creative skill of true artificers, and both were the product of craftsmen of unbounded integrity. The longevity of these boats under exacting conditions eloquently attests the manual expertness and the fidelity of their makers. A seventy pound guide boat, built by Dwight Grant in 1884, is still in service locally and appears staunch enough to continue its usefulness for many years to come. A twelve foot boat weighing thirty-four pounds, built by Riley Parsons in the early nineties, still plies the Fulton Chain seemingly impervious to the infirmities of age. Many other boats of both models, ranging in age from thirty to forty-five years, continue to withstand seasonal usage throughout the Adirondacks.

That materials of such lightness could be fashioned staunchly enough to buffet the waves of nearly half a century constitutes a real achievement in boat building, and the contribution of the guide boat furnishes a distinct chapter in the history of lake and inter-lake transportation in the Adirondacks. A series of slender ribs of graduated lengths, cut from naturally crooked spruce roots, supply the framework. To these are fastened strips of siding in a single layer one-eighth to one-fourth of an inch thick. Native pine was formerly used for this purpose but has been replaced by California sugar pine due to the present difficulty of obtaining native material of desirable quality. Twenty-five hundred brass wood-screws and four thousand copper tacks are utilized in the construction of a sixteen foot model. These are all inserted by hand, for the entire boat is a hand-made product.

Dwight Grant's sons, Lewis and Floyd, both skilfully adept in their father's vocation and in woodsmanship, continued to build boats in Boonville for a number of years following the death of their father. In 1923 they discontinued their construction because of the greatly decreased demand. The use of motor boats on the lakes, the opening of new roads and trails, and other innovations of travel have been contributing factors in the failure of this type of craft to remain in general use. Today, guide boat building in the Adirondacks is a dying craftsmanship. In the Fulton Chain region it has taken its last refuge in the boat shop of Ben and Ira Parsons. At this writing both brothers retain the skill and deftness of hand acquired in youth, and both retain a devotion to the art of fashioning inanimate wood into forms of beauty and usefulness. Each winter they build a few guide boats which go into service the following spring or summer. They are modeled as of old, buoyant, dainty vessels that stand the gruelling test of time, glad things to the eyes of lovers of water trails, but sadly reminiscent of a day that has passed—the heyday of the guiding fraternity in the closing decades of the nineteenth century.

Facilities for communication by telephone penetrated the western foothills of the Adirondacks in 1881. During that year Henry J. Botchford constructed eleven miles of line reaching from his home in Port Leyden, Lewis County, to his tannery store at Moose River Settlement.   Five years later a line from Boonville to the Settlement was extended along the Brown's Tract Road to the Forge House.   This consisted of rather makeshift equipment with a single wire strung from tree to tree beside the thirteen miles of narrow road.   It effected an appreciable saving of time in periods of fair weather, espe- cially when the services of a physician were urgently needed. But fair weather and the telephonic needs of the Fulton Chain community did not always coincide.   Frequently, the line went out of commission with exasperating abruptness.   High winds lashed the heavy growth of woods that crowded the wire, and the toppling of decayed trees often broke the connection in one or more places in a single day.   In time the line became a public charge.   Its maintenance devolved upon the good offices of passers-by who chanced to detect a broken strand of wire trailing at the roadside.   If the traveller happened to be a Good Samaritan with the mechanical well-being of his fellow men at heart he stopped long enough to join the loose ends and fasten the wire to a tree by such means as he could hastily im- provise.   Buckboard drivers or their passengers usually per- formed this service.

In the autumn of 1888, an all day storm worked havoc with the line in several places and caused an indefinite suspension of service.   It also caused an aggravated buckboard driver to taint the evening air of the forest with profane invective. Delayed by the storm, the driver started from the Forge House in the afternoon, several hours behind schedule.   His vehicle was heavily laden with a consignment of freight, two passen- gers and their personal baggage.   He was a seasoned veteran of the road, pridefully aware of the responsibility vested in him of maintaining a high standard of service, and he grasped the reins with muttered impatience to make up for lost time.   Being a public spirited citizen he could not ignore the broken strands of wire that lurked along the way.   He stopped long enough to connect them and replace the wire, but each successive bit of repair work was undertaken with growing resentment against the institution of the telephone. Half way to Moose River Settlement darkness overtook the travellers, and the storm's damaging effect on the line faded from sight. Beyond Six Mile Hill a twisted wire reached out to the center of the road and awaited, like a snake in the grass, the arrival of the buckboard. It fastened itself to a spoke of a rear wheel and coiled tenaciously in and out from hub to rim weaving a circular network similar to a spider's crumpled web. Finally a loop of wire settled around a metal projection at the rear of the vehicle and slowly drew taut, thus producing a braking effect which retarded the revolving motion of the wheel. At twenty rods the buckboard stopped. Lantern in hand, the driver descended from his seat to ascertain the cause, and a brief inspection revealed it. Passengers reported later that if the pithy expletives he employed in stating his opinion of wire communication could have been broadcast at the moment they would have discouraged telephone construction for all time.

The badly disrupted line remained out of use forever after. Not until the organization of the Fulton Chain Telephone and Telegraph Company in 1892 did the region enjoy the luxury of uninterrupted telephone service. This company was formed by Dwight Sperry who was identified with several local development and building projects. Associated with him in the telephone enterprise were Clarence Sperry, Frank Sperry, Dennis Cannon, Mrs. Daisy Glenn and Mrs. Francena Higby. The area served by the new company extended from Thendara to the head of Fourth Lake, and sixteen subscribers were listed during the first year's operation.

Steam navigation took its place among Fulton Chain transportation methods in 1883—an early date to introduce this medium of travel considering the scarcity of camps and visitors then prevailing and the consequent dearth of ready patronge. In spite of its prematurity, the enterprise survived and eventually returned a profit, and steamboating gradually rose to dazzling heights as a local industry. For a quarter of a century it flourished and prospered, churning the waters of the Fulton

Chain in gala arrays of tourist-laden decks. Then it succumbed suddenly before the swift onslaughts of the more adaptable gasoline-propelled launches and motor vehicles.

The first steam driven vessel to ply the lower four lakes of the Fulton Chain became known to the travelling public through printed advertisements as the "Steam Yacht Hunter." It was owned and operated by Jonathan Meeker, a veteran Adirondack woodsman who has been presented to the reader in a previous chapter. Jonathan had spent thirty-five years in the Central Adirondacks and was widely known as a guide of marked ability and integrity. After launching his pioneer enterprise in 1883, he became known as "Captain Jonathan," an appellation of distinction which he bore with his usual solemnity and unassuming dignity.

The Hunter was screw propelled, thirty-five feet in length, with an eight foot beam. Its upright, six horse power, wood-burning boiler generated a driving power of from seven to eight miles an hour. From its canopied top waterproof curtains could be lowered in protection against rain and wind. The cost of construction, delivery and launching slightly exceeded eight hundred dollars but the undertaking returned a profit that fully justified the investment.

The vessel was designed and built by Dwight Grant in his Boonville boat shop in the winter of '82 and '83. In the spring of '83 it was skidded on horse drawn sleds along the Moose River and Brown's Tract Roads into the deep woods, and then along a narrower bark road to Minnehaha on the Moose River, five miles below Thendara. There it took to the water, unacclaimed and unchristened, and under its own power navigated the freshet-swollen river to the old forge where it was skidded around the dam and launched again in Old Forge Iake. The latter launching was almost as sensational a procedure locally as Robert Fulton's launching of the Clermont in the Hudson River seventy-six years before.

It is not improbable that Captain Jonathan Meeker never beheld the sea, but in mannerism and appearance he was a

CAPTAIN JONATHAN MEEKER

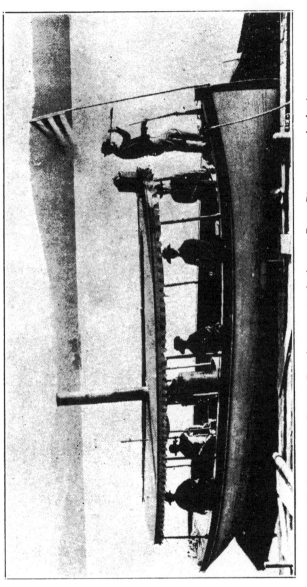

The Steam Yacht Hunter.   Captain Jonathan rests in the bow as Peter Giroux scans the horizon for storm signals and belated patrons.

striking counterpart of the traditional weather beaten **New** Englander who has toiled a lifetime on the briny deep. At the wheel of a Gloucester fishing trawler he would have blended in grim harmony with the environment of deck and rigging and the mingled smells of fish and salt air. Stern visaged, close mouthed, tall and sturdy, he possessed the resolution and inflexible honesty of his sturdy forebears who had settled in America years before the Revolution. He looked upon life with quiet, unvarying seriousness, and had scant time for its frivolities and vices. The meagre tuft of beard that drooped from his firm chin seldom moved in conversation, for its owner, being given to contemplation rather than to loquacity, had little to say, and a curt manner of saying it. Tobacco lured him to his only display of weakness. He chewed it wholesale and incessantly, tremendous quids of the juicy leaf that bulged his cheek far beyond normal proportions and required real dexterity to shift from side to side. The habit had its virtue, for the shifting of so bulky a cargo consumed time, and the Captain seldom spoke before shifting. This afforded an opportunity to deliberate, and many hasty, ill-advised retorts had been avoided by the Captain because of his routine performance of thoughtfully re-locating his quid before giving answer.

The advance announcement of the Hunter's proposed launching failed to inspire Fulton Chain guides with the same enthusiasm which the debut of Dwight Grant's guide boat had aroused. They viewed it as progress in the wrong direction, as an impudent intrusion into a sylvan region of oarlocks and open camps which Providence had consecrated as a land forever free from the contraptions of modernity that afflicted the outside world. The whistle alone, they argued, would frighten deer and other wild life from the waterfront, and cause a scarcity of game in the adjacent woods. Incoming sportsmen would resent the spectacle of a steamboat brazenly disturbing the placid surface of the lakes and contaminating the mountain air with shrill sounds and noisesome belchings of smoke. All in all, they declared emphatically against the innovation of steam and screw, and many of them openly vowed that the prosperity of the new enterprise would never be enhanced by their patron-age. A few of the more excitable muttered subtle threats against the Captain's person should he persist in going through with his project.

To a certain extent, the widely voiced antagonism toward the introduction of steam craft had birth in intelligent vision. But it was by no means infallible vision. The large majority of sportsmen who employed guides at that time differed con-siderably from the present day type of vacationists who insist upon conveniences of travel. Early visitors were attracted to the region by its primeval aspect of virgin wilderness despite its lack of transportation facilities. While they gloried in its charm of unspoiled forests and clear waterways, they also found relaxation in its immunity from mechanical conveniences. The steamboat offered a double threat against the security of these allurements, and the guides, in turn, regarded the steam-boat as a damaging threat against their vocation. Pride and prestige also had their place in the general discontent. For what woodsman of the early eighties, to whom were entrusted the safety, and the satisfying of adventurous cravings of a party of sportsmen in his charge, could complacently climb aboard a thirty-five foot steamer of modern design and sail in luxury up the lakes, at the same time representing the surround-ing country to his charges as an uncharted section of the wilder-ness, the very heart of the great rolling sweep of the Adiron-dacks, gloriously remote by virtue of its position from the despoiling hand of civilization.

Despite the outspoken hostility to his project, Captain Jonathan stolidly blazed the trail of progress and launched his Steam Yacht Hunter. The guides, firm in their resolve to ignore the unwelcome craft, stuck to their oars in adherence to the time honored means of locomotion. The Captain, equally firm, stuck to his ship and resolutely plied the Fulton Chain in majestic though unprofitable splendor. But as time passed, the guides relaxed from their antagonistic attitude, and, one by one, began to patronize the Hunter. To be sure, its shrill whistle still desecrated their Eden, but if it had frightened the deer those adaptable creatures had soon adjusted their brute temperaments to the phenomenon and could again be seen of an evening along the shores of the four lakes. Then, too, the steamer had quickly demonstrated its efficiency as a time and labor saver, two achievements that are inevitably welcomed by even the staunchest advocates of the old order. Rowboats gradually disappeared from long distance transportation on the lower lakes, and the worthy Captain and his sturdy craft were soon breasting the waves of the Fulton Chain in triumph.

Comprehending the value of advertising as a business stimulant, Captain Jonathan posted the following notice after a few seasons' operation:

FULTON CHAIN

Cheap Rates!   Staunch Boat!   Quick Passage!

On and After August 1, the Fast

STEAM YACHT HUNTER

Will carry passengers at the following rates from
Old Forge:

To de Camp and Stickney Camps_____10 cents
To Johnnie Vann's Camp_____10 cents
To Robert Perrie's Camp _____20 cents
To Clarke Camp _____30 cents
To Alexander Camp _____30 cents
To Arnold Camp _____40 cents
To Lawrence Camp _____40 cents
To Big Moose Landing_____50 cents
To Lon Wood's Camp _____50 cents
To Cedar Island, Fred Hess Camp_____50 cents

RETURN TRIPS AT SAME RATES

Boat will leave Cedar Island at 6 A. M. and arrive at Old Forge at 8 A. M. Will leave Old Forge upon arrival of teams at night.

CAPT. JNO. MEEKER

Of the eleven landings listed in the foregoing schedule, six were public camps, four were private, and one, Big Moose Landing, was not a camp but merely a landing dock maintained for the convenience of passengers travelling to Dart's and Big Moose Lakes.   Emil Meurer erected a public camp near the Landing about a year after the publication of the schedule.

Captain Jonathan fueled the Hunter from a woodlot on the present site of the hamlet of Eagle Bay.   Both he and Fred Hess felled enough trees in that locality to make room for the little settlement that grew up there.   The Captain built a cot-tage nearby which he occupied during the boating season, and each evening at the end of his trip up the lakes he tied the Hunter up at the small dock in front of this camp.   For winter storage of his boat he built a combined shed and camp on the upper shore of Big Island (Alger's Island).   Like the majority of his contemporary woodsmen, Captain Jonathan utilized various fuel sources and building sites with only a squatter's right to the premises.   In 1895, however, he purchased a plot on the North Shore of Fourth Lake for the erection of Camp Meeker, a cozy public camp which he conducted for several years and which is now owned and managed by his daughter, Mrs. Ida Peterson.   The Big Island boat house was moved sectionally to this location and incorporated in the camp struc-ture.   The Eagle Bay cottage is still tenanted at this writing. It is located a short distance east of the Eagle Bay Hotel and is owned and occupied seasonally by Frank Anderson of Brooklyn, N. Y., who has summered in the Adirondacks for nearly half a century.

The Hunter enjoyed a monopoly of the transportation busi-ness until 1887 when a second vessel steamed its way into the lake service.   The newcomer, a twenty-two foot boat with a three-quarter horsepower engine, bore the name "Etta S."   It was built by Theodore Seeber about 1880 for use on the Black River and Black River Canal.   With its limited carrying capacity and leisurely rate of speed the *Etta S* hardly menaced Captain Jonathan's supremacy of the waves.   By sitting rigidly upright and grooving their knees between the knees of fellow passengers seated opposite, eight cheerfully disposed travellers could make the best of its accommodations on each trip up or down the lakes. It was put into local service by Will Sperry, not as a competitive gesture against the Hunter, but as a transportation feature in connection with Will's and his mother's public camp operations on Fourth Lake. In 1888 it retired to its home port on the Black River. There it served in various capacities until an unfortunate collision with a coal barge caused its permanent retirement to Davy Jones' inland locker.

Storm clouds of more ominous aspect mottled the Captain's business horizon during the winter of '87 and '88. Jack Sheppard was at work building a steamboat which current rumor intimated would excel the Hunter in capacity, speed and all-round trimness. A temporary shed erected on the shore of Old Forge Lake near the State dam housed the undertaking which was carried on under the direction of Theodore Seeber. Current rumor did not err. In the summer of '88 the "Fulton" slid gracefully into the lake, a far tidier craft than the five year old Hunter. Fifty-five feet in length and equipped with an engine powerful enough to attain a speed of fifteen miles an hour, it gave promise of formidable competition. Instead of a canopied and curtained superstructure similar to that of its older rival, the Fulton carried a spacious, well fitted cabin of wood and glass which guaranteed protection against the severest buffetings of storm and wave. After a modest launching ceremony Jack Sheppard became known as "Captain Jack," and the Fulton Chain proudly boasted two steamboat Captains instead of one. To acquaint the public with the superior character of steamboat service he had inaugurated, Jack posted copies of the following notice:

STEAMBOAT FULTON
E. L. Sheppard, Captain.
From
OLD FORGE
to the head of
FOURTH LAKE, FULTON CHAIN
The only steamboat in the Adirondacks with first class
cabin accommodations!

An imposing photographic likeness of the steamer appeared on the poster, together with a group of satisfied looking passengers who contributed their silent testimonials by posing before the camera in the company of the new craft. The launching of the Fulton and the subsequent business rivalry between the two Captains caused no ill feeling on the part of either man. Captain Jonathan was a fair minded skipper, capable of recognizing the just claims of competition without harboring resentment against the competitor. Furthermore, the men had been friends for more than a quarter of a century and had shared many wilderness adventures in each other's company. The senior Captain, however, could not banish the perplexity and misgivings which beset him as he scanned Captain Jack's illustrated poster from time to time. That the Fulton outclassed the Hunter he readily admitted. It was faster, roomier and handsomer, to say nothing of the superior penetrating quality of its whistle. But the fact that so seasoned a frontiersman as his friend, Jack Sheppard, should introduce the elegance of first class cabin accommodations in an isolated wilderness struck him somehow as an unfair blow below the business belt. Considered nautically, it seemed a deliberate fouling of the other fellow's craft. Fair or foul, however, the travelling public could be expected to extend liberal patronage to any vessel of such luxurious appointments—and the Hunter's cabin accommodations, alas, were distinctly not first class.

Captain Jonathan was correct in apprehending his own early demise as a dominant figure in Fulton Chain transportation affairs. Many of his former patrons availed themselves of the Fulton's excellent service, leaving the Hunter to ply the lakes with a steadily dwindling passenger list. For some time the Captain pondered this loss of patronage in stoic silence. He chewed his mighty quids as deliberately as ever, and spat as precisely, (he could sink a floating leaf at ten feet). Finally he sought out Captain Jack. The latter received his old friend, not with the triumphant bearing of an Admiral who views the lowering of an adversary's colors, but with the simple friend-liness that invariably marked his social contacts. He listened attentively as his visitor outlined a proposition. When the interview ended, Captain Jack had acquired the Hunter as an auxiliary freight and passenger carrier, and Captain Jonathan's career as a Fulton Chain ship owner had come to an honorable end.

With two steamers at his command, Captain Jack may be said to have been the first local operator of a fleet. He main-tained his commanding position on Fulton Chain waters until 1893, but the coming of the railroad with its sudden influx of visitors and camp builders led him to dispose of his business. He sold out to David Pierce and left the Fulton Chain to make his home in the far west.

In the meantime, an extension of the local transportation service was effected under the direction of Charles Bennett to include the territory between upper Fourth and lower Raquette Lakes. Charles was the proprietor of The Antlers on Constable Point, Raquette Lake, a hotel which had become famous under his personal management. The new service which he inaugu-rated utilized small steamers on the upper lakes of the Fulton Chain and on Brown's Tract Inlet, a slim, tortuous stream that zig-zagged a four mile course between Eighth and Raquette Lakes. Horse-drawn wagons were employed to transport pas-sengers and baggage over the carries between lakes and streams on the route.

With the organizing of the Fulton Navigation Company, steamboating on the Fulton Chain attained its greatest distinction and prosperity. Until 1920 this company operated a fleet of vessels between Old Forge, Eagle Bay and Inlet which included freight and mail boats as well as excursion and regularly scheduled passenger boats. Among their carriers were the Nehasane, Clearwater, Uncas, Mohegan, Old Forge and Irocosia. The first three were double decked vessels with a combined carrying capacity of more than three hundred passengers.

Local road construction, and the use of automobiles and gasoline propelled launches exercised an adverse effect upon steamers as they previously had upon guide boats. Patronage accorded the steamers gradually diminished until the Fulton Navigation Company was left with a fleet of commercially stranded vessels which were no longer adapted to local needs. Today, a steamboat on the Fulton Chain or on Big Moose Lake is almost as rare a novelty as the wrath-provoking Hunter must have been in the summer of 1883.

Shades of Jonathan Meeker, and of Captain Jack, the early sports and the old guides! If the shattering echoes of an outboard motorboat could stir their sleeping forms today, with what glad acclaim would they declare the whistle of the long departed Hunter to have been no more than a ripple of melody upon the vast sea of Adirondack silence. How genial would be their congratulatory handclasps all around ere they again sought refuge in the quiet solitude of eternal sleep!

Steam navigation on Big Moose Lake began in 1901 with the formation of the Big Moose Transportation Company by Dwight Sperry, Jim Higby and William Glenn. The company's first vessel to serve the needs of that community was the Zilpha, a thirty-five foot, wood burning steamer capable of carrying twenty-five passengers. It came to Big Moose in the manner of a hoary old sea Captain who seeks an easy berth in a pleasant environment in which to spend his declining years. It had seen service on numerous lakes, rivers and canals, but

The Steamboat Fulton, launched at Old Forge in 1888. Photo of the same year. Included in the group, left to right, (several unidentified) are the following: Chris Goodsell, Joseph Harvey, Jack Sheppard (in bow), Henry McCormick, Emma, Gertrude and Sadie Harvey, Mrs. Joseph Harvey with daughter Anna in arms, Nettie Harvey, Dan Gookins, Frank Sperry, William Weedmark, Engineer John Sprague (extreme right). The juvenile group was the only family of children in the region at that time, and the eight months old Anna was the pride and curiosity of the entire woodland community. The Adirondack guide boat resting in the stern travels as free baggage.

had never been honored or dignified with a name. Will Sperry brought it to Old Forge from Beaver River in 1896, overhauled and christened it, and as the "X-10-U-8" it rendered faithful service on the Fulton Chain for six years. Later, Will renamed it the "Zilpha" in memory of Nat Foster's daughter. In 1901 the Big Moose Transportation Company sledded it overland from Eagle Bay and launched it near Big Moose Outlet the following spring.

The Zilpha became an object of public curiosity in 1906 when the spotlight of national attention focused on Big Moose as the result of a heinous crime committed in South Bay. In July of that year Chester Gillette, accompanied by Grace Brown, his fiancee, (as the girl properly supposed herself to be) registered at the Glenmore Hotel on the westerly shore of the lake for the ostensible purpose of enjoying a few days' outing. In reality, the young couple had left their Cortland County homes for more momentous reasons, differing one from the other as graphically and tragically as death contrasts to life. The girl had set out upon a journey which she hoped would lead to marriage and the honorable birth of her baby. The young man had accompanied her with the intention of ridding himself of her claim to his fidelity through the agency of murder.

Grace Brown was a gentle, home loving girl, trustful and guileless. With more affection than discrimination she had responded to Gillette's seemingly sincere advances, and had welcomed his declaration of love and proposal of marriage without skepticism. Her suitor was of a rather dashing type, not highly intelligent, but plausible in his amorous utterances, and clever in finding his way to the feminine heart. He either utterly lacked the wholesome moral fibre of manliness, or it was slow in knitting itself into the fabric of his character, for the facts of his brief life reveal but little that popular estimate regards as commendable.

Having registered at the Glenmore, Gillette procured a boat and rowed with his companion up the lake and into South Bay.

When they failed to return, a searching party aboard the Zilpha explored the shore line, discovered the overturned boat near the south shore of the bay, and quickly recovered the unfortunate girl's body.

Gillette, meanwhile, satisfied that he had relieved an embarrassing situation by the brutal expedient of murder, walked through the woods to Eagle Bay and thence to Inlet where he registered at the Arrowhead Hotel. He joined gaily in the pastimes of the summer colony there, exhibited no apparent signs of remorse for his crime, and seemed to be thoroughly enjoying himself when taken into custody a few days later. His trial on the charge of first degree murder, held at Herkimer, was a bitterly fought proceeding, and through the medium of the press gained the attention of the entire country. It terminated with the jury's verdict of guilty and the Court's imposition of the death sentence. In spite of the mass of convincing evidence presented against Gillette, his mother stoutly averred his innocence and espoused his lost cause to the extent of delivering a series of public lectures in his behalf. Although she succeeded in injecting an element of doubt in the minds of her more credulous listeners, her efforts went for naught. Gillette, cooly denying his guilt to the end, paid the penalty for his crime in the death house of Auburn Prison. His spiritual adviser admitted later that the execution represented no miscarriage of justice. Theodore Dreiser's widely read novel, "An American Tragedy," is based on the facts of the Gillette-Brown careers and the double climax of the girl's death and her betrayer's unavailing attempt to escape the vengeance of society.

The laboriously travelled and verbally abused Brown's Tract Road has been drawn into this story in several previous chapters, perhaps more often than the road's inferior character has reasonably merited. The nearest approach to a complimentary mention of its thirteen uncomfortable miles comes from a traveller of the early eighties who described it as "better than no road at all." However, its long abandoned, overgrown length cannot in strict justice be shunted to oblivion without the consolation of a brief eulogy. In a cumbersome sort of manner it served its purpose for more than three-quarters of a century. It withstood the vituperation of outraged travellers as it doggedly continued to furnish the region's only inlet and outlet on the west. Finally it became the forerunner of the railroad. It extended from Old Forge Lake to Moose River Settlement where it joined a road leading to settlements in Lewis and Oneida Counties. This road forked at Porter's Corners, four miles beyond Moose River, one branch leading to Port Leyden and the other to Boonville. Both villages served as ports of entry to the western area of the Adirondacks, Boonville being the more prominent of the two.

Several buckboard lines maintained scheduled passenger, freight and mail service over the old road from Boonville to the Fulton Chain between the years 1865 and 1892. Early owners of these lines included, among others, Charlie Phelps, Frank Barrett and George Goodsell, and drivers numbered nearly one hundred during the continuation of the buckboard era. Charlie Phelps pioneered in this service in the sixties, and his commercial association with the Brown's Tract Road continued until the railroad conclusively disposed of both the road and its slow moving vehicles. His freight wagon transported the body of Otis Arnold to Boonville in 1869 after it had been recovered from Nick's Lake. In 1882, Charlie passed out cards advertising his transportation business. He referred to it as "The Old Line" offering daily service in season from Boonville, on the Utica and Black River Railroad, to the Fulton Chain of Lakes "on the John Brown's Tract side of the Adirondacks." According to Charlie's advertisements, the scheduled travelling time between the two points was eight hours. Theoretically, the buckboards left Boonville at 8:00 A. M., reached Moose River Tavern at noon, and the Forge House at 4:00 P. M. According to the same published schedule, a buckboard leaving the Forge House at 9:00 A. M. could be expected to reach Boonville at 5:00 P. M. An unwarranted degree of optimism entered into the publication of this schedule. Only the most favorable driving conditions, freedom from mishaps and skilful handling of the reins enabled a driver to traverse the twenty-five mile route in reasonable conformity with the time-table.

The conveyances employed in this service were strongly and flexibly constructed, designed to withstand the necessarily grueling contact with an unkempt wilderness highway. Their floor boards were unsupported, except at the two extremities, to produce a pliant quality which enabled the vehicles to yield pacifically when a wheel encountered a rock obstruction or dropped to its hub in a deep rut. The safety and equilibrium, if not the comfort, of feminine passengers were made reasonably certain by fastening them in with leather straps secured at each end of the seat. Although vehicles of this type were in general use on other roads of exceptional roughness, they were known locally as "Brown's Tract Buckboards" due to the region which they served.

Buckboard drivers were essentially a hardy class of men, dexterous in handling their teams and in improvising temporary repair parts for their damaged wagons. They were, as a rule, a philosophic group, exhibiting a laudable fund of patience in enduring their rough lot, but capable of unleashing a robust vocabulary whenever that patience became exhausted. They also possessed fathomless imaginations which they put to good use by fabricating strange tales of the wilderness for the innocent beguilement of gullible passengers.

As a source of self-encouragement on the long arid journey from Moose River Settlement to the Forge House and return they arranged a refreshment cache near Six Mile Hill, midway of their route. This consisted of a sizeable stone jug immersed and concealed in the cool waters of a spring that gurgled from the base of a huge boulder. It existed solely for the benefit of the drivers' craft, members of which kept it filled with a supply of high proof liquor. The supply was maintained by freight haulers who, with the aid of hammer and nails, tapped the portly casks entrusted to their care for delivery at Old Forge, and withdrew enough of their contents to replenish the jug's depleted stock, with, perhaps, a drop or two extra for themselves by way of compensation for their trouble. A gentlemen's agreement existed among the drivers to the effect that none would consume more than a normal thirst and a day's tribulations warranted, and that none would reveal the secret of the spring to persons outside the craft. Being men of discretion and not without honor, they rigidly observed the spirit and letter of this pact—particularly its latter clause. Admittedly the practice constituted a clear breach of ethics to thus violate the confidence reposed in them of hauling valuable merchandise intact to its destination. But the way was hard and long for the weary drivers, and the need for a heartening stimulant great. Furthermore, the practice instilled in the minds of buckboard passengers a high regard for the efficacy of Adirondack spring water. Jaded drivers who left their vehicles and slouched into the woods with the announced intention of getting a drink at the spring soon returned with a jaunty air and a brisk step to resume the journey in noticeably better spirits than they had previously exhibited. This startling rejuvenation impressed the passengers immensely as an incontrovertible testimonial to the vitalizing power of the region's water, and it is said that, as a result, many of them cultivated the wholesome habit of patronizing woodland springs to the detriment of the local bar trade.

The buckboard regime faced the handwriting on the wall in the spring of 1888 when newspaper dispatches reported a proposed innovation in travel facilities between Moose River Settlement and the Fulton Chain. This involved the building of a narrow gage railroad between the Settlement and Old Forge Lake which would reduce the running time between the two points at least three hours and, incidentally, eliminate the discomforts of buckboard travel. The plan originated with G. H. P. Gould, of Lyons Falls, and Samuel F. Garmon and Dr. Alexander Crosby who, as the firm of Garmon and Crosby, owned the Forge Tract at that time. Current news dispatches also informed that an estimated total of fifteen hundred persons had visited the Central Adirondacks the previous year, and that the future of the region loomed bright due to improved methods of transportation and a growing appreciation for the woods.

True to the predictions of journalism, construction work on the new road progressed rapidly during the spring and summer of 1888, but it failed by a matter of several miles to reach Old Forge Lake. William Scott de Camp interposed serious objections to its proposed route. He viewed the scheme with a mixture of approval and well founded skepticism, recognizing the need for superior travel facilities, but also apprehending the tendency of wood-burning locomotives to shower the landscape with destructive firebrands. Without undue conservatism he felt concerned for the security of Township Seven's timber land and refused to grant the railroad builders a right of way through the de Camp property. Stumped, as it were, by this objection, the partnership of Gould, Garmon and Crosby regarded their project of an all-steam route to the Fulton Chain impossible of attainment until the objector himself came forward with a solution. William Scott de Camp agreed that if the partnership would complete their road to the western border of Township Seven near Minnehaha on the Moose River, he would provide the connecting link of transportation by operating a steamer on the river as far upstream as navigable water permitted. The steamer, like the locomotive, would be a wood burner and consequently a fire hazard, but its owner could be assured of an adequate water supply at hand in the event of a threatened conflagration. This offer effaced the only serious obstacle in the path of the enterprising builders, and both parties to the agreement pushed their construction work to rapid completion.

Service on the seven mile length of the Moose River-Minnehaha Railroad began in the late spring of 1889, and

William Scott de Camp's steamer, the Fawn, waited alongside the Minnehaha terminus to convey passengers up the scenic river that led to the Fulton Chain. The Fawn had been built by Theodore Seeber the previous winter on the Hatchery grounds below the Forge Dam. It was a double decked side wheeler with ample deck space for passengers, freight and baggage. Its two wheels were independently reversible. Either could revolve in a forward direction as the other back paddled, thus permitting the vessel to accomplish a quick, pivotal turn as a means of avoiding obstructions suddenly encountered in the river. A log and board dam thrown across the river at Minnehaha created a navigable depth of water as far upstream as the present site of Thendara. At the latter place a lock and dam were built to enable the Fawn to proceed farther up the river to its eastern terminal dock near the present site of the State highway bridge between Old Forge and Thendara. From that point buckboards carried passengers and freight to Old Forge Lake. The dams and lock were built by Dwight Grant and maintained and operated by Dana Fraula.

The narrow gage railroad became a celebrated bit of trackage despite its abbreviated length. It was built in a single season, in much the same manner that a wooden sidewalk might be laid along the rough floor of the forest. After a swath of timber had been felled to open the right of way, a portable sawmill followed the grading crew and cut from the fallen trees sufficient lumber to provide material for the track structure. The stringers, rails and cross ties were fashioned wholly of wood, the rails being two by four lengths of hardwood secured to the ties with six inch wire nails. At the curves, strips of band iron protected the rails against abrasion by contact with the iron wheels of the locomotive and its train of cars. Although the route followed a path of least resistance wherever possible, several trestles were required to carry the track over depressions or ravines. One trestle bridged a gap twenty feet deep.

In addition to the engine, the train included a combination

freight and baggage car, and one passenger coach, roofed but open at the sides, with a seating capacity of thirty persons. It carried no separate fuel or water tender as these materials were available at both ends of the seven mile run. The locomotive was a diminutive, black creature of the mechanical world, equipped with most of the power-generating and noise-making appliances common to its bigger brothers of the iron rails, and, like them, smoky and belligerent in appearance. Its ten foot length of cab and boiler were set upon six chubby wheels that scurried through the forest with all the ferocity of a band of pigmy warriors. Persons lingering beside the right of way to observe its approach were delighted at the incongruous spectacle of a puffing, panting little train hurrying upon important errands through the somber depths of virgin forest. Sometimes their cheers of mock encouragement brought a humorous response from those aboard, and sometimes they didn't. Passengers could often be seen clutching the wooden seats in trepidation lest the impetuous engine should send them headlong into the depth of a chasm or against the wall of stalwart trees that bordered the track. The confusion of sound engendered by the contact of iron wheels with wood and the echoes awakened in the surrounding forest created an impression of wilder speed than the train actually attained, and the effect on timorous passengers sometimes approximated the excitement provoked by an amusement park "thrill ride." Mishaps occurred at intervals, but all of a minor character. Occasionally the train left the track and the combined efforts of crew and passengers were required to pry it back upon the rails. Passengers were also called upon to push the train, when heavily freighted, up the sharp grade that confronted the engine after it had left Moose River Settlement.

The road became known as the Wooden Legged or Peg Legged Railroad, and finally by the contemptuously familiar term "The Peg Leg." These names were suggested by the wooden rails. Newspapers, including several metropolitan journals, printed humorous feature articles about the road and

THE FAWN

DR. WILLIAM SEWARD WEBB

the humiliating predicaments its little train experienced because of the unstable type of track construction. Regardless of all the good natured ridicule to which it became subjected during its four years' operation, it served as a really valuable link in the transportation chain from the west. An appreciable increase of travellers resulted from its operation in conjunction with the Fawn, and the elimination of the tedious pilgrimage on the Brown's Tract Road brought the outside world considerably closer to the Fulton Chain than the mere time saving of three or four hours indicated.

After serving the public four consecutive years, the road passed to the discard upon completion of the Adirondack and St. Lawrence Railroad in 1892. The Fawn also faded from the transportation scheme. For a few years it steamed up and down the river as an excursion boat carrying picnic parties to Minnehaha, but it eventually found a permanent mooring beside the lock and dam at Thendara where it slowly rotted away from disuse.

Abandoned by its owners as well as by the travelling public, the Peg Leg gradually gave way before the encroaching growth of woods which hemmed it. It had screeched its smoky swan song while hauling materials and supplies for the new road under construction. Today, its vaguely marked trail may be followed by an alert explorer for at least part of the seven miles between the deserted terminus at Minnehaha and the abandoned Moose River Settlement. Birch and cherry trees, rooted between the wooden rails nearly forty years ago, have attained mature membership in the sedate tree family that borders its route. The rails have long since disappeared, and decay has flattened the stringers and cross ties to nearly shapeless contours, but from their green moss coverings long rows of six inch wire nails protrude, erect, defiant and rusty, exotic growths of the forest that recall the story of a very small railroad that bowed humbly to the dust before the advent of a greater one.

The construction of the Adirondack and St. Lawrence Railroad by Dr. William Seward Webb takes its rightful place among epic achievements of American railroading—one hundred and ninety-one miles of standard gage track pushed to completion through the rocky heart of the Adirondacks within eighteen months of the date of the original survey. When the last spike was driven, connecting the northern and southern divisions into a through road at Twitchell Creek Bridge, October 12, 1892, Chauncey Depew hailed the enterprise as "the fairy tale of railroading." It was the first road to penetrate the Adirondacks from border to border, and is still the only trans-mountain line.

Prior to its construction, four standard gage lines had been built wholly or in part within the foothills of the mountains. The first of these, the Whitehall and Plattsburg, completed in 1868, extended from Plattsburg to Point of Rocks, a distance of twenty miles. It was subsequently lengthened to reach Ausable Forks. The Adirondack Railroad, a sixty mile line connecting Saratoga and North Creek, was built in 1871, and the Chateaugay Railroad inaugurated service between Plattsburg and Saranac Lake, a distance of seventy miles, in 1887. This road reached Lake Placid via Saranac Lake in 1893. Hurd's Road, with sixty miles of rather flimsy trackage, built and owned by John Hurd, a lumber man of Bridgeport, Conn., began operating between Tupper Lake and Moira in 1889. Two years after its completion, Dr. Webb offered Hurd the magnificent sum of $600,000.00 for the line, intending to improve it and to incorporate it as a segment of his own road. Scenting the possibility of a still larger offer, Hurd engaged in a series of foxy trading tactics, hoping to realize an extra hundred thousand or so by exploiting the Doctor's eagerness to push ahead with his building project. But to Hurd's deep chagrin and heavy financial loss, the exasperated Doctor abruptly withdrew his offer, halted all further negotiations regarding the deal, and one year later the sixty mile Hurd Road was paralleled and eclipsed by the Adirondack and St. Lawrence. These four lines of prior origin were all built for service between certain local points only, and none was ever extended the entire length or width of the Adirondacks.

Perhaps the most noteworthy circumstance in connection with the building of the Adirondack and St. Lawrence Railroad is the fact that it was conceived, financed and directed by a man who had spent years in the study and practice of medicine. In that respect, Dr. Webb's career closely paralleled that of another physician of Central Adirondack fame—Dr. Thomas C. Durant, a Raquette Lake camp owner who built the Adirondack Railroad in the late sixties. Dr. Durant had practiced medicine but a few years when the lure of railroading led him to abandon his profession. He became prominently identified with the building and financing of the Rock Island, Michigan Southern and the Mississippi and Missouri railroads. Finally, he became a leading factor in the building and management of the Union Pacific—the first trunk-line to inaugurate trans-continental railroad service between the Atlantic and Pacific.

Dr. William Seward Webb was born in New York City in 1851, the son of General James Watson Webb. The family has been prominent in American business and social life for three centuries, the first of that name, Richard Webb, having settled in the colonies in 1626. Dr. Webb's education included courses of study in London, Paris and Vienna, and in Columbia College and the New York College of Physicians and Surgeons, both of New York City. He practiced medicine in New York for a number of years, served as an interne in St. Luke's Hospital there, and later retired from practice to begin a more lucrative and probably more interesting career in Wall Street. His marriage to William H. Vanderbilt's daughter, Lila Osgood Vanderbilt, stimulated his interest in transportation affairs, and at the suggestion of his father-in-law in 1885 he undertook the reorganization of the Wagner Palace Car Company, the forerunner of the Pullman Company with which it merged in 1899. During his management of this company he developed it from a frail concern with 170 cars to a highly prosperous organization with 800 cars. Other big business affairs claimed his attention, and in each he attained a conspicuous success which eventually characterized his every undertaking.

Early in life he developed a fondness for the Adirondacks. This led to the establishment of Ne-ha-sa-ne Park, a contiguous tract of 115,000 acres in Herkimer and Hamilton Counties, 40,000 acres of which are still held by the Webb family as a private preserve. While piecing this acreage into a unified tract and developing it as a game preserve, Dr. Webb conceived the possibility of a railroad traversing the Adirondacks north and south. The commercial value of a direct rail route between New York and Montreal through the mountains, often talked of but never undertaken, appealed to him as a consideration of paramount importance in his conception of the project. A further incentive lay in the fact that the added accessibility of the Adirondacks by the projection of a road through them would materially speed their development and enhance their value. The conception was a bold one, for the rough region which the road would penetrate offered but slight inducements in the way of population and industry at that time which are vitally essential to a public carrier's prosperity. But the Doctor possessed a fund of practical vision which enabled him to foresee an influx of traffic if the means of transportation were provided. Convinced of the successful outcome of such an enterprise, he outlined his plan to the New York Central Railroad Company and to his father-in-law who at that time held a commanding position in the railroad world. Whether or not both concurred is not known, but it is believed that the Central encouraged him to undertake the project and possibly offered financial assistance. At that time the company had no rail connection with Montreal, and two or three of its competitive lines were handling the bulk of Canadian traffic. Sometime after negotiating with the Doctor, however, the Central leased one of its rival lines, the Rome, Ogdensburg and Watertown, and thereby acquired control of a connection with

the Canadian metropolis effective March 1, 1891. That put
an end to the Central's interest in the Adirondack route.
Meanwhile the Doctor had already spent a small fortune in
preliminary surveys and in acquiring property along his proposed right of way. The withdrawal of his ally from participation in his scheme clouded the prospect of its favorable
consummation and burdened him with a momentous responsibility. He could proceed with his plan entirely on his own
initiative or he could bow to the alternative of failure and
abandon his project with a substantial personal loss. Retiring in the face of serious difficulty had never been characteristic of the Doctor's business and professional careers,
and he chose the former. By mid-summer of the same year,
men, machines and money were hewing their way swiftly
across the Adirondacks under his personal direction, and the
ultimate success of his visionary scheme was shaping itself into
reality.

Dr. Webb possessed a keenly analytical mind and an extraordinary versatility. His aptitude for new undertakings, and
the enormous energy and high degree of intelligence with
which he pursued them to successful conclusions marked his
lifelong activities. Born into the Social Register by virtue of
an eminent ancestry, he easily maintained the prestige of his
family tradition, and even added to it. At the same time an
ever-widening range of practical affairs claimed his attention,
and he experienced real satisfaction in constant association
with people and transactions in numerous strata of society and
in contrasting spheres of activity. The aggressive intellectual
curiosity he exhibited in analyzing the fundamentals of every
problem under consideration led to his early success in such
dissimilar pursuits as the practice of medicine, business and
finance, literature, forestry (and the study of wild life), military and governmental affairs and a wide range of civic,
philanthropic and social activities. No lost motion hampered
his fast moving mental processes. He thought rapidly and ac-
curately, seldom overlooking a detail of even slight significance

that might bear on the outcome of a current project or situation. This trait characterized his humorous utterances which often attended his inconspicuously rendered charities.

In the spring of 1890, he had occasion to stop overnight at the Forge House. Before retiring to his room he sauntered about the premises on a tour of inspection which included the barn and stables, and a Jersey cow which Joseph Harvey, the proprietor, kept to supply milk for his five young children. In the morning the Doctor was informed that the cow had died during the night. Sympathetically comprehending the loss of the children's milk supply, and realizing that the animal's death represented a financial loss to the proprietor, he replied with mock gravity, "This is an evil coincidence for which I am clearly at fault. The poor creature could not survive a single night's proximity to a physician. I will buy another cow."

Vainly the proprietor protested his generous offer, and equally futile was his attempt to exonerate the facetious Doctor of culpability. In reality, the only coincidence in the affair lay in the fact that it was the first time that Doctor Webb had stopped at the hotel, and, of course, it was the first time the cow had died. Nevertheless, no inconvenience resulted from the animal's death. The proprietor received the purchase price of another cow, with instructions to buy a good one, and the unsmiling Doctor departed, heartily enjoying his joke.

Hon. E. C. Smith, former Governor of Vermont, expressed an enlightening tribute to Dr. Webb in a recent letter to Charles H. Burnett who had been closely associated with the Doctor in his various Adirondack enterprises:

"It is given to some men to be born with a quality of mind which carries their vision to the outer rim of human knowledge, to stab the unknown, so to speak, with the shaft of their intellect; and this applies to most great men in the realms of art, science, commerce, statesmanship, diplomacy and war. But such outstanding ability is usually at the expense of other qualities of mind and character, which remain mediocre. With a few there is an expansion of intellect in a dual or triple sphere.

In recalling Dr. Webb's life, there has never been in my experience any other man who possessed so many shining characteristics, in all of which he travelled far beyond the multitude.

"Far beyond the many he possessed vision to see, courage to act, tenacity of purpose and loyalty to his ideals and friendships. His sincerity and honesty commanded the respect of all. He had a generosity of heart and soul that held his friends irrevocably, and a wonderful charity that enabled him to overlook the mistakes of those whom he had trusted and who had not lived up to his own high standards.

"He was possessed of a nature that was full of vigor, and a mind that was intuitive. He could grasp a subject instantly and reach a conclusion at once that was in a great majority of cases accurate, while the exercise of these qualities was always predicated upon the highest sense of honor. There is one word that is always associated in my mind with Doctor Webb, that best describes his dominant characteristic, and that word is valor. The attributes mentioned fairly radiated from his personality all during the period of his active life, and even toward the end, when infirmity sapped his strength, the valor of his character remained unchanged.

"Aside from the qualities of mind and heart already alluded to, he possessed an exquisite artistic sense. In whatever direction his mind turned, whether to railroading, farming, architecture, flowers, fruit or trees, or even to organizing an excursion to Europe, Alaska or the West, a breadth of vision and perfection of detail were immediately manifest, and the consummation was flawless.

"When he passed away the homage of affection and sorrow was rendered by a real multitude, comprising the highest and the lowest, who had grown to love and respect him sincerely as a friend."

The corporate history of the Adirondack and St. Lawrence Railroad had its beginning in 1880 with the incorporation of the Herkimer, Newport and Poland Narrow Gage Railway Company which was opened for traffic in 1883. In 1890 the

Mohawk Valley and Northern Railway Company came into existence for the purpose of building a road from Poland to Hinckley. A consolidation of these two roads was effected in 1891 under the corporate name of The Herkimer, Newport and Poland Railway Company. By authority of an Act of Legislature the gage was changed to standard in 1891. During the same year the Mohawk and Adirondack Railroad Company was incorporated for the purpose of building a road from Poland to Malone. A reorganization in the same year resulted in the formation of two companies, the Herkimer, Newport and Poland Extension Railway Company to operate between Poland and Remsen, and the St. Lawrence and Adirondack Railroad Company to build and operate a road from Remsen to Malone. From Malone, trackage rights could be leased to extend the Company's service to Montreal. In June, 1892, these three companies consolidated as the Mohawk and Malone Railway Company to operate between Herkimer and Malone.

The building of the Remsen-Malone Division required less than eighteen months, an amazingly brief period of time considering the mountainous character of the region penetrated, and the severity of winter weather encountered during the progress of the work. Dr. Webb's stimulating personality chiefly accounted for this record-breaking speed under adverse conditions, and the success of the whole project exemplified the usual fund of energy which he brought to bear on all of his undertakings. Contracts entered into with several building firms permitted the work to proceed in a number of disconnected sections of the right of way at the same time. These sections were finally joined into northern and southern divisions which were projected swiftly northward from Thendara and southward from Childwold to meet at Twitchell Lake Bridge. A young engineer drove the last spike, lustily but erratically, while a group of experienced negro trackmen of the southern division and a band of equally experienced St. Regis Indians of the northern viewed his efforts with obvious mirth.

Practically all the contracting firms concerned with construction within the mountains went broke on the job, yet none suffered financial setbacks. Dr. Webb, realizing that they had grossly underbid due to ignorance regarding the natural obstacles to be encountered in the Adirondacks, came to their rescue with considerable more magnanimity than railroad builders of that day were suspected of possessing. He financed their work to completion, wiped out the accrued indebtedness which they were unable to liquidate, and procured more profitable contracts for them on other construction projects.

One of these firms, engaged in building the southern division, imported contract gangs of negro laborers from Tennessee with a view to reducing construction costs. Inexperienced in the complexities of nature, human and otherwise, beyond the region of their nativity, the negroes started northward upon a happy excursion of steady work and good pay. Work and pay awaited their arrival, but so did the severity of an Adirondack winter. Snows, deeper than their imaginations had ever conjured, and temperatures, fifty degrees lower than an untraveled Southerner could reasonably anticipate, cooled their ardor for the task at hand. They were well fed and warmly housed, but after a few days' toil at ten or twenty below zero the urge to earn vanished. Singly and in groups they deserted camp until only about fifty of them remained to finish the job. Fidelity to agreements previously made with their employers proved as ephemeral as a June breeze compared with their longing to return to the friendlier climate of Tennessee. They straggled down through the Black River and Mohawk valleys, telling tales of hardship and harsh treatment at the hands of stony hearted foremen. Sympathizers helped them on their way and repeated the brutal stories to their neighbors. In a short time the partially constructed railroad acquired an unsavory and undeserved notoriety as a burial place for negroes who had succumbed to inhuman treatment by their white employers. As a matter of fact, the fugitive Tennesseans had no just cause to complain of anything except the folly of their employers in transporting them to a country of such climatic rigor. No semblance of cruelty or brutality was employed by the foremen to force their wills upon the disheartened and homesick negroes. Occasionaly an exasperated foreman rounded up a group of deserting laborers at the point of a gun and frightened them back to work, but as he never pulled the trigger this intimidating gesture soon lost its effectiveness. No fatalities occurred among the men beyond those normally resulting from the hazards of railroad building, yet twenty-five years after the road began operating, a gruesome tale still went the rounds to the effect that a colored laborer lay buried beneath every cross-tie between Remsen and Beaver River.

The Mohawk and Malone inaugurated service between Herkimer and Fulton Chain Station (Thendara) on Friday, July 1, 1892. At 5:30 A. M. Train Number Seven, hauling two cars, left Herkimer in charge of Conductor John C. Brennan, with engineer Charles Sweet at the throttle. Lucky Seven apparently neutralized the sinister threat popularly attached to Friday inaugurations, for the train proceeded without serious mishap to within one-half mile of its destination. Its starting passengers were principally railroad officials and press representatives together with a few sleepy eyed citizens of Herkimer who arose at dawn to enjoy a historic train ride. Other passengers climed aboard at Newport, Poland, Trenton Falls and Remsen. A sink hole caused by the settling of track ballast halted the train a half mile below Fulton Chain Station, but the passengers cheerfully continued the journey on foot to the waiting stages which carried them to the Forge House.

This first and highly successful run from Herkimer into the heart of the Adirondacks was heralded by the state press as a significant achievement that foretold an inpouring of the masses who could now conveniently indulge their taste for mountain beauty. Columns were devoted to the story of the road's construction, and to the natural attractions of the Central Adirondacks. As a revelation to many readers came the news that no less than thirty camp structures, public and private, had already been erected on the shores of the Fulton Chain and Big Moose

Lake.

Visitors who had never undergone the hardships attending the former devious route to the mountains now came pouring into the region in trainloads. A new patronage sprung suddenly and eagerly from the populous confines of the cities. Swift as the sunrise, a new era dawned upon the Adirondacks, and puzzled old guides found themselves viewing askance the railroad and its heterogeneous human influx. To them, the new order came as a mixed blessing, as a revolution that spelled the doom of the good old days. Logically enough, they preferred the even tenor of existence in their beloved haunts of a lifetime—the quiet, unpeopled byways of the forest.

Hand in hand with his railroad building operation, Dr. Webb stimulated the development of the region by acquiring large tracts of land which he sub-divided and marketed in small plots. Waterfront lots on the Fulton Chain and on Big Moose and other lakes were sold as camp sites, and the interior timber land, remote from the lake shores, was sold to the State with certain restricted lumbering rights retained for a period of years. When Dr. Webb completed his program of acquisition his holdings approximated something more than two hundred thousand acres, and, aside from his Nehasane Preserve, included nearly all lands adjacent to Second, Third and Fourth Lakes of the Fulton Chain, Rondaxe, Dart's, Cascade, Moss, Big Moose and Twitchell Lakes, and a score or more of smaller bodies of water. In tracing the many ownerships of this vast tract, Dr. Webb instituted a search which led across the United States, England and France. Titles, complicated by time and taxes, by obscure transactions and by a lethargic attitude on the part of equity holders, were sought out in a successful endeavor to piece the scattered realty parcels into a contiguous tract under a single ownership. Titles were found vested in both distinguished and obscure families on either side of the Atlantic. Through the ingenious efforts of Dr. Webb's legal staff to gather the loose ends of ownership into a single strand there came to light remarkable human stories of family heritages and fortunes, as well as misfortunes, which included all the stirring elements of drama, romance and humor. Since the time of Alexander Macomb's historic purchase in 1792 many fingers had found their way into the Adirondack pie. Few, indeed, had plucked plums, but all had added to the confusion of equities by leaving a tracery of their speculative interest. It was this comprehensive search that inspired Charles E. Snyder, of Herkimer, one of Dr. Webb's attorneys and managers, to write the first authentic account of early days on the Brown's Tract.

Dr. Webb began disposing of his waterfront acreage in 1894 and continued until 1902. During the latter year between ten and eleven thousand acres of his original purchases remained unsold. This acreage was acquired at that time by William J. Thistlethwaite who had entered the Doctor's employ in 1894 as an assistant manager in connection with land sales and lumbering. Still actively interested in local land developments, Mr. Thistlethwaite has set an unusual record for physical and financial longevity of a business man concerned with the development of Adirondack realty. His record of thirty-seven years, extending from 1894 to the date of this writing, has probably never been excelled or even equalled. In fact, very few men have survived for even half that period the mysterious affliction that has so often constituted commercial association with Adirondack soil an ordeal rather than a business enterprise.

To further stimulate local development activity, Dr. Webb purchased an interest in the Fulton Chain Transportation Company, the Fulton Chain Railway (Thendara to Old Forge) and the Raquette Lake Transportation Company and its little subsidiary, the Marion River Railroad. He served as president of these companies for a number of years. Effective May 1, 1893, he leased the Mohawk and Malone to the New York Central for the term of its corporate existence. A second lease, effective April 17, 1902, continued this leasehold arrangement until 1913 when the lessor company merged with the Central.

Having disposed of his various holdings except Nehasane Park Preserve, Dr. Webb continued to manifest a lively interest in Adirondack affairs until his death in 1926. He died at Shelburne, Vermont, where he had maintained a beautiful home near the shore of Lake Champlain for many years. His grave is marked with an inscribed boulder transported, in compliance with his request, from Nehasane Park shortly after his death. His memory is perpetuated locally by the Town of Webb, so named at the time of its incorporation in 1896 in appreciation of his railroad building achievement. Incidentally, the events leading to the enduring use of this name resulted in the disappearance of another name from the roster of Herkimer County Towns. The area now included within the Town of Webb formerly comprised a portion of the Town of Wilmurt which was then the largest political subdivision of the County. Simultaneously with the partitioning of Webb from Wilmurt, the remainder of the latter Town was divided and the two divisions were incorporated in the Towns of Russia and Ohio. By three quick slashes the Town of Wilmurt thus lost its corporate identity and sank to political oblivion.

A two mile spur, laid in 1895, leading from Thendara to the foot of Old Forge Lake, provided rail connections between the Mohawk and Malone Railroad and steamboat service on the Fulton Chain. This insignificant length of trackage furnished the missing link of an all steam transportation system between New York City and Inlet at the head of Fourth Lake. It was built by the Old Forge Company, owners of the Forge House and Forge Tract, and acquired by the New York Central several years later. Until motor cars and launches came into popular use locally, this little road did a passenger and freight business in summer seasons. Week-end and holiday excursions from Herkimer swelled the volume of traffic handled by the road, and added considerably to the excitement and color then prevailing at the foot of the Fulton chain. Passengers leaving the train at that point could conveniently embark on lake steamers which docked nearby. The improvement of highways through the region gradually lessened the volume of business handled by the road until it became an undesirable though very small white elephant on the hands of the New York Central. The Inter-State Commerce Commission and State Public Service Commission have recently granted the Central's petition for permission to abandon the road.

The Raquette Lake Railway, nineteen miles in length, was built in 1898 through the joint enterprise of several wealthy Raquette Lake camp owners who desired the convenience of through railroad service in reaching their camps. Their combined wealth mounted to the staggering total of hundreds of millions of dollars which was vastly more than was needed to finance their small project. The builders and directorate included J. Pierpont Morgan, Dr. William Seward Webb, Alfred G. Vanderbilt, Collis P. Huntington, William West Durant, Harry Payne Whitney, William C. Whitney and Chauncey M. Depew. A survey for the road had been made by Dr. Webb in 1892. It extended from Clearwater (now Carter) on the Mohawk and Malone to the shore of Raquette Lake. Except for a very slight deviation, this survey formed the right of way when construction began six years after the date of its projection.

The first President of the road, Collis P. Huntington, who was also the President of the Southern Pacific, promoted the enterprise from motives of personal comfort. He became a summer resident of Raquette Lake in 1895 when he purchased Camp Pine Knot from William West Durant. To reach this camp he left his private car at Fulton Chain Station and embarked on a small steamer at Old Forge which carried him to Eagle Bay near the head of Fourth Lake. From there he proceeded by stage along the Uncas Road to South Bay of Raquette. Mileage considered, the trip involved an inordinate amount of time and personal discomfort. The Fulton Chain steamers were not spacious, and vacation crowds usually taxed their capacity to the point of overcrowding. On one occasion Mr. Huntington was forced to make the trip up the lakes sitting on a keg of nails on an uncanopied portion of the aft-deck. The warm summer sun broiled him above, and the sharp, circular rim of the up-ended keg galled him below as the steamer plowed a rolling, zig-zag course from camp to camp. Certainly the accommodations were out of keeping with the customary modes of travel enjoyed by so prominent a railroader as the President of the Southern Pacific, and upon reaching Eagle Bay, Mr. Huntington vowed that the Raquette Lake Railway should be built without further delay. Several of his Raquette Lake neighbors had experienced similar vicissitudes of travel, and they joined readily in the project. After its completion, the New York Central assumed the management of the road. Like the Fulton Chain Railway, it proved unprofitable from an investment standpoint; in fact, its gross revenues have hardly equalled its annual operating and maintenance costs.

A striking illustration of the sterility of certain Adirondack business enterprises from a profit making standpoint is to be found in the appraisal of J. Pierpont Morgan's stock and bond holdings in the year 1916. Mr. Morgan died that year leaving an estate valued at seventy-eight million dollars. Among his securities listed by the appraisers as "cats and dogs," or worthless stocks, were the following investments: the Fulton Chain Railway Company, the Raquette Lake Railway Company, The Fulton Navigation Company and the Raquette Lake Transportation Company.

XII
THE ADIRONDACK LEAGUE CLUB

WITH steam trains rumbling swiftly across the Adirondacks on orderly schedule, the tempo of life in the Fulton Chain-Big Moose region quickened immeasurably. Tiny hamlets sprouted in the dense woods and gradually grew into permanent little trade and social centers. A tremendous increase of visitors created new needs, and new settlers arrived to supply them. Old hotels were remodeled and enlarged, new ones were built; roads and trails were cut through the forest to supplement the water routes that imperfectly linked the scattered communities of the region. The railroad that brought the incoming host of visitors also brought the carloads of freight essential to their comfort. Conveniences formerly regarded as luxuries became commonly associated with camp and hotel life. The rough edges of wilderness life were fast disappearing. The pioneer days had gone.

Oddly enough, while the railroad opened vast tracts of forest for the public's enjoyment, it caused the posting of other tracts as private preserves from which the public found itself excluded by the barriers of private ownership. For the most part these came into existence through the initiative of individuals or associations whose personal or collective wealth enabled them to acquire and maintain extensive mountain estates for their exclusive occupation. They were little empires of lake and forest carved from regions of great natural beauty that had been difficult of access prior to the building of the railroad. This setting apart of choice areas of game haunts and trout waters to the exclusion of the rank and file of sportsmen caused no slight sense of exasperation among Adirondack guides. Having roamed the woods in unrestricted freedom since their earliest association with them, they resented this sudden circumscription and its inhospitable array of "no trespass" signs. The signs themselves formed no forbidding barriers, for the guides' rifles quickly perforated them to meaningless jumbles of punctuation marks.   But back of the signs loomed the restraining disciplinary threat of the law—too impalpable a barricade to be shattered by a barrage of lead—and the guides were forced to soothe their outraged feelings by levelling a barrage of invective against the institution of real property, privately owned on a large scale, in the Adirondacks. In a few isolated cases they went farther, and the mysterious killing of one or two estate owners of unneighborly disposition caused general uneasiness among other landed proprietors who had ensconced themselves in the leafy depths of posted domains.   Often the guides overlooked the fact that for nearly a century the major portion of the Adirondacks had been privately owned and that the owners could have enforced their legal right to privacy had they cared to do so.   But the long established precedent of the free use of the wilderness for hunting, fishing and trapping purposes had become, in the minds of the guiding fraternity, a fixed and seemingly logical conception of the future status of the mountains.   With this faulty though honestly held opinion, the guides were not unreasonable in assuming a hostile attitude toward the possessors of large tracts from which they were peremptorily excluded. Time and understanding, however, have long since dispelled the old rancors, and private preserves today are not only an accepted fact but a welcome one as well.   The perspective of years clearly demonstrates their value to the animal and arboreal life of the forest.   Whatever the motives that led to their establishment forty or fifty years ago, they have served admirably as bulwarks against the despoiling advance of axe and gun. Within their own boundaries there have been promoted standards of game and forest preservation which have beneficially influenced the public attitude toward these important subjects. Contributions to the piscicultural and forestry sciences are justly credited to the large estate owners in view of the special character of their lumbering and recreational activities, while the guarded fastness of the estates themselves offered an in violate haven for the normal propagation of wild life long before State supervision had attained its present effectiveness.

Among the earliest associations, and, incidentally, the largest, to hold extensive preserves for recreational purposes was the Adirondack League Club which controlled a magnificent area of forest in Herkimer and Hamilton Counties. Its organization was effected simultaneously with the announcement of Dr. Webb's plans for the building of his railroad; and it was from Mills W. Barse, the Club's first President, that Dr. Webb acquired control of the Herkimer, Newport & Poland Narrow Gage Railroad which formed the first span of his trans-mountain route. The group of League Club organizers included Mills W. Barse and O. L. Snyder of Buffalo, Mark M. Pomeroy, Brooklyn, and Robert C. Alexander and Henry C. Squires of New York City. The objects of the Club were set forth in Article II of its constitution as follows:

> "I—The preservation and conservation of the Adirondack forests and the proper protection of game and fish in the Adirondack region. II—The establishment and promotion of an improved system of forestry. III—The maintenance of an ample preserve for the benefit of its members for the purposes of hunting, fishing, rest and recreation."

In August, 1890, the Club acquired by purchase a tract of 104,000 acres lying in Townships 2, 5, 6, 7, and 8 of the Moose River Tract for $475,000, and by lease a 75,000 acre tract adjoining on the east. The whole formed a contiguous area of 179,000 acres—certainly a playground of impressive dimensions on which the members could happily begin their recreational life. Three years later the Bisby Club property on first Bisby Lake was added to this preserve, and in 1894 the 12,000 acre Wager Tract became part of it also. With this last acquisition, the total area of the preserve nearly approximated the Brown's Tract acreage which had come into the unwilling possession of John Brown of Providence a hundred years before. The passing century, however, had evolved a more practical and profitable use for the Adirondacks than prosaic mining and agricultural activities.

The Club's 1892 and 1893 Year Books, the earliest of a series of annual issues, uninterrupted to date, described the newly acquired preserve as an "Adirondack Empire" of 275 square miles, eight times as large as Manhattan Island, three times as large as Richmond County, and the equivalent of one-sixth the area of either Herkimer or Hamilton County. Of the 104,000 acres acquired originally, 93,000 were covered with virgin forest, the largest contiguous tract of its kind then remaining in the Adirondacks. From its northwest boundary near Little Moose Lake, three miles southeast of the village of Old Forge, the preserve extended in a southerly and south-easterly direction to a line in Hamilton County below West Canada Creek and First and Second Stillwaters. The 179,000 acres contained sixty lakes and ponds, the whole area being drained by innumerable rivers and streams bountifully alive with trout. Club houses were built and maintained on Honnedaga, Bisby and Little Moose Lakes. The A. D. Barber camp, built on the Honnedaga shore prior to the organization of the League, served as the first Club rendezvous there. Mountain Lodge, the club house on Little Moose Lake, was completed in 1892. The administrative headquarters of the League are now maintained at this lake.

For four years after the organization of the Club, members gained access to Mountain Lodge by steamer from Old Forge to Little Moose Landing on the South Shore of First Lake, and thence by foot or buckboard along the old three-quarter mile trail leading to Little Moose Lake. The present road, which affords a more direct and convenient route to the lake, became available to vehicular traffic in 1894.

The club house on Bisby Lake, erected by General Sherman and his associates of the Bisby Club in 1878, provided the early headquarters for the League's membership on that lake following the merging of the two Clubs in 1893.

To the credit of the local guiding fraternity, as well as to the caliber of the League Club organizers, it must be said that a large majority of Central Adirondack guides evinced no hostility toward the establishing of so large a private preserve. From the Club's inception the relationships between members and guides were invariably harmonious. The exceptionally high average of intelligence among local woodsmen and the commendable purpose underlying the formation of the Club easily precluded the reign of contention which had marked the introduction of private preserves in certain other sections of the Adirondacks.

Early in its history the League adopted a stringent policy of game preservation designed to perpetuate the prevailing status of wild life on its preserve and to encourage a general public interest in the conservation of the Adirondacks. Its by-laws, drafted by the committee on club rules, incorporated more rigid protective measures than were imposed by the State game laws. They shortened by fifteen days the legal season for taking deer, prohibited the killing of does and fawns, and discontinued the destructive practice of "jacking" or "floating." This method of hunting involved night shooting from a boat and led to the loss of wounded game that escaped the hunter under cover of darkness and died, unrecovered, in a place of concealment remote from the water front. The Club also discouraged the use of hounds for deer running, and maintained a vigilant patrol to insure the enforcement of its rules and to prevent poaching.

A number of years ago the Club disposed of certain lease and fee holdings which substantially reduced the extent of its preserve. At this writing it controls 99,000 acres, of which 23,000 acres are held by lease and the rest by ownership vested in the Club. This tract contains thirty-three lakes. On fourteen of them well equipped camps have been erected for the common use of members, and nearly one hundred specially designed fishing boats are moored on streams and lakes for the convenience of anglers. One hundred and forty miles of completed trails, twenty-three miles of motor roads, and thirty miles of telephone lines combine with miles of picturesque water routes to form the preserve's network of communication.

The present membership of the Club exceeds two hundred and fifty people hailing from fifteen states and the District of Columbia. Residents of New York State compose more than one half the membership total, and the most distant member travels across the continent from his California home to enjoy the Club's facilities. Approximately six hundred persons are employed on the preserve during the summer season. A fish culturist, forester, and fire and game patrols are included in the regular personnel in addition to a year round administrative and maintenance staff.

A noteworthy contribution to the esthetic side of Adirondack life is found in the forty years' development of a harmonious architecture on the preserve. In the vicinity of Little Moose Lake this development is due in part to the cooperation and good taste of the members and to the genius of Augustus D. Shepard, the Club architect.

As a boy, Mr. Shepard roamed the Adirondacks and acquired an early and zealous affection for their rough wild beauty. Following the formation of the League Club in 1890, he became one of its earliest members. His fondness for the woods has deepened through the years, and at this writing he continues to plunge into wilderness "roughing" expeditions with the same unbounded enthusiasm that he exhibited as a youth. By a fortunate choice of the art and science of architecture as a profession, he attained a conspicuous measure of success in the metropolitan area of New York City and, at the same time, bestowed a lasting gift of beauty and utility upon the material properties of Adirondack camp life. Camp building, with Mr. Shepard, has always been a fine art. His instinctive and cultivated ability to sketch wilderness experiences and impressions of natural beauty into architectural designs has evolved a community of summer dwellings on the shores of Little Moose Lake that embodies the highest degree of rustic harmony. It is a colony of vacation homes which observes on

a grand scale the early Adirondack tradition that color, location and design of habitations and their auxiliary structures
should blend with their environment—but never conflict with
it.   Many of these structures are pictured in Mr. Shepard's
recently published book of designs, "Camps In The Woods,"
a handsome volume which depicts the artistic achievements of
a true woodsman.   A leisurely browse through its one hundred
expansive pages is a pleasant journey through a field of human
enterprise where discord between man and Nature is conspicuous by its refreshing absence.   The book's foreword, which is
partially quoted below, comes from the pen of Robert W.
Chambers.   It utters a graceful tribute to the builder and a
subtle comment on the virtue of conforming architectural
effects with natural settings:

> "It is easy to deface nature by building intrusively.   It
> is difficult to build leaving the landscape unvexed.   But
> to build and enhance is genius.
>
> "Wild growth, usually, is faultlessly composed.   But
> one must not only care for it but also understand it, as
> does Mr. Shepard, to produce so delicately and undis-
> turbingly the work of which he is naturally, as well as
> professionally, a master.
>
> "His forms, construction, textures are as graceful, and
> yet as clever and professionally sophisticated as are the
> intuitive constructions of our lesser brethren whose
> world is the woods and fields."

That the League Club has cherished the fine conceptions of
usefulness which were voiced by its founders more than forty
years ago is evidenced by the declaration of principles contained in its 1931 Year Book, the fortieth consecutive annual
publication.   Following a reprint of Article II of the Club
Constitution, the declaration continues:

> "The above extract from our Constitution implies the
> rendering of useful and beneficial service to the State in
> return for privilege.   This is in accordance with our
> American system which exacts with the grant of every

privilege some compensating duty or service. It is assumed that all members endorse the principle of linking
duty with privilege and that as good citizens and good
sportsmen they wish the Club to render service to the
State."

XIII

THE BROWN'S TRACT GUIDES' ASSOCIATION

THIS virile band of woodsmen began its organized existence in Boonville, March 8, 1898. Its active membership included experienced guides not only of the Brown's Tract, as the name might imply, but of the entire Central Adirondack region. Many of these guides had formerly been affiliated with the Adirondack Guides' Association which had been organized seven years before with headquarters at Saranac Lake. The need of an alliance of this character, designed to function locally, outweighed the appeal of the larger and more unwieldy association to the extent of inducing local woodsmen to with-draw from it and cast their collective lot with the newly formed guild. A small group of men, meeting by invitation in Dwight Grant's Boonville boat shop, effected the organization. Count-ing the host, the group included the following "baker's dozen," all of whom were Adirondack woodsmen of long experience: Garry Riggs, Peter Rivett, Ira Parsons, Nelson Chandler, John Cummerford, Artie Church, Frank Williams, George Barber, Merrill White, Robert Roberts, William Cummerford, H. Dwight Grant and Richard Crego. Richard Crego was chosen to serve as President, Garry Riggs, Vice-President, and Artie Church, Secretary and Treasurer.

The stated objects of the Association included provisions "to aid and secure a better enforcement of the game and forest laws of the state, to secure wise and practical legislation on all subjects affecting the interests of the game regions of the state; to secure to the sportsmen who visit the Brown's Tract region competent and reliable guides, and to maintain a uniform rate of wages for guides."

A tang of the locally historic flavored the proceedings of the thirteen guides whose deliberations in the little boat shop gave birth to the Association. The celebrated Adirondack Guide Boat had been conceived and perfected in that shop

ARTEMUS (ARTIE) M. CHURCH

"Few men have loved the woods more dearly, or treated them more graciously"

nearly twenty years before, and there the Hunter, the first steamer launched on the Fulton Chain had been built by Dwight Grant in 1882.   Keel, bow and stern designs were pencilled on the yellowing folds of paper that embellished the unpainted wooden walls.   Sharp edged tools, bright with use, hung in orderly arrangement awaiting the deft manipulations of the craftsman.   On the overhead rafters, lean strips of pine, fragrant with the seasoning of years, bided the time when the fitting process would make them a part of the shapely boats under construction and a buoyant part of life on the water' ways of the Adirondacks.   The setting proved to be an aus' picious one, for the guides launched a craft of their combined making that easily outrivaled the usefulness of the graceful vessels surrounding them.   It was a craft of conscientious service that made its way into the current of Central Adiron' dack affairs.   After serving its high purpose with admirable effectiveness, it dropped anchor in the region's history, leaving in its wake a trail of far better sportsmanship than the moun' tains had known before.

The Association attained immediate prestige.   Hon. Garry A. Willard, editor of the Boonville Herald, long a friend of Fulton Chain guides and an interested observer of Adiron' dack affairs in general, announced the birth of the new organi' zation with narrative and editorial enthusiasm.   He became one of its first associate members, vigorously championed its several projects undertaken on behalf of forest and game con' servation, and by virtue of his political and personal influence materially advanced the cause of the Association during its fifteen years of active existence.   Other newspapers followed suit, and in a short time the guides' activities became matters of lively news interest throughout the state.   Practically all the woodsmen of the region applied for membership.   Their qualifications were carefully scrutinized by an executive com' mittee, and only men of good repute and recognized ability were accepted.   The privilege of associate membership swelled the Association's roster to several hundred names.   These in' cluded sportsmen who frequented the region, business and professional men and women (living in or out of the state) and native Adirondackers other than guides, all of whom professed a direct personal interest in the Central Adirondacks. The inclusion of the gentle sex on the list of associate members added a gay touch of color to the annual festivities of banqueting, speech making and dancing. This program of socialities became known as "The Guides' Banquet" and was usually held during the month of February in Old Forge, Inlet or Boonville. It was the gala social event of the local midwinter season, and many in attendance travelled hundreds of miles to be on hand.

The Association's first Secretary and Treasurer, Artemas M. Church, filled his important office for twelve consecutive years, and a large measure of the organization's prestige and achievements has been attributed to his love of the forest and public spirited devotion to the cause of conservation. Modest of stature and mild of voice and manner, he possessed a scholarly, analytic mind, an unlimited fund of good comradeship and a mighty love for the Adirondacks and their diverse families of wild creatures. The name "Artemas," of course, failed to survive the rigors of his camp mates' affectionate familiarity and soon gave way to an unromantic "Artie." But it was all the same to him. He pursued his tranquil way into the forest's remotest holy of holies, amassed an invaluable store of Nature's secrets, and, in the doing, probably experienced more actual romance in the wilderness than any woodsman of his time.

Artie was born in Morristown, N. Y., on the banks of the St. Lawrence in 1852. He descended from a colonial family of the same name who had crossed to America in the seventeenth century and who had taken part in many of the Country's pre-national adventures. From them, no doubt, he inherited a natural tendency to penetrate the unexplored. As a child, he moved with his parents to Lyons Falls, Lewis County. He attended the local school there, and later the

Lowville Academy in the same county.   Although he acquired
a liberal institutional education, photography, taxidermy and
excursions into the surrounding forest dwarfed his interest in
the more classic but less entrancing halls of learning.   At the
age of twenty he was an experienced woodsman. ·. In 1879
he built the first permanent camp erected on the shores of
Seventh Lake, a picturesque spruce log and slab-shingled cabin
partially hidden from the water by a growth of cedars.   Like
its owner, it served as an excellent example of unobstrusive
good taste and good woodsmanship.   As an amateur photog-
rapher he ranked high among the region's pioneers.   His duffel
seldom failed to include a huge box-like apparatus and tripod
with a goodly supply of 5 x 8 glass plates.   From these fragile
records many interesting pictures of local historic value are still
available which portray natural scenes of the seventies and
eighties as well as the products of a number of early improvement enterprises.   Guide, business man, sportsman and a
true friend, he won a remarkable measure of affection from
his associates of the Central Adirondacks.   His persistent and
intelligent advocacy of conservation and good sportsmanship
in relation to the Adirondacks, however, carried his name far
beyond the foothills of the mountains.   Harry V. Radford,
editor of *Woods and Waters*, a magazine devoted principally
to the welfare of the Adirondacks, expressed the following
tribute to him and the Guides' Association in reference to the
successful attempt in 1905 to restock the forest with beaver:

> "Too much can not be said in praise of the public spirit
> and intelligent zeal of the members of the Brown's Tract
> Guides' Association, and particularly of their painstak-
> ing and indefatigable secretary, Mr. A. M. Church, to
> whose influence was due largely the success of the plan
> for keeping the beavers at Old Forge through the winter.
> Mr. Church is a woodsman of long and wide experience,
> and, also being a taxidermist, his practical knowledge of
> wild animals is very great.   His services to the cause of
> Adirondack game and forest preservation have been

legion.

"It is a pleasure to record the universal esteem in which this association of woodsmen and guides is held in the section over which it operates."

Many a venerable hemlock has tottered in decay to the waiting earth since Artie made his quiet debut as an Adirondack woodsman. But Time has dealt gently with him, for eighty years have not stifled his profound interest in the destiny of the forest, nor have they dimmed his glowing memory of more than half a century's association with the woods and waters and good companions of the Adirondacks. To be sure, his step has slowed perceptibly as the infirmities of age have crept upon him like a thief in the night and stolen his once buoyant stride of a woodsman. But the warmth of his hand and the clear, friendly twinkling of his eyes belie the weight of many years that have piled up to bow his frame in tribute to the mastery of Time. Ten years or more have passed since he closed his shop in Old Forge and bade goodbye to the Fulton Chain, but taxidermy is still his vocation, and he is still an Adirondack woodsman at heart. Skilfully, though slowly, he plies his craft in a little shop in Boonville. Old men, friends of his younger days, climb the stairs to visit and chat with him of the North Woods of long ago. Their visits are infrequent, for not many friends of his youth remain. Often he is alone—alone but not lonely—for his thoughts and memories must surely be good companions. A family of birds and beasts surround him, all creatures of his artistic mounting. Shapely deer look down from the walls, and it requires but scant play of the imagination to observe with what trustful affection they follow his every movement. They are watching a staunch old friend whose voice was raised in their behalf, a friend who demanded —and still demands—that they and their kind be given a fair chance in the game of life. Perhaps if they possessed thoughts and the power to voice them they would echo the fervent utterance of one of Artie's former associates who said of him, "few men have loved the woods more dearly, or treated them more graciously."

Having effected a compact organization that immediately attracted the best class of the region's guides and sportsmen, the Brown's Tract Guides' Association lost no time in formulating a program of improvements. The vigorous practicality with which it struck at existing evils, and the constructive character of the reforms which it advocated and practiced, won the admiration of Governor Theodore Roosevelt, himself a naturalist and sportsman of distinction as well as an enthusiastic devotee of Adirondack camp life. (While serving his first term as Vice President of the United States Roosevelt was vacationing in the Adirondacks on September 6, 1901, when he received the tragic news of President McKinley's assassination at the Pan-American Exposition in Buffalo). One year after its organization, Governor Roosevelt invited the Association to send a committee of guides to Albany for the purpose of conferring with him regarding proposed amendments to the conservation laws. A delegation of seven well informed members journeyed to the Capital and an interesting conference ensued. The committee included the following guides: Dwight Grant, Artie Church, Garry Riggs, Merrill White, Bill Dart, Henry Covey and Bill Cummerford. A frank exchange of views and ideals resulted in mutual profit for all concerned. Governor Roosevelt proved to be not only a cordial host and an interested and sympathetic auditor, but a fascinating companion of the trail and camp fire whose familiarity with the ways of the wilderness endeared him to the assembled guides. That conference marked the beginning of several years' beneficial influence exerted by the Association upon legislative enactments affecting the Adirondacks.

The efforts of the Association were directed chiefly toward preserving the primeval aspect of the woods and insuring a generous perpetuation of its fish and game. It subscribed emphatically to the State's protective laws, urged their strict enforcement, and even upheld the dignity of the law to the extent of hiring trustworthy guides to patrol the woods in the role of enforcement officers. It advocated the enactment of stringent legislation designed to protect does and fawns during the entire year, and the shortening of the legal season for taking bucks and other game. The use of hounds for deer running met with its vigorous disfavor, as did the practice of "jacking" or night hunting.

Although a hounding law, prohibiting the use of dogs as auxiliaries in deer hunting, had been enacted and supposedly become operative a short time before the guides organized, its actual operation remained in the experimental stage for several years. Its passage had not won the unanimous approval of guides and sportsmen throughout the Adirondacks. In fact, until comparatively recent times flagrant violations of the act have persisted in several sections of the mountains and elsewhere. A widespread clamor for its repeal and numerous reports of its violation prompted the Association to go on record as strongly favoring its continuance. For several years a rather sharp controversy raged anent the measure, but it finally won out and is now a secure and popular edict among New York's prohibitory statutes.

The Association wisely took issue with opponents of the measure on the grounds that hounding constituted a destructive and unsportsmanlike practice which would eventually diminish the number of Adirondack deer to the point of near-extinction. Although dogs had been the companions and servants of men since the first white hunter roamed the Adirondacks, their presence in the forest had never before seriously menaced the survival of its wild life. But the tremendous increase of hunters resulting from the railroad and other improved means of transportation had brought the deer hound to the front as a dangerously obstructing factor in the path of conservationists.

Adirondack deer hounds were not actually a classificatory branch of the canine family especially adapted to, or employed in, the running of deer. Rather, they were a species of keen scented fox hounds of various colors, black and tan predomin-

ating. A pungent secretion from the inter-digital glands of
the deer enabled the dogs to pick up and follow the scent of
their quarry with comparative ease. Once on the trail they
gave voice to their exultation with a prolonged musical baying
that resounded through the forest carrying vibrant good tidings of the chase. Sportsmen, stationed on the shores of
neighboring lakes, equipped with boats and rifles, were warned
of the proximity of game and awaited its approach in expectant readiness for the kill. In the meantime, the hunted deer,
also warned by the baying of the hounds, sought safety in precipitous flight or in a circling counter movement designed to
maneuver its pursuers off the scent. Failing in these tactics
it took to the water as a certain avenue of escape. This was
a fatal jump from the frying pan into the fire. Alert watchers
quickly rowed to within easy range, rifles swung into action,
and whining steel joined the chase to beat the swimmer in its
race for life. It was all very thrilling for the hunter, very safe,
and comparatively effortless. It was profitable, too, from the
standpoint of venison and handsome heads to be carried home
as trophies of the huntsman's prowess. Up to a certain point
even the deer may have enjoyed the game for they are reputed
wily players at hide-and-seek. But the poor creatures never
had a chance. The odds of men, dogs, boats and guns were
too great against them, and the game conspicuously lacked the
element of good sportsmanship. The dogs were not squeam-
ish in the matter of sex or age; neither were some of the
hunters, and does and fawns went the way of bucks in providing targets for the slaughter.

Without question, the Association took a wise and public
spirited stand in declaring against this form of so called sport.
It did more than take a stand, for it literally took up arms. Its
members declared an open season on dogs employed as game
runners in violation of the law, and the number of these lawless canines killed by local guides became items of record in the
Secretary's annual reports to the Association.

The terms "jacking" and "floating" were used synonymously

in reference to the sport of night hunting with the aid of artificial light. This method of taking deer involved the use of
boats (and guides to propel them) and small jack lights
equipped with strong reflectors. The guide, seated in the
stern, pushed the nose of the boat slowly along the wooded
shore under cover of darkness. The sportsman sat comfortably in the bow while the lantern or jack light attached to his
cap threw a glaring illumination of small circumference upon
the fringe of trees and shrubbery at the water's edge. Across
his knees the omnipotent rifle lay in readiness to take part in
the sport. Fascinated by the curious phenomenon and unaware of the lurking danger, the deer would stand gazing at the
gleaming reflector, its motionless body bathed in light and presenting a perfect target for the unseen enemy. Of course,
it was only one more demonstration of superior intelligence
and deadly mechanical odds pitted against the instincts of a
dumb animal, and the unsophisticated creature usually paid
for its curiosity with its life. Sometimes the hunter's excitement or the tilting motion of the boat deflected the rifle and
the deer escaped with injuries of more or less severity. Darkness precluded the possibility of following its bloody trail, and
many animals thus fatally wounded were never recovered.

So diverse and practical were the policies adopted and advocated by the Association that it rapidly won recognition as a
standard bearer in the fight against improper exploitation of
Adirondack resources. It vigorously opposed the political
strategists who endeavored to throw open state-owned timber
land for the commercial advantage of large lumbering companies, and it urged the purchase by the state of additional
tracts within New York's forested areas. Its wide influence
may be traced to the fact that its active membership included
only woodsmen of long experience rather than uninformed
theorists or forest devotees whose alliance with the cause of
conservation sprung from purely sentimental promptings.
Every voice helped, of course, during the formative period
when policies vital to the future welfare of the Adirondacks

were being shaped, and the Association was by no means the only influential group dedicated to the shaping process. But its utterances came with a distinct, unmistakable voice of authority. The forest was its laboratory. Its members were engaged in daily research, comprehensive in scope and intimate in detail. Their collective experience contributed a huge fund of accurate working knowledge essential to an intelligent administration of Adirondack affairs, and the fruits of their efforts are discernible today in nearly every phase of the region's sporting and recreational activities.

Perhaps the most interesting, if not the most profitable responsibilities assumed by the organized guides were their efforts to stock the Central Adirondack region with wapiti, moose and beavers. The race of beavers at that time was tottering on the brink of complete extinction; moose had entirely disappeared forty years before, and wapiti had never been known to inhabit the region within the memory of white men. Of the three species, beavers alone survived the experimental stage of the replenishing enterprise. Climate, topography and vegetation favored the survival of the two others, but the regrettable human factor intervened to blast the experiment almost at its inception.

In 1902, the city of Binghamton offered the Brown's Tract Guides' Association five wapiti to be used as parent stock in establishing the species as native game animals of the Adirondacks. Wapiti are a variety of deer, similar in appearance and habits to the European stag which, since time immemorial, has been esteemed the noblest quarry of English and Continental sportsmen. In America they are commonly though erroneously referred to as "elk." Fully matured, they attain a shoulder height of five feet and a weight range of from seven hundred to nine hundred pounds. The antlers develop to a towering symmetry with a spread of four feet and weigh from twenty to thirty pounds. They are hardy, versatile animals, capable of adaptation to a variety of environments including regions of severe cold and deep snow. Cognizant of their superior worth as additions to the wild life of the region, the Association promptly accepted Binghamton's offer, and several guides journeyed to that city to prepare the animals for shipment.

Four cows and one bull were crated and, attended by the guides, were transported by rail to Big Moose Station. From there they were hauled in wagons to Dart's Lake where Bill Dart had improvised winter quarters in which to shelter and feed them until Spring. They wintered well, and in late March were released from their detention camp thoroughly acclimated to their mountain environment. Free to range the great wooded reaches of the Adirondacks at will, and displaying considerable animal enthusiasm at the prospect, they set out in a body to explore the world of lakes and forest that had been the habitat of their ancestors centuries before. Bill Dart also displayed noticeable enthusiasm at their departure. The task of maintaining them safely through the long winter months had added heavily to his responsibilities as well as to the routine of daily chores.

Needless to say, the eyes of the meagre population of the Central Adirondacks and of the outside public followed the rovings of the newly released animals in a figurative sense. Newspapers published information at regular intervals regarding their condition and whereabouts. These reports were uniformly encouraging and led to the general belief that the experiment would undoubtedly succeed. The five wapiti represented a fascinating test in the adaptation of exotics to local conditions, and their survival would logically presage the successful propagation of a new and highly desirable life line in the animal kingdom of the Adirondacks. The Brown's Tract Guides' Association voiced a public appeal in their behalf, entreating all to cooperate in the experiment by refraining from acts of violence or other treatment detrimental to their welfare.

For several months all went well, and the huge strangers browsed their way to a state of sleek contentment. They roamed the region from Dart's Lake to the foot of the Fulton

Chain, pausing enroute to enjoy the innumerable watercourses and succulent forage grounds that lay between. From time to time, concurring reports, based on personal observations of guides and other interested witnesses, indicated their complete satisfaction with life in the wilderness and their willingness to remain as guests of the Association.

But the creatures refused to "go native." They sought and enjoyed the companionship of man, and accosted travellers in the forest in mute appeal for tasty morsels to be eaten from the hands of the donors. Their visits to the clearings were social events which delighted local householders. In keeping with true mountain hospitality, their calls were rewarded with an assortment of tid-bits which added variety to the menu pro' vided by the woods. But the social instincts that endeared them to native woodsmen proved their undoing. In the late autumn, the five wapiti were found dead in the woods at the foot of Moss Lake. They had been shot by a disgruntled guide, so rumor intimated, in reprisal against the Association, and their bodies were found lying within an area one hundred yards square. Apparently they had faced the slaughter in meek submission, making no effort to escape the danger which they could not comprehend. All mankind had been their friends, and nothing in their Binghamton or Adirondack ex' periences had taught them to discriminate between members of the race.

Indignation at the outrage reached a high pitch, but circum' stantial evidence only could be adduced against the suspected killer. No retributive action could be taken by the Associa' tion to avenge the loss, and the guides, individually, were averse to taking the law into their own hands. The guilty woodsman, therefore, escaped punishment. The antlered head of the bull was placed in Dart's Camp where it remained for many years—the only tangible product of the Association's praiseworthy experiment. Artie Church had mounted it, caustically reflecting, the while, upon the magnitude of human degeneracy that could encompass so despicable an act. At the guides' annual banquet which was held in Old Forge the following January, David Charbonneau was called on by the chairman to express his opinion of "the man who shot the elk." David possessed a vocabulary all his own. It was distinctive, curt and emphatic. But ladies were present, so, being always a gentleman, he contented himself with a conventional response to the invitation by saying, "I don't care to mention the matter at this time for the reason that what I think of that fellow is not fit for public expression."

The liberation of moose in the Adirondacks resulted as unprofitably as the wapiti enterprise so far as it concerned the permanent establishment of an exotic species. A group of these creatures were released to browse and multiply in the woods, but the devastating pot hunter asserted himself in time to render the experiment null and void. One by one, they were shot from the experimental stage into Kingdom Come of the brute world. Instead of adding their progeny to the region's family of attractive game, they only added to the general conviction that drastic protective and disciplinary measures on the part of the State alone could secure the perpetuation of wild life in any form. Despite its unqualified failure, however, a certain interest attaches to the experiment if for no other reason than that it brought the vivid personality of Harry V. Radford, chief instigator of the enterprise, to the foreground.

When the first moose were liberated in 1902, Harry was only twenty-two years old. But among the voices raised in behalf of New York's vast forest lands at that time his was the most vibrant and far reaching—and probably the most effective. Born in New York City in 1880, his education there included courses of study at Manhattan College from which he was graduated in 1901 and 1906 with B. S. and C. E. Degrees. Between terms he travelled extensively through Europe with his widowed mother who was a woman of independent means. As a boy, he had spent several summers vacationing in the Adirondacks and had grown to love and understand the woods more dearly than any other environment.

So deeply rooted, in fact, became his interest in the well-being of the forest that he undertook the publication of a small maga- zine in 1898 which he styled *Woods and Waters*. Harry was then eighteen, and a college freshman. Published quarterly, the new magazine entered the field as a disseminator of news pertaining to the great out-of-doors, particularly the Adiron- dacks. The fluent literary style and intimate knowledge of wild life exhibited by its youthful editor, together with his inspiriting enthusiasms for a variety of worthy projects, imme- diately attracted the attention of a wide circle of readers. *Woods and Waters* grew steadily in size and circulation until it won a position of prestige at least comparable to that of older contemporary publications of like character.

Harry crusaded in new fields of enterprise as ardently as he explored remote nooks of the wilderness. Having launched his magazine upon a receptive public, he lost no time launching a project that had been near and dear to him since boyhood— the restoration of moose to the Adirondacks. This objective assumed an importance of the first magnitude in his editorial columns, and he quickly stirred public interest to cooperative proportions. For three years he waged a vigorous campaign designed to influence the State Legislature into passing a "moose bill" with sufficient appropriation to finance its several provisions. He enlisted the aid of the Brown's Tract Guides' Association and of numerous other woodsmen throughout the Adirondacks. All were in sympathy with the proposed meas- ure and heartily advocated its passage.

Men and organizations of wide influence were subjected to the wizardry of Harry's irresistible salesmanship and became zealous allies in the cause. (Prominent among this group was the Association for the Protection of the Adirondacks, an or- ganization dedicated to the preservation of forest, fish and game. It was organized in 1901 chiefly through the initiative of Hon. Warren Higley, president of the Adirondack League Club. Its membership included, among other notables, Gov- ernor Benjamin B. Odell, Jr., and Lieutenant Governor

Timothy Woodruff). The group most directly concerned
with the moose movement owed its formation to Harry's personal solicitations and genius for organization. This was the
Association For Restoring Moose To The Adirondacks, organized in 1900 for the specific purpose indicated by its name.
Its officers included Hon. Warren Higley, Frank S. Gardner,
Harry V. Radford and a formidable array of no less than
eighteen distinguished vice-presidents—more officers in all
than there were moose to be liberated.

Needless to say, Harry won his fight eventually. In 1901,
the Legislature passed a bill appropriating $5,000.00 for the
purchase and transportation of wild moose to be released in
the Adirondacks, and Governor Odell promptly signed it. The
three year campaign to achieve this result had captured the
public fancy to a remarkable degree, and its termination in victory commanded numerous headlines in the country's press.
All eyes were turned upon the Adirondacks and upon the
twenty-one year old college youth whose buoyant, dominating
personality had guided a boyhood ambition to reality through
a labyrinth of legislative procedure and public opinion.

The first shipment of moose arrived in the Adirondacks in
1902, a bull, a cow and a bull calf. They came crated and in
excellent physical condition, consigned to Game Protector Ned
Ball. Ned, whose real name was John Edwin Ball, was an
active member of the Brown's Tract Guides' Association and
one of the region's most capable woodsmen. Born in England
in 1854, he came to America while still a young boy. He began frequenting the Fulton Chain country in 1879, and in
1886 built a permanent camp near Bullhead Rock on the river
between Old Forge Lake and First Lake of the Fulton Chain.
This was the third dwelling erected in the vicinity of the "old
forge," and Ned occupied it continuously until his death in
1927. His comprehensive knowledge of wild life prompted
Harry V. Radford to write of him:

> "Ned has had more experience than any other person in
> handling and liberating live game animals in the Adiron-

dacks for the state—moose, wapiti and beaver. What he doesn't know about the Adirondack woods and their inhabitants is not generally learned in the course of a lifetime."

A good deal of fanfare and excitement attended the liberation. The site chosen lay near Uncas Switch, several miles east of Eagle Bay, and on July 7 a cavalcade of woodsmen and spectators moved upon the scene in obvious anticipation of an event. Several guides furnished by the Browns Tract Guides' Association were present to assist in the operation; a group of photographers climbed to points of vantage to record the affair pictorially; an assembly of vacationists and visitors were on hand to represent the public's interest in the liberation, and the jubilant editor of *Woods and Waters* had travelled from New York City to be present in the capacity of Master of Ceremonies. To Ned and Harry fell the honor of opening the two crates. Owing to its tender age, the calf had been left to mature in a specially constructed pen on the state hatchery grounds in Old Forge.

The three animals had been captured in the Canadian woods several months before. When taken, they were in a wild state and extremely difficult to handle. Following their capture, they had spent a good deal of time in a number of detention camps and had been subjected to several hundred miles of railroad transportation. Somewhere along the line they had renounced their wild ways, turned over a new leaf in the matter of moose ethics, and had settled down to enjoy the companionship of men from whose friendly hands they had nibbled many savory morsels. When the crates were opened they refused to escape. Both animals stood contentedly within their wooden prisons, docile and gentle as dairy cows. This amiable behavior disappointed the wide-eyed spectators who had come in the hope of witnessing a frenzied rush from crates to woods. Even Harry Radford, a master showman on such occasions, seemed baffled by the stupid lack of dramatic instinct exhibited by the two until Ned coaxed them forth with a handful of lump sugar. Observers later reported that the cow, having devoured her portion of the sweets, attempted to climb back into her crate and was prevented from doing so only by a sharp kick on the rump administered by one of the guides. The dense wall of forest seemed to intimidate them, and they were plainly reluctant to play a part in restocking the region with their kind. Eighteen vice-presidents to the contrary, they would not take to the woods. It required the employment of strategy on the part of the resourceful Ned and Harry to coax them into the fringe of forest, and additional strategy for the strategists to escape without being detected and followed. Instead of the moose attempting to evade their captors, the captors were hard put to evade their moose. But the creatures finally wandered off among the trees, and thus, tamely enough, the long awaited experiment began.

The importation of moose continued during the summer of 1902, and by autumn of that year a half dozen of the huge animals were ranging the Central Adirondack forest. On July 13, a yearling cow was set at liberty near Bug Lake, a few miles south of Uncas Road Switch. (Bug Lake is tributary to the outlet of Eighth Lake of the Fulton Chain). Others were liberated in the same vicinity on July 14 and August 1. With these importations from the Canadian wilderness disposed of successfully, and more to follow, the Moose River country gave promise of again coming into its own as the natural habitat of the species from which its name derives. In the meantime, the calf which had been confined at Old Forge retired from participation in the experiment. Its care had been entrusted to Henry Davidson, foreman of the state hatchery. Henry ministered to its creature comfort with skill and devotion, but the hardships of travel to its new home and subsequent separation from its kind proved to be the little fellow's undoing and it died soon after arriving—to the deep regret of Henry and his fellow villagers.

Woods and Waters kept its public informed of developments. Each quarterly issue carried detailed accounts of the

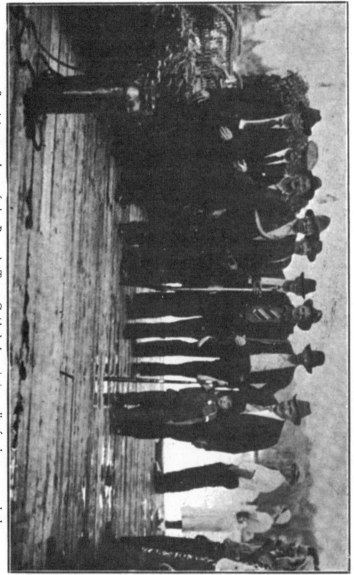

Surviving members of the Brown's Tract Guides' Association, all of whom roamed the Adirondacks in pre-railroad days. Left to right: Peter Rivett, Will Sperry, William Weedmark, Emmett Marks, Charlie Puffer, Ben Parsons, Dana Fraula, Ira Parsons and Dave Charbonneau. The tiny huntsman is Keith Hollister of Old Forge.

Mr. and Mrs. Benjamin Harrison at their camp on Second Lake of the Fulton Chain

peregrinations, habits and condition of the moose, together with photographs of them as they browsed in the clearings or loitered at camp doors in mute appeal for edible handouts. Hoof prints made by the liberated animals as they stepped for the first time on Adirondack soil, and even the empty crates in which they had been transported were subjects for pictorial reproduction in the magazine.

Like the ill-fated wapiti, all the liberated moose had become domesticated to the danger point. They ranged an extensive area of forest, visiting several lakes of the Fulton Chain, Big Moose and Raquette Lakes and other smaller lakes and a number of streams. Camps en route were honored by their visits and so were travellers in the woods to whom they made overtures of ingenuous friendliness. Food and water abounded; the hungry wolf pack—arch enemy of North American animal life—no longer inhabited the region; all mankind seemed affably disposed toward the trustful creatures, and the law protected them. For some time they thrived in the manner of contented, well fed dairy stock, and each passing month added its welcome assurance that the restocking enterprise would result in abundant fruition.

Suddenly a regrettable though logical series of reverses set in. Partly deprived of their self-preserving instincts, the moose began falling victim to the superior killing power of man—the one species of animal life they trusted implicitly. Less than a year after their liberation, a woman armed with a rifle sighted a cow moose while sauntering through the woods near Seventh Lake. Simultaneously, the moose sighted the woman. It paused from its browsing to amble genially toward her in expectation of a friendly caress and, perhaps, a bite or two of food. Now a moose, genial or otherwise, is a fear inspiring spectacle to a solitary lady when suddenly encountered in the deep woods— especially when it insists on approaching without first giving evidence that its motive is without guile. The huntress had but recently arrived in the region and had no knowledge of the harmless nature of the imported animals. In vain she endeavored to frighten the oncoming apparition. Undaunted by her screams and frantic gesticulations it continued to advance until the lady, in self defense, resorted to her rifle. The first shot took effect, and experimental moose number one lay dead in the forest.

Other fatalities followed. Some time later a moose was discovered lying dead near the shore of Eighth Lake where it had been shot in wanton sport and left to rot in the woods. The identity of the killer never came to light. Two more were shot near Raquette Lake, and their deaths swelled the list of unsolved mysteries. The bull got by for nearly two years before a pot hunter laid it low beside the Brown's Tract Inlet. Of the fifteen or more animals liberated along the water courses extending from the Fulton Chain to the Saranacs, none survived the experimental stage. For several months a friendly old cow moose frequented the village streets of Newcombe. It was a favorite with the children who vied with one another in feeding it the tastiest viands that could be secretly extracted from the family larder. But eventually it went the way of its mates and was found dead in the adjacent forest.

Having won his editorial campaign to restore the exiled moose to the Adirondacks, Harry Radford turned the force of his pen and personality to effecting the rehabilitation of the nearly extinct beaver. Since its inception, the Brown's Tract Guides' Association had advocated their restoration, and it now joined heartily with Woods and Waters and other periodicals of outdoor life in espousing the cause and pushing it to a swift and successful issue. Artie Church, the Association secretary, had conducted a comprehensive survey of the Adirondacks in an effort to determine as nearly as possible the exact number of beavers inhabiting the mountains. The results were discouraging so far as rehabilitation by native stock was concerned. A rather feeble colony existed in St. Lawrence County, and a few isolated specimens were discovered in other sections. Artie brought his findings to the attention of the Legislature and strongly urged immediate action by the State to

save and strengthen the life line of the dwindling race. Legis-
latures are notoriously reluctant to further a good cause unless
it be also a popular cause, and to popularize this one Harry
Radford took up the cudgel on behalf of the beavers by institut-
ing a systematic series of public appeals through the columns
of his magazine.

Since the introduction of American furs as factors in European commerce early in the seventeenth century, the fortunes
of the American beaver had receded to a deplorably low ebb.
In 1609, when Henry Hudson and Samuel de Champlain explored the river and lake which now bear their names, the
Adirondacks and their foothills were known to the Five
Nations of the Iroquois as *The Beaver Hunting Grounds*—a
designation plainly indicating the regional abundance of that
species at the time. It has since been estimated that nearly a
million beavers then flourished in the Adirondacks. Following the bold explorations of the intrepid Hudson and Champlain, there came the no less intrepid and far more ruthless
adventurer, the fur trader. The advent of this commercially
inclined pioneer upon the wilderness frontier inaugurated an
era of unprecedented activity among Indian fur hunters.
Iroquois and Algonquin tribesmen who had never exploited
the beaver habitat beyond the satisfaction of their modest needs
plunged suddenly into a campaign of massacre, spurred to the
heights of destructive cunning by the competitive offers of
English, Dutch and French traders. Then came the beaver
hat—adopted in the mid-seventeenth century as the ultra-
fashionable article of masculine headwear. That was Fashion's
most destructive innovation for the beaver. For two hundred
years their sleek fur maintained its prestige atop the heads of
well dressed gentlemen in Europe and America. The ominous
hum of hat makers in England, France and Holland echoed
drearily across the Atlantic to sound the little animals' death
knell. White trappers joined the hunt, for the beavers were
easily captured and the rewards great, and in a comparatively
short time the Adirondack branch of this defenseless family

was swiftly approaching the portals of oblivion.

From the tenth annual report of the Forest, Fish and Game Commission comes the story of the beaver's decline in figures which were first published in *Woods and Waters*. The year 1800 found but an estimated 5,000 inhabiting the Adirondacks. Twenty years later this number was reduced to 1,000, and in 1850 only 100 remained. During the mid-century period, the capture of a single beaver became so rare and delicate an accomplishment that the few successes in this employment were achieved only by trappers of exceptional skill and patience—all this in face of the fact that beavers are among the most prolific propagators of American wild life. The decayed remnants of beaver dams were still discernible in the Central Adirondacks seventy-five years ago, but their builders had vanished many years before and no newcomers had put in an appearance to replace them.

The slaughter continued until 1895 when no more than ten beavers could be found in the entire Adirondacks. Obviously, the species at last tottered on the brink of utter extinction. Spurred to action by this disconcerting revelation, the State Legislature passed a protective law that year—the first of its kind to be enacted in the State—prohibiting the taking of beavers by any method during all seasons. It was belated legislative recognition of their desperate plight, but it helped, and the furry creatures at once began a progressive program of rehabilitation. Their number increased for the first time in two and one half centuries. The numerical upward climb proceeded slowly, to be sure, for game hogs still haunted the watersides in illegal quest of precious skins. Eight years after the protective measure became operative not more than twenty-five beavers were known to inhabit the Adirondacks.

In the meantime, the hue and cry for the improvement of their lot gained momentum. The public added its voice to the demands of leaders in the movement, and in time the restoration of these animals to their former high estate became as popular a topic as the previously proposed liberation of moose

had been. In 1904, an enactment more specific and stringent
in its provisions, replaced the beaver law of 1895. At the
same time the Legislature voted an appropriation for the purchase of beavers and for their liberation in the Adirondacks
as a means of speeding the propagation of the species.

The first purchase, consisting of seven beavers, was made by
the State Forest, Fish and Game Commission in December,
1904. The seven animals came to the Adirondacks from
Canada via St. Louis where they had been guests of the
Louisiana Purchase Exposition as exhibits of the Canadian
Government. As the deep snow and frozen condition of the
lakes and streams rendered them temporarily incapable of providing for themselves, the Brown's Tract Guides' Association
volunteered to maintain them comfortably through the winter.
Their debut as Adirondackers occurred under rather humiliating circumstances—considering the fact that they were distinguished international travellers and objects of wide public
attention. Upon arrival, the seven were consigned to the
cellar of Game Protector Robert Moore's home at Thendara
to await the completion of suitable quarters in Old Forge. Ned
Ball and Henry Davidson hurriedly constructed a small house
on the hatchery grounds which duplicated, as nearly as possible, the architectural features traditionally approved by its
prospective tenants. A two-story structure, nine feet long,
four feet wide and four feet high, it stood in a cement rearing
pond beside the main hatchery building. A wire fence surrounding the pond prevented the captive animals from escaping, although they made persistent efforts to leave the enclosure. Ned fed them once a day, and a goodly crowd of villagers
usually managed to be on hand at meal time to enjoy the sight.
Vegetables, bark and cuttings from branches formed the menu.
The vegetables, which they consumed at the rate of one bushel
a week, included apples, carrots, turnips, cabbage and potatoes.
Several kinds of trees were used to supply the woody items of
their diet. They consumed about a cord of freshly cut brush
each week in addition to the bark from a cord or more of small

logs. Ned knew his business as a dietician, and his seven charges passed the winter without exhibiting a single known beaver symptom of digestive disturbance or malnutrition.

The opportunity for releasing the beavers came with the warmth of Spring and the rapid thawing of ice and snow. Although they had wintered well from a standpoint of physical well being, their number was no longer seven, but six. The blight of social snobbery had descended upon the colony to divide the captives into two cliques. Five of the seven had banded themselves into a definite group determined to occupy the nine foot house to the exclusion of their fellows. The attempts of the ousted pair to occupy the little dwelling were savagely repulsed by the numerically superior band, and the two were saved from the relentless teeth of the snobbish five on several occasions only by the timely intervention of Ned or Henry. Failing to effect a reconciliation between them, Ned divided the rearing pond with a high wire fence and built a second house to shelter the minority faction. Restrained thus from intimate contact, the two groups abandoned their contentious attitudes, and for some time thereafter the house divided against itself thrived and waxed fat. In early March one of the outcasts succeeded in breaking through the wire barrier and entering the enemy domain where it was promptly set upon and killed. Outcast number two prudently refrained from emulating its comrade's rash feat, and to this exercise of discretion, no doubt, its numerous progeny now inhabiting the Adirondacks owe their existence.

The task of distributing the six beavers and others that arrived later rested with a volunteer group of Association guides who were thoroughly familiar with the lakes and streams of the Central Adirondacks. Harry Radford left his editor's desk and travelled from New York to join each of the expeditions. The activities of this group in carrying the State's experimental project to a successful conclusion brought them into the limelight as "The Army of Liberation." By this name they became known to a large circle of readers who followed their expeditions through the columns of newspapers and magazines. The group included Ned Ball, Frank Sperry and his son, Ben, Edward F. Abbott, Eri Delmarsh, E. J. Van Arnam, Stanley Weedmark and Harry Radford.

Frank Sperry, the oldest member of the Army in point of association with the mountains, had first roamed the Central Adirondacks shortly after the Civil War—while still a very young boy. Like several other Lewis County residents at that time, he kept returning until the mountains captured his affec-tions to the exclusion of all other geographic environments. In 1889 he built a camp opposite Bullhead Rock just below the Ned Ball cabin. With this as a home base, he inducted his two small but enthusiastic sons, Louis and Ben, into the mys-teries of woodcraft. The youths, themselves, were something of a mystery to the forest, for the region's supply of small boys at that time was almost as negligible in quantity as its families of beaver. Frank's bent for adventure led him on long expeditions through the Canadian and Alaskan wilds. Before the height of the gold rush had peopled the Klondike with fortune hunters, he boated into Dawson, cater-ing to that growing settlement's food needs with cargoes of fresh-killed game. He acted as Benjamin Harrison's personal guide during the ex-president's several years of camp life on Second Lake of the Fulton Chain.

On April 27, the Army of Liberation set out for the South Branch of the Moose River carrying two of the six captive beavers on a specially constructed litter to perform the first act of liberation. Leaving their boats at Inlet at the head of Fourth Lake, the party marched through the woods to the cabin of Frank Gray, a hermit-like woodsman who lived on the South Branch twelve miles from Inlet. After resting overnight in the cabin, they proceeded, accompanied by their host, to Otter Brook which a beaver (also a hermit) had inhabited for the past three years. This animal had escaped from the estate of Lieutenant Governor Woodruff at Lake Kora in 1902. After making its way overland to Otter Brook, which is tributary to the South Branch, it had dammed that small stream and set up a bachelor housekeeping establishment in the flow. Subsequent developments demonstrated that the Army employed winning diplomacy by availing themselves of the cordial relations existing between members of the brotherhood of hermits. The hermit beaver welcomed Hermit Gray and his party, and signified its willingness to receive their furry charges into its domicile. Released from their crates, the two creatures accepted the solitary one's watery hospitality. Unaware that their respective fates were matters of interest to thousands of people, they casually entered the stream and swam out of sight around a wooded point of land.

This diffusion of new blood into the Otter Brook colony—if the former lonely inhabitant may be termed a colony—inspired a program of community improvements. The following year a new and more pretentious house rose above the surface of the flow. In a letter to Harry Radford, written that year, Frank Gray described the house as "about ten feet in diameter on the ground floor, six feet high, shaped like a haystack, gothic on the outside. Don't know what is inside—suppose popular finish." Two years later, the population of the colony numbered a dozen plump citizens, and the original dam, built by the pioneer beaver in 1902, had been replaced by a more substantial barrier four feet high.

The day after their return from Otter Brook, the Army of Liberation started for Big Moose Lake carrying the four remaining beavers on two litters. These were released near a small stream flowing from the south into the main inlet to the lake. The four separated into two couples, and both spent a good deal of time looking the country over before settling down in permanent quarters. Eventually they and their offspring occupied sections of Big Moose Lake and smaller bodies of water lying to the east. Some of their number also migrated as far away as the Beaver River region where they established flourishing colonies.

In 1906, the Forest, Fish and Game Commission purchased

from the Federal Department of the Interior twenty-five beavers which were captured in Yellowstone National Park. These were shipped to the Army of Liberation at Old Forge in small groups for distribution between the Fulton Chain and Tupper Lake. Altogether, thirty state-owned beavers were thus released by the Army. Fourteen others were released by private agencies or escaped from private preserves which brought the total number of the species introduced from outside habitats to forty-four. These, added to the estimated twenty inhabiting the Adirondacks at the time, swelled the total native population to about sixty. With their domestic security safeguarded by stringent laws and close State supervision, they lost no time in exemplifying the well known tendency of their kind to proliferate. The several colonies rapidly increased in size and number. Evidence of beaver occupation appeared on numerous lakes and streams throughout the entire mountain area. A conservative survey conducted in 1915 placed their number at from 15,000 to 20,000. They continued to increase until the year 1920 found them inhabiting practically every body of water in the mountains—and looking about for more.

During the century intervening between the decline and subsequent rise in the fortunes of Adirondack beavers local conditions changed to the extent of transforming the diligent and highly interesting creatures into an embarrasing element of the wilderness population. Generally speaking, large contiguous tracts of forest lands concentrated under individual ownerships had gradually given way to smaller privately owned plots which had been improved by the erection of resort hotels, camps, boathouses and other adjuncts of human occupancy. These represented substantial investments of time and money, and the owners were reluctant, of course, to place their improved real estate at the disposal of the State as beaver feeding grounds. But the increasing hordes of beavers took no such restricted view of the matter. They swarmed across the mountains, trespassing upon real property that promised comfortable livelihoods, posted or otherwise, fed heartily, built, reared their young, and made themselves complacently at home as their race had done in the prosperous days of old. They dammed small streams and ponds, creating flow grounds which drowned adjacent standing timber. Their voracious appetites for juicy twigs led them to gnaw down trees on artistically landscaped camp grounds, and as they dined they gnawed the hearts of prideful owners who were restrained by law from retaliatory action against them and their dams and lodges. Eventually, their rapacious communism provoked an avalanche of claims and protests which deluged the Conservation Department, whereupon the Department relaxed its rigid protective attitude. Permits were issued in 1920 authorizing aggrieved land owners to dynamite dams and lodges as a means of causing the creatures to migrate from the afflicted neighborhoods. For a time this policy partially alleviated the hardships complained of, but beavers continued to increase despite the opposition of dynamite. In 1923 the Legislature amended the Conservation law to the extent of delegating to the Conservation Department absolute authority to regulate the number of Adirondack beavers by subjecting them to open trapping seasons at departmental discretion. The subsequent judicious exercise of this authority by the Department has apparently solved the problem. The first open season, from March 1 to March 31 inclusive, was proclaimed in 1924 and repeated in 1925. With prime beaver skins commanding a price of more than thirty dollars at that time, an army of trappers eagerly cooperated with the Department and plied their craft with telling effect. Too telling, in fact, for the results approximated those achieved by Iroquois and Algonquin trappers during the beaver hat era. In two years the number of beavers declined to the point of scarcity, and the flow of complaints received by the Department concerning their activities subsided in like ratio. Three years of protection followed, during which the subdued animals exhibited astounding recuperative powers. In 1928 they were again too numerous and migratory for the comfort of the

Department which found its daily mail cluttered once more with a rising tide of complaints. A third open season was proclaimed that year and the results were sufficiently gratifying to establish the periodic capture of beaver as a permanent Department policy.

By their habits and unique individuality beavers have deservedly won the official recognition and protection of the State as desirable citizens. They share with deer on equal terms the center of the Adirondack stage as fascinating exhibits of the region's wild life. Many thousands of visitors are annually attracted to the scene of their labors. A view of the fat little fellows instinctively working out their destiny in their peculiar, industrious manner, an intimate scrutiny of their social behavior, or even a simple inspection of their dams and lodges offer bounteous recompense for the negligible effort expended by sightseers. With the scope of their colonizing activities properly restricted, they can never be excluded from an adequate enumeration of Adirondack charms.

Aside from furnishing attractive subjects for the zoologist and amateur observer of animal life, beavers serve a number of more palpably useful purposes. Oddly enough, while their destructive tendencies have aroused a host of Adirondackers to a state of righteous indignation, they are really untiring contributors to the cause of conservation. Flowed lands, resulting from their instinctive urge to build, provide excellent rearing ponds for trout which seldom fail to reward inquisitive anglers with goodly catches. Beaver dams also create natural reservoirs whose impounded waters, often conveniently located, are invaluable aids in extinguishing forest fires.

After fifteen years of constructive activities, the Brown's Tract Guides' Association discontinued its organized existence. The urgent need for an alliance of its peculiar type had diminished with the passing years due to the public acceptance of a clearly defined policy of conservation in relation to the Adirondacks. But during its brief lifetime it realized its fine ambitions to the full. It achieved the admirable purpose which brought it into being, served the locality and the State unselfishly and effectively, and bequeathed to posterity a more wholesome appreciation for the Adirondacks, as well as for their problems and possibilities.

The Association's appearance upon the scene of the forest was fortunate and timely beyond question. It made its influence felt through the crucial formative years during which the public attitude toward the forest became crystalized into enduring policies. The voice of authority gave vigor to its pronouncements, and added emphasis came in its own scrupulous practice of its published doctrines. Its members were acknowledged experts in their craft, and no vague or delusive recommendations found a place in their program of forest protection. Sentiment, of course, played a part in holding them to their charted course of service. The sinewy, weather-bronzed members of the Association harbored a deep, unspoken affection for the wilderness. They loved it as dearly as a justly proud householder esteems his small estate of lawn and shrubs and garden, and, like the householder, they considered it their right and duty to protect the sanctity of their wilderness home.

Harry V. Radford's interest in the Adirondacks continued until his death which occurred tragically and permaturely in the Canadian woods. In 1910, accompanied by Thomas Street, a congenial young adventurer, Harry set out upon an expedition through the Canadian wilderness to the Hudson Bay country. After a year spent exploring the region and compiling data pertinent to the journey, the two men started for home, guided by a small group of Eskimos who had joined them early in the expedition. The party had proceeded but a short distance on the homeward march when a trivial misunderstanding arose between Harry and one of the guides. Neither of the two was well versed in the language of the other, and consequently both failed in their hasty attempts at intelligible communication. Verbal expressions gave way to manual gesticulations, and the Eskimo, needlessly fearing for his personal safety, attacked and killed Harry with his spear. Thomas, valiantly hurrying to his comrade's aid, was mortally wounded by a spear in the hands of a second Eskimo who had become panicky at the prospect of the white man's wrath. News of the double tragedy reached civilization a year or more after its occurrence and caused general regret. The fateful expedition had been given wide publicity by the press and numerous periodicals and had aroused a good deal of interest among thousands of readers who had followed Harry's colorful career from his boyhood days at Manhattan College. His tragic death was a distinct loss to the Adirondacks. Perhaps more than any man of his time he directed the attention of the nation to the glories of New York's vast forest area. His enthusiasms were wholesome and contagious, his interests sincere, and his knowledge sufficiently profound to command the respect of well informed nature lovers. The brief span of his activities has long since blossomed and borne rich fruit—a more dearly beloved and zealously guarded land of lakes and forest.

XIV

OLD FORGE

OLD FORGE, the miniature metropolis of the Central Adirondack area, is an unpretentious little mountain village that makes
no claim to municipal grandeur or commercial importance.
Its charm, like that of its picturesque sister village, Inlet, and
other neighboring settlements, lies in its environment and in
the unostentatious friendliness of its people. The environment
is an entirely natural one, a handsome concession of Nature
for which the villagers are duly grateful and sometimes par-
donably boastful, and on which they necessarily depend for
their modest livelihoods. The fortunes of the village are inex-
tricably rooted in the forest which surrounds it. Neither farms
nor dairy lands relieve the dense growth of woods beyond its
borders, and no industrial enterprises thrive within. Framed
in the natural barriers of the Moose River, Old Forge Lake
and a long sweep of tree covered ridge flanking on the south
and east, it forms an irregular pattern about one and one-
quarter miles long and one-third of a mile wide. According
to a recent census, eight hundred permanent residents dwell
in this area.

As a trading center, the village is no more than forty years
old, and many of its population are comparative newcomers
to the Adirondacks. Their social and family traditions, and
in some cases their material interests, lie mainly beyond the
borders of the mountains. Very few local adults can claim
the distinction of being native born mountaineers.

Typical of adolescent settlements, particularly those of a
semi-frontier character, Old Forge is a community of good
fellowship and generous charities. It still clings to a fine old
heritage which descends from its woodsmen founders—that of
a quick, unselfish cooperation in every wholesome local enterprise, and a considerate interest in the well-being of its
individual members. Despite the conflicting multiplicity of

interests which claim the attention of the modern, this heritage continues to survive to a unique degree. Totally lacking in community traditions directly connecting its people with the region's past, the village also lacks crystalized strata of local society with the inevitable by-products of upper and lower "crusts" and uncertain "in betweens." The result is a free and easy social commingling that adds charm and reality to the adventure of living. The laundress enjoys an afternoon of bridge with the merchant's wife while the merchant and his friend, the woodcutter, exchange woeful confidences anent the village tax rate as they companionably probe the mysteries of a favorite trout stream. If an aristocracy exists to a recogniz-able degree it is a purely natural one, not consciously main-tained, yet popularly acknowledged. It is composed of the few surviving old guides who inhabited the region before the coming of the railroad.

Like the inflammable phenix, Old Forge has had its uncertain ups and downs. Three times it has risen from the floor of the forest, striving eagerly toward municipal being, but unfriendly forces have twice toppled it, decayed and unpeopled, back to the soil which gave it birth. By deviating slightly from de-scriptive accuracy, it may be said to have been, in turn, a mill, a factory and a resort community. The first two identities were conspicuously ill-conceived and ephemeral, but as a resort center the village has achieved a substantial measure of fame and prestige dispensing its marvelous product—the mountains.

Its history dates to 1799 when John Brown, after acquiring title to the 210,000 acre Brown's Tract, built a dam, mills and cabins at the foot of the Fulton Chain. These were designed to form the nucleus of a flourishing agricultural colony. John possessed the winning qualities of business acumen and dip-lomacy, but he failed to conciliate the hostile mountains and mold them to his purpose. His enterprise failed, and after his death in 1803 desuetude and decay replaced the feeble life spark which he had endeavored to fan into flames. A few years later, his son-in-law, Charles Frederick Herreshoff, attempted to rehabilitate the deserted settlement with a mining and forging venture. Aside from the historical interest attached to his brief regime, nothing of his labor survives except the name of Old Forge, the abandoned mine at Thendara and a few remnants of the mill and forge equipment which are now preserved as relics on the State Hatchery grounds. For a half century following his death, the knowledge of his and his father-in-law's failures acted as a deterrent to local business, and gentlemen of promotive tendencies prudently refrained from exploiting the Brown's Tract. They ignored its vast undulating sweep of wooded valleys and ridges and its endless waterways—to the deep satisfaction of sportsmen and nature lovers who were the only accurate appraisers of the region's worth.

The State dam at Old Forge is the only tangible survival of the earliest attempts by John Brown to colonize the wilderness. During the past one hundred and thirty years ownership of the dam has changed hands several times. It has been built and re-built in adaptation to changing needs, and, although it no longer functions as a direct agency of motive power, it continues to occupy, approximately, the original site selected for the first dam in 1798 or 1799. Since 1900 it has been maintained by the State solely as a reservoir dam to impound the waters of the lower four lakes of the Fulton Chain. Its history in this role dates to 1872 when it became the object of legislative attention which eventaully led to its present use and to the exclusion of local industrial operations depending on its falling water. Several transportation projects undertaken beyond the borders of the mountains have influenced legislative enactments affecting the status of the dam, and a brief summary of these are given here.

In 1834 and 1835 the Legislature authorized the survey and construction of the Black River Canal as a navigable route between Lyons Falls, Lewis County, and Rome, Oneida County. This canal was also designed to serve as a feeder for the Erie Canal into which its water and traffic emptied at

Rome. Concurrent legislation provided for the construction of a Black River Canal feeder which would tap the headwaters of the Black River near Forestport and empty into the canal at Boonville. A third legislative project known as "The Black River Improvement" provided for the dredging and maintenance of the Black River for navigation purposes between Lyons Falls and Carthage. Following the completion of this improvement, several steamers plied the river towing fleets of canal boats upstream to Lyons Falls where they were locked into the canal and enabled to proceed southward to Rome and thence to New York City. The Black River Canal from Boonville to Rome was completed in 1850, and the continuing section from Boonville to Lyons Falls in 1855. The feeder, diverting the water of the Black River at Forestport into the canal at Boonville, was completed in 1849, but it failed to provide adequately for uninterrupted canal navigation, and the State sought other sources of water supply which could be conveniently utilized.

In the meantime, the wheels of industry had been turning for half a century along the banks of the Black River between Lyons Falls and the mouth of the river near Sacketts Harbor on Lake Ontario. The diversion of water at Forestport for canal purposes seriously handicapped numerous mill owners whose prosperity depended upon an equable flow of the river, and their caustic protests accelerated the State's quest of a method for overcoming the deficiency. In 1851, the Legislature authorized the construction of reservoirs of sufficient capacity to insure a uniform flow in the Erie and Black River Canals and at the same time to meet the needs of industrial operations along the river. Between the years 1857 and 1894 ten reservoir dams were completed upon the headwaters of the Black River. Three of these, Bisby, White and Chubb Lake Reservoirs which were built in 1881 and 1882, have since been abandoned. The seven other lakes, in the order in which their waters were impounded for industrial and navigation purposes, include North, Woodhull, South, Sand, Canachagala, Twin and Forestport Lakes. The abatement of the headwaters of the Black River during seasons of light rainfall rendered the earliest constructed of these reservoirs incapable of supplying both the Canal and the Black River Improvement area, and the latter suffered accordingly. Whereupon, in casting about for other lakes adaptive to storage purposes, the legislative eye settled upon the abundant waters of the Fulton Chain. In 1872, the Legislature voted a provisional appropriation of $18,000 for the construction of a dam at the "old Brown's Tract forge," the impounded waters to be held at the disposal of the Black River industrial plants—"if, in the opinion of the Canal Board, the State is under equitable obligations to construct said dam." In reporting its opinion, the Board absolved the State from legal liability but recommended the building of the proposed dam as an equitable obligation. The following year, the State Engineer and Surveyor concurred with the finding of the Board. The $18,000 was reduced to $10,000 by an Act of 1879 authorizing the State Superintendent of Public Works to construct dams at the old forge and at the outlet of Sixth Lake. The Act also carried an appropriation for the purchase of necessary lands for the State adjacent to the proposed dams.

The first State dam at the forge site was built in 1879. It was a crib structure formed of two log walls paralleled across the stream and filled with sand and stone. This was replaced with concrete in 1901 and 1905, and in 1927 the wooden gates were dismantled in favor of cast iron sluice gates. Six years after the building of the log dam the State acquired by purchase about ten acres of adjoining land from Alexander B. Lamberton of Rochester. It lies on both sides of the highway and includes the Hatchery grounds, park and a portion of the bathing beach. The storage area created by the dam extends to the head of Fourth Lake and is known as the *Old Forge Reservoir*. It includes a water surface of about five square miles and an approximate capacity of 700,000,000 cubic feet. The Sixth Lake Reservoir, which includes Sixth and Seventh

Lakes, was created by the building of a log dam in 1880. This dam was raised one foot in 1900, and twenty years later was replaced with a concrete structure of the same elevation.

The outlet of these reservoirs is through the Middle Branch of the Moose River at Old Forge. The Middle Branch is joined by the North Branch at the southerly border of the village, and is confluent with the South Branch ten miles below. At Lyons Falls it descends a rocky precipice into the Black River and there joins forces with its larger sister stream to power the industrial plants along its northerly way to Lake Ontario.

In its three branches the Moose River has long been a favorite haunt of experienced woodsmen and lovers of tree-bowered seclusion. It is a river of wondrous beauty, flowing its pleasant way between walls of green forest that branch protectingly over its quiet surface. So intimate and natural is its blending with the surrounding woods that it seems a harmonious part of the great forest rather than a divider of it, and its unaffected charm utterly belies the industrial mission that awaits its confluence with the Black River.

Both the Old Forge and Sixth Lake Reservoirs are under the direct supervision of the Board of the Black River Regulating District. This Board was authorized by the State in 1920 to assume the regulatory functions pertaining to the Black River which were formerly performed by the Conservation Commission. The Board and Commission, each in turn, have been considerate of the recreational character of the Fulton Chain region. Although the authority delegated to them by the State is an arbitrary one, and the mid-summer needs of the Black River power owners are often pressing, they have exercised their discretionary powers to the best possible advantage and have persistently refrained from withdrawing the impounded waters during the summer vacation months.

The building of the Forge House and its neighboring cottage at the foot of the Fulton Chain in 1871 may be said to have definitely marked the site of the future village of Old Forge.

Eighteen years passed, however, before other building operations enlarged the little settlement with additional dwellings.
Meanwhile, a series of economic vicissitudes had beset the
owners of the 1358-acre Forge Tract which resulted in a succession of shifting equities and several fruitless efforts toward
development.   The first to meet with appreciable success in
promoting the growth of the settlement were Dr. Alexander
H. Crosby and Samuel F. Garmon who purchased the tract
and hotel from Eunice B. Lamberton of Rochester in 1888.
Both men were residents of Lowville, Lewis County, and both
had become familiar with the region during the early eighties.
As the firm of *Garmon and Crosby,* they undertook the development of a year round community.   They relied for their
success chiefly upon the established patronage accorded the
Forge House and neighboring lake resorts, and upon the increasing volume of "through traffic" passing up and down the
Fulton Chain.   Progress was slow, of course, but their enterprise was rewarded with a greater measure of success than
any predecessor had enjoyed.   From an embryo village in 1888,
consisting of one hotel, a cottage, saw mill and hatchery, Old
Forge began to spread slowly over the landscape and assume
an appearance of permanency.

Garmon and Crosby sold several building lots during their
first year of ownership.   These were priced at less than one
dollar a front foot bordering the Brown's Tract Road, and
easy time payments were made available to buyers as an incentive to home building.   The buyers were principally guides
and others who found seasonal employment in the woods.

In 1888 and 1889, Josiah Wood erected a dwelling house
on a plot of land a short distance south of the dam which is
now occupied by the David Codling residence.   Josiah, known
locally as "Si," was the son of Alonzo Wood and was employed at the time by Emmett Marks in the hatchery.   About
the same time, Theodore Seeber, a boat builder and skilful all
round mechanic, erected a dwelling nearby which is now the
Charles Wilcox residence.   Concurrently with the building

of these two houses, Sylvester Whetmore erected a third dwelling on a plot adjoining Si Wood's home. Sylvester had come to the Brown's Tract in 1889 to supervise the re-building of the Forge House which Garmon and Crosby considered inadequate to supply the growing demand for hotel accommo- dations. Due to their business initiative and unbounded con- fidence in the future of the region, a more commodious and attractive hotel structure supplanted the old hostelry erected by Buell and Desbrough in 1871. The improvement found immediate favor with vacationing travellers and contributed noticeably to the early growth of the community.

In 1889, Fred Rivett and John Sprague built homes on the west side of the Brown's Tract Road (Main Street) a short distance south of what is now the busy corner. Fred was a well known woodsman of the Central Adirondacks, while John, with Jack Sheppard and Will Sperry, was engaged in the steamboat business.

With five new houses built within a period of two years, congested living conditions must have threatened the locality; so building operations moved across the river. Ira Parsons built the first dwelling north of the dam in 1890. It stands on a knoll overlooking Old Forge Lake and is still occupied by its builder. Two years later, Ira's father, Riley Parsons, built the second house on that side of the lake on a lot adjoin- ing Ira's It has since been enlarged and is now conducted as a resort hotel.

After the completion of the Forge House improvements in 1890, George Deis leased the saw mill beside the dam for the production of finished lumber to be used in local dwelling and hotel construction. George was a native of Germany who had emigrated to America as a boy and settled in the Fulton Chain region in 1884. A skilled mechanic and builder, he became identified with a number of construction projects in the woods, including the building of the first water power mill at the foot of Sixth Lake in 1890 for Fred Hess.

In 1888, George was joined in the mill business by his sixteen year old son, Charles. From 1891 to 1900, father and son conducted the Old Forge milling enterprise as *George Deis and Son.* The bulk of their logs was procured from a tract adjoining the southerly shore of the lower lake chain. These were sledded upon the ice during the winter months and boomed down stream to Old Forge Lake during spring thaws. A large sales and storage yard gradually spread out along the shore adjacent to the mill as building operations increased throughout the locality. In 1900 the mill and yard were re-located at Fulton Chain (Thendara), and three years later the company incorporated as *George Deis, Son and Company,* under which name it continues to operate at this writing.

In 1891, Dave Charbonneau busied himself with hammer and nails building a house near the Sylvester Whetmore cabin a few hundred feet up the dirt road from the dam. In the same year the suffrage franchise became a local political exer-cise. Prior to 1891, qualified voters inhabiting the northern portion of the Town of Webb were compelled to undergo a tedious journey to the village of Wilmurt to express their political preferences at the polls. But in 1891 the northern portion of the Town was designated as an election district and a polling place was set up at the Fourth Lake House on the lower South Shore. The Election Board included Joseph Harvey, Jack Sheppard, Ben Parsons and Dave Charbonneau. The sparse population hailed the forthcoming election as an achievement in the cause of local political expression, and all native voters attended. In fact, most of them remained until after the polls closed to assist the Board in tabulating the bal-lots and to ascertain the results. The count was sensationally close. Eighteen votes were cast—eight Republican, eight Democratic and two Prohibitionist. After a brief but appro-priate celebration by all voters present, Dave Charbonneau set out on foot that night for Moose River Settlement whence he could proceed by horse to Boonville and then by rail to Herkimer to deliver the sealed ballot pouch to the elec-tion commissioners. The night was dark and the way rough, and Dave's mission was not a pleasant one. But the hardships of travel were petty compared to the strange, inscrutable problem which harrassed him on his lonely thirteen mile journey. Ponder as he would, he could bring the mystery to no logical conclusion. When he reached Moose River Settlement in the early morning darkness he confessed himself utterly baffled in his attempts to solve the identities of the Adirondack woodsmen who had cast two votes for prohibition!

The completion of the railroad in 1892 stimulated the growth of Old Forge during that year to the extent of two dwelling houses and a general store. The latter—the first of its kind to be established—was housed in a combined store and dwelling house structure erected for the purpose on the east side of the Brown's Tract Road about one hundred feet south of the busy corner. The builders and merchants were Edmund F. Abbott and Gideon Kilmer, both of Forestport, who conducted the business under the firm name of *Abbott and Kilmer*. Edmund Abbott brought his wife, Lucy, and their two small children, Harold and Luella, to live in Old Forge, and Gideon brought his wife, Elizebeth. The addition of six congenial newcomers swelled the population perceptibly and enlivened the social life of the tiny community. Although the store was a comparatively small and modestly stocked establishment, the natives welcomed it as an emporium of good things which could be procured conveniently and quickly.

During the same year, Peter Rivett, one of the best of the region's guides, erected a dwelling a few rods south of the store on the opposite side of the road.

A few months after Abbott and Kilmer began business, a second general store opened its doors to cater to the needs of the community. Its proprietor, Joseph Harvey, a brother-in-law of Sam Garmon, had moved from Watson, Lewis County, in 1888, to become proprietor of the Forge House. He brought with him his wife, Ellen, and five small daughters. One of his daughters, Nettie, later taught the first district school to be established in the locality. Joseph Harvey was a man of fine character who possessed more than average educational advantages, and he soon became prominent in social, business and political affairs. Failing health forced his retirement from the hotel business at the end of the 1891 season, and the firm of Alger and Kitts succeeded him in the proprietorship of the Forge House. The Harveys then purchased the newly built Charbonneau dwelling near the dam and the Sylvester Whetmore house which stood nearby. The latter building they converted into a retail store which they conducted until 1898 when Joseph Harvey's death ended his influential career of ten years as a local resident.

In 1893, Dave Charbonneau erected a second dwelling house beside the Brown's Tract Road which he located diag- onally across the road from the Abbott and Kilmer store. At this writing the Charbonneau family continues to occupy it. At the same time, Joseph Perkins, a well known guide, built a house on the opposite side of the road. In 1894, the Parsons family lost their four-year monopoly of their side of the river when John C. Woodruff built a dwelling near the Riley Parsons home. John, a native of Watertown, had come to Old Forge that year to fill the position of State gate keeper of the Old Forge and Sixth Lake Reservoirs. His wife, Ada, and their four children came with him. One of his sons, Fred, then a youth of eighteen, became a prominent local merchant in after years.

With several families of children in the locality, the need for a regularly conducted district school made itself felt —among all except the children. The younger set, especially the male members, took a lukewarm attitude toward this form of progress and steadfastly refrained from encouraging the promotion of a local seat of learning. In 1893, Wesley Earnshaw, the son of a Lewis County clergyman, volun- teered to instruct the community youngsters in the three R's. For several months he conducted a school without pay in a small building which Emmett Marks had erected on the hatch- ery grounds for storage purposes. The classes were irregularly attended although the teacher was very popular among his students. The boys, in particular, suffered prolonged periods of aberration while en route to school and frequently ended up at a picturesque trout stream or swimming hole—to the appreciable detriment to their scholarship.

In 1894, the community considered the problem of education seriously and officially. It elected its first school trustee, Dave Charbonneau, authorized to provide a permanent school building, hire a teacher, and keep a sharp lookout for forgetful members of the student body who were oversensitive to the Waltonian influence. Dave hired Jeannette (Nettie) Harvey to teach the school. During the earlier terms the classes were held in the same building that Wesley Earnshaw had utilized the previous year. At the same time, the district began the erection of a larger frame building better adapted to the purpose on the site of the present school structure in Old Forge. This site proved admirably conducive to the cultivation of such academic virtues as concentration and application. An eighth of a mile of dense forest intervened between the schoolhouse and its nearest neighboring structure along the road leading to the dam.

Schoolmistress Jeannette faced an arduous task during her 1894 term. Several of the pupils had never attended a school before and they plotted with their more experienced classmates to devise an infinity of subtle or forthright methods of escaping the irksome routine of school life. But their teacher mingled winning patience with persistence; so did Director Dave, and eventually the pupils, being good children, settled down to the quiet tenor of schoolroom existence which marks the dutiful assimilation of knowledge. The little institution grew rapidly, and in 1895 the register of attendance disclosed the following names: Anna, Leila and William Christy, Edna and Josie Fraula, Cora and Edwin Galle, Bertha, Pearl and Frank Wakely, Ella and Jay Shafer, Anna Harvey, Jennie Rivett, Matilda, Stella, Mary and Charlie Sprague, Ethel Codling, Laura Charbonneau, Ben Sperry, Carrie and Mary

Murer, Florence Zimmer, Louis Tennis, Grace Perkins, Harold and George Sperry, Rose Hames, Eddie Shafer, Herman and Charlie Brockway, Earl Glenn, Luella Abbott and Jimmie Kennedy.

The growth of Old Forge dragged slowly until the year 1895 when Garmon and Crosby revised their methods of handling their development project. They included several new members in their company, and incorporated under the name of *The Old Forge Company*. Stimulated by new business blood, the company's affairs progressed at a considerably brisker pace in the attempt to colonize the Forge Tract. The Forge House was again remodeled and enlarged. In 1896 it emerged from a network of scaffolding—a more pretentious and commodious hostelry and a still greater asset to the growing resort community. Several streets were cut through the woods within the proposed limits of the village, and all were designated by appellations chosen principally from the family names of the members of the Old Forge Company. These included Adams Street, Crosby Boulevard, Garmon Street, Gilbert Street and Sheard Street. The name "Park Avenue" was applied to the street bordering Old Forge on the southeast. Not all of these streets were inhabited, nor even threatened with human occupancy at the time of their christening, but the names gave them a certain prestige despite their rutty surfaces and numerous mud holes, and added to their attractiveness as residence addresses. The old Brown's Tract Road, risen to a new distinction as the main thorofare of a bustling hamlet, was renamed *Harrison Avenue* as a mark of respect for ex-president Benjamin Harrison who at that time was the most prominent yearly visitor to the locality. His name furnished a distinguished addition to the nomenclature of village streets, but somehow, in retrospect, it seems ungrateful treatment to have thus shorn the aged road of its identity after its nearly a century of faithful service.

Described by Henry L. Stoddard as "able, wise and cool" and by Chauncey M. Depew as "the profoundest lawyer ever at the head of our government," Benjamin Harrison made no effort to live up to these impressive characterizations during his several summers as a Fulton Chain resident. After enjoying the beauties of the Adirondacks at irregular intervals, he decided to make summer vacationing in the region an annual affair. In 1896 he built a handsome camp on the lower South Shore of Second Lake of the Fulton Chain which he occupied seasonally with his wife, Mary Lord Harrison, until his death in 1901.

Like other summer visitors in search of relaxation, the Harrisons lived unostentatiously while in the mountains. They boated, fished and hunted, and enjoyed camp fire picnics where steak and pancakes vied for favor as the piece de resistance of a woodsy repast. The ex-president was a crack shot, especially with his favorite firearm, a double barrelled shotgun. Many tales of his prowess with this weapon were related by his admiring guides, most of whom were, themselves, expert marksmen. Although his aloofness and lack of a winning personality in public were nationally discussed, he conducted himself while in the Adirondacks in the manner of a friendly, well disposed neighbor. His sincerely cheerful greetings to acquaintances along the lake shores and his companionable visits with them gave convincing proof of the innate friendliness of his nature. The corps of press representatives that besieged his camp in daily quest of significant political news were received hospitably by a dignified host who submitted affably to their questioning before he dismissed them with polite effectiveness.

In 1896, Harrison accepted an invitation to speak at a Fourth of July celebration and flag raising at the newly remodeled Forge House. The participation of so distinguished a guest as an ex-president of the United States inspired the program committee to their utmost. They imported a small brass cannon from Little Falls and mounted it on an improvised rampart beside the hotel in readiness to fire a presidential salute. Gay draperies of flags and bunting adorned the hotel and the speaker's stand at the east veranda. An expectant crowd of natives and visitors gathered on the lawn. The political atmosphere of the country was surcharged with uncertainty that year—not to be clarified until the conclusion of the memorable McKinley-Bryan campaigns in November—and the audience could reasonably anticipate a significant discussion of major political issues by the speaker of the day. Promptly at the appointed time, Harrison disembarked from his naphtha-propelled motor boat at the Forge House dock, and accompanied by such notables as the committee had mustered for the occasion, climbed the path leading to the hotel. The brass cannon boomed its smoky tribute, a field of human necks craned sharply toward the oncoming party, and a mighty hush enveloped the crowd. Then a bizarre, impromptu bit of mimicry suddenly claimed the center of the stage. Out from the hotel barroom, and into the thick silence, staggered George McCabe, lumberjack, teamster and for many years denizen extraordinary of the Adirondack forest. George had been celebrating in advance and had successfully reached that alcoholic goal where proprieties are submerged and lost in a tremendous surge of hilarity. Stiffening himself in imitation of the unmistakable and widely caricatured bearing of the approaching ex-president, he trod a hob-nailed course to the front of the speaker's stand. There he bowed several times in mock dignity, and then executed a series of rigid-armed gestures as though to punctuate an imaginary address of profound governmental import. His performance continued only a moment or so when harsh hands were laid upon his person and he was dragged from the scene of his triumph. But Harrison had witnessed the pantomime long enough to recognize himself as the subject of the ludicrous impersonation. To the relief of the embarrassed spectators, he not only laughed heartily but actually applauded the performer. Although his ensuing address did not touch on controvertible policies, it was a rousing success nevertheless.

After Harrison's death the Second Lake camp passed to the possession of Mrs. Harrison. The ex-president's will, made shortly before his death, referred to the place in affectionate terms and recalled the happy summers which he had spent there with his wife. Some time later, Mrs. Harrison disposed of the camp to Frank Green of New York, who, in turn, sold it to its present owner, Horace de Camp, the son of the late William Scott and Julia Lyon de Camp. Many of Harrison's personal effects and vacation duffel are still in the main camp building. Not the least interesting of these is a long barrelled fowling piece which was used by Benjamin's illustrious grand-father, William Henry Harrison, the ninth president of the United States.

Although religious services had been held each summer in the Fulton Chain locality since the coming of Dr. Niccolls in the sixties, no formal church body was organized in Old Forge until 1897. During the year 1895, religious services had been conducted at irregular intervals, often "without benefit of clergy," in the district school house. The annually increasing flow of visitors to Old Forge and the steady growth of the community emphasized the need for a permanently established local church organization. At the request of the Utica Presbytery, Reverend R. Howard Wallace of the Presbytery of Bismark, N. D., came to Old Forge in 1896 to conduct services throughout that year. Rev. Wallace, a refined elderly man whose devotion to mission work had prompted him to leave his long established New York pastorate for the mission fields of the West, was born in the Hudson Valley, the son of a Presbyterian minister. His father held the pastorate of a small church on the shore of the lower Hudson for fifty years, and the son, R. Howard, succeeding him, served the same church for the next twenty-five years. Father and son successively held the pastorate for three quarters of a century —a long and eloquent testimonial to the family popularity.

On June 28, 1897, a group of Old Forge and Fulton Chain (Thendara) residents met in the school building and organized the *Old Forge Presbyterian Church*. Rev. I. N. Terry presided at the meeting. Rev. H. H. Allen of the Home

Mission Committee of the Utica Presbytery and Rev. Wallace were present in an advisory capacity. Members received into the Church during that meeting included the following local residents: Dana Fraula, Frank Peck, Harry Brown, Mrs. Hattie Sperry, Mrs. Laura Thompson, Miss Clara Brown, Mrs. Esther Seeber, Mrs. Hattie Fraula, Louis Sperry, Mrs. Mary Newton, Mrs. Susie T. Codling, Mrs. Ella Brown, Mrs. Kittie Marks, Miss Jennie Parsons and Miss Edna Fraula.

At the same meeting, plans were made for the erection of a church building, and the work of construction was begun less than a month after. The Forge Company donated land for the purpose on Crosby Boulevard, a few rods west of the busy corner. On November 30 of the same year, the building and contents were dedicated, Rev. A. V. Wallace, the pastor's son, delivering the dedicatory sermon. The following year a manse was erected on a lot adjoining the church.

Mr. Wallace remained as pastor of the Church until 1904 when the infirmities of age forced his retirement from the ministry. He had been an indefatigable worker in behalf of the infant parish during his eight years' residence in Old Forge and his departure caused deep regret. The original church structure remained in use until the present building was erected in 1918 during the pastorate of Benjamin B. Knapp (1909-1919). The name was changed at that time to Niccolls Memorial Church in memory of Dr. Niccolls.

St. Bartholomew's Catholic Parish had its beginning in 1895 with the arrival of Father Hugh N. Byrne. Like his Protestant contemporary, Rev. R. Howard Wallace, Father Byrne's attachment to mission work had led him far afield from his first parish charge which was in Ireland. His Adirondack pastorate embraced an extensive area in the southern and central portion of the mountains with headquarters in Wells, Hamilton County. His visits to Old Forge were necessarily infrequent due to the prevailing lack of travel facilities, but in 1895 he celebrated the first mass in the village at the home of Joseph Harvey. From then until the summer of 1896 he continued to visit Old Forge at intervals of several weeks. Word of his coming was usually announced a week or two in advance in order to inform his parishioners of the date and place of worship. In July, 1896, he began a program of weekly services in the school house.

Cognizant of the growing religious needs of the community, several parishioners met with Father Byrne in the autumn of that year to establish St. Batholomew's Parish. The first board of trustees named to handle the business of the Parish included Bishop Henry Gabriels of the Ogdensburg Diocese, Very Reverend Thomas E. Walsh, Vicar General, Father Byrne, Joseph Harvey and Alexander McIntyre. (Alexander McIntyre also served as the first Supervisor elected from the Town of Webb. He succeeded Joseph Harvey who held the office by appointment until the first Town election was held.)

A bazaar and fair, held at the Forge House in August, 1896, netted the newly formed parish a substantial amount to be used in acquiring suitable church property. This sum was applied to the purchase price of two lots and a dwelling house at the corner of Park Avenue (then Railroad Street) and Crosby Boulevard. The dwelling served as a rectory and, for the time being, as a chapel.

In December, 1896, Father John G. Fitzgerald succeeded Father Byrne as the local pastor, after which the latter returned to his birthplace in Ireland. The following year the Old Forge parish was incorporated, Bishop Gabriels, Father Walsh, Father Fitzgerald, Alexander McIntyre and David Charbonneau acting as incorporators.

Like his predecessor, Father Fitzgerald was a native of Ireland. He was born there in 1853, studied at Black Meath, England, and later at Troy Seminary, Troy, N. Y., where he was ordained for the Ogdensburg Diocese in 1874. After twenty years in the Diocese he filled pastorates in Minnesota and Arkansas until called to Old Forge in 1896. In mannerism and appearance he was one of the most eccentric and colorful Adirondack clergymen of his time. Physically and

intellectually robust, possessed of a resonant speaking and sing-
ing voice and a commanding stature, he plunged into the manifold activities of the parish and community with all the gusto
of a youthful novitiate despite the fact that his years had
already passed the half century mark. He loved the woods
with a poet's fervor and proclaimed their scenic charms with
poetic emphasis upon every plausible occasion.

In 1898, St. Bartholomew's Parish completed the building
of a church structure on one of the lots purchased from the
Old Forge Company in 1896. This building was formally
dedicated on August 27, 1899, with Bishop Gabriels officiating.

Father Fitzgerald filled the local pastorate until 1925. He
died in March of that year and was buried in the Old Forge
Cemetery in compliance with his frequently expressed wish.
Father James E. Joy took charge of the parish later in the year.
During his pastoral charge several improvements have been
effected in the original church structure and a new parish house
has been erected.

The arrival of a resident physician, Dr. Stuart W. Nelson,
in Old Forge in 1897 caused a good deal of satisfaction among
the villagers. The procuring of medical aid had been a laborious undertaking for the isolated settlement, and an especially
vexatious one in times of urgent need. Physicians were usually
summoned from Boonville, Forestport or Remsen. Dr. Nelson,
a native of Boonville, graduate of New York University and
staff physician of King's County Hospital, Brooklyn, came to
Old Forge in search of health rather than in search of a location for the practice of his profession. The salubrious Adirondack climate cooperated to speed his recovery, but instead of
returning to Brooklyn to resume his hospital post he remained
in Old Forge to cooperate with climate in effecting the recovery
of others. He carried on his early practice in the mountains
under a variety of conditions that offered distinct contrasts
to professional life in the metropolis which he had quitted.
These were especially marked in the modes of travel which

he utilized to make distant calls. They included guide boats, snowshoes, saddle horses, sleighs, freight trains, railroad hand' cars and plain pedestrianism.

In 1904, a second physician, Dr. Robert S. Lindsay, a grad' uate of Albany Medical College, began the practice of medicine in Old Forge. Reasons of family health led Dr. Lindsay to abandon an established practice at Brockport, N. Y., and begin anew in the Adirondacks. Both physicians became influential figures in the early development of the village. Dr. Lindsay's son, Robert N., a graduate of Syracuse University, began the practice of medicine locally in 1922. His arrival brought the total of practitioners to three and raised the community to the dignified status of a miniature medical center.

In 1903, Old Forge was incorporated as a village, and its less than three hundred permanent residents faced their civic future with ambition and confidence. The first village board met in October, 1903, with the following officers present: President, George Goodsell; Trustees, Ben Parsons, Sam Smith, Dr. Nelson and Justin Reed; Secretary, Walter D. Marks.

The need of the community for an adequate water system was chiefly responsible for the incorporating of the village, and the newly created Board immediately turned its attention to the problem of locating a source of supply. Strange to relate, although springs and ponds in open view abounded on all sides, the Board discovered the most satisfactory water source in no less remarkable a hiding place than the mystic arms of Morpheus. During a meeting of the Board in the autumn of 1903, the deliberations of the village fathers were interrupted by the arrival of a local resident who carried a report to the effect that on the previous night Ned Ball had dreamed of the existence of a conveniently located spring whose cool waters gushed forth from a mountainside in sparkling abundance. Although professing a good deal of official skepticism concerning the truth of the report, the trustees pondered its Morphean intelligence with due gravity, and then set out in a body to investigate. A search of the locality re' vealed the spring. True to predictions, it gushed from a wooded mountainside in a situation easily adapted to reservoir purposes. The find brought Ned into the limelight as a master of divination and he was hailed by his townsmen as the community's most successful dreamer of practical dreams. In fact, several of his tax-paying friends importuned him to go to sleep again and dream a painless method of defraying the cost of installing the water system, but Ned prudently refused to engage in mercenary drowsings. He was less familiar with the financial structure of the village than with the geography of the woods, and he preferred to do his dreaming in the realm of the latter. The spring was dammed and the water piped to Old Forge. Ned never confirmed or denied the truth of the report of his alleged inspiration. But if it really had birth in Slumberland it was, at least, no "pipe dream," as the slangily facetious might infer, for the cool water of Ned's Moulin spring supplied Old Forge villagers for many years.

In 1904, Northwoods Lodge 849, F. & A. M., was organized under a dispensation with twenty-two charter members, Dr. Stuart W. Nelson serving as the first Master. The following year the lodge erected a spacious temple on Crosby Boulevard which is still in use although the present membership exceeds two hundred. Old Forge Chapter, O. E. S., was organized in 1909 with eight charter members. Mrs. Robert S. Lindsay of Old Forge, a former District Grand Officer of the Order, served as the Chapter's first Matron, and Ben Parsons as its first Patron.

During the years 1910 and 1911, William J. Thistlethwaite of Old Forge and Daniel F. Strobel of Herkimer, acquired the corporate stock and realty holdings of the Old Forge Company. The new owners continued the company's development operations until 1915 when Mr. Thistlethwaite organized the Adirondack Development Corporation. This Company purchased the land holdings of the former company, which consisted chiefly of the unsold portion of the Forge Tract and a number of scattered parcels in the Town of Webb. The

Forge House and Forge Tract parted company in 1915 when C. I. and R. E. Thomson purchased the forty-four year old hostelry and several acres of adjacent land from the Development Corporation. Since his earliest association with Dr. Webb in the nineties, Mr. Thistlethwaite has carried on without interruption the program of improvements which the energetic doctor began more than forty years ago. The realty transfers in which he has personally figured total several thousand at this writing and include such well known developments as the Joy Tract, Gray Lake Park, the Brooklyn Section of Old Forge (north of the State dam), the Eagle Bay Road and Little Moose Road projects, and several tracts within the village of Old Forge.

In 1917, a sturdy, gilt-edged little war baby made its appearance in the form of the First National Bank of Old Forge— the only financial institution ever organized in the Central Adirondacks. It began its useful and highly successful career with a modest capital of $25,000.00 which was increased to $50,000.00 the following year. The officers and directors of the bank for the year 1917 were Maurice Callahan, President, Walter D. Marks, Vice President, Carl O. Pfaff, Cashier, Charles Williams, Patrick J. Foley, Charles M. Barrett and Frederick A. Potter. Soon after its organization, Moses Cohen, Frank E. Tiffany and Dennis Dillon became members of its directorate. The territory served by the bank extends from Forestport to Long Lake.

The incorporators exercised a distinctive choice in selecting for the presidency of the bank one of the very few commercial leaders of the region who were born within the borders of the mountains. Maurice Callahan emerged upon the business clearings of the Adirondacks from the hamlet of *Adirondack* on the easterly shore of Schroon Lake in Warren County. Having exhausted the baseball and educational possibilities of his humble birthplace, he left home as a boy to embark upon a commercial career as bellhop in the Leland House, a neighboring resort hotel. Between hops he applied himself studiously to mastering bookkeeping and telegraphy and for several years found employment in both of these important agencies of commerce. His early experiences admirably fitted him for the business leadership in several branches of commercial enterprise which he was eventually called upon to assume. In 1895 he became associated with William West Durant in a clerical and later in an executive capacity at Raquette and Blue Mountain Lakes. The Durant operations at that time were varied and elaborate almost to the point of the spectacular, and furnish one of the highly interesting chapters in the history of the Raquette Lake region. They included a number of construction, development and transportation projects which brought Mr. Durant to the fore as the most noted Adirondacker of his day. Mr. Callahan was appointed assistant superintendent of the Raquette Lake Transportation Company at the time of its incorporation in 1901, and the next year was appointed to the same office in the management of the Fulton Navigation Company and the Fulton Chain Railway Company. He became superintendent of the three companies in 1903, and in 1923 with several associates he purchased both boat lines. Since 1902 he has resided in Old Forge although his business interests extend throughout the entire Central Adirondacks. He is a member of the Raquette Lake Railway Company's board of directors, and since 1912 has served continuously as a member of the Town of Webb school board.

The year 1917 and America's entry into the World War found Old Forge and the Towns of Webb and Inlet swinging into quick step with the nation in its swift march to victory. Liberty Loan drives went over the top with astounding suddenness; feminine sociability fashioned itself into knitting clubs that wove love and patriotism into warm woolen fabrics; young mountaineers eagerly answered the call to duty, and the entire Central mountain area cooperated with the nation by doing its helpful bit. The local Liberty Loan Committee functioned under the direction of Dr. Robert S. Lindsay.

Hon. E. Burt Pullman served as local Food Administrator, John A. Given as Fuel Administrator, and Howard Weller as chairman of the local draft board unit. The draft board made its headquarters in the Given drug store where the proprietor also did duty as recruiting officer for the country's rejuvenated mercantile marine. Between drafts, drugs and distribution of fuel Mr. Given spent an exceptionally busy wartime.

William Covey Post of the American Legion became a welcome and interesting factor of Old Forge and Central Adirondack community life in 1920. ‚ It was organized by Ernest Hauptli, a convalescing veteran and native of Syracuse, who served as the first Commander. The Post was so named in memory of William Covey of Twitchell Lake who died while in service. The accidental death in December, 1921, of Stephen Bazyliv, a charter member of the Post, brought the Old Forge Cemetery into use as a burial ground for the first time. (The Old Forge Cemetery Association was incorporated in December, 1921, by William J. Thistlethwaite, J. G. Hoffman, Carroll A. Thompson, John J. Ryan, Leon Eldridge and R. E. Thomson, and the plot of land acquired by the association was named the *Riverside Cemetery*).

Stephen Bazyliv, a native of Ukraine, had emigrated to America a short time before the outbreak of the World War and had made his home in Syracuse. Upon America's entry into the war in 1917, he enlisted, was severely wounded at Verdun, and upon returning to America was invalided to Old Forge. While hunting in the woods in October, 1921, he suffered a serious injury from the accidental discharge of a twenty-two caliber rifle, and died in a Utica hospital on the third day of December. His last request, made to his chum and fellow Ukrainian, Stephen Welychko, also a convalescing war veteran, was that he be buried at Old Forge. In compliance with his wish, a plot was hastily prepared in the unpopulated cemetery of the village, and a military funeral arranged by the local Legion Post. On December 6, an improvised caisson drawn by two white horses bore the dead soldier through the snow-covered streets of Old Forge to the waiting grave. Despite a bitterly cold wind that lashed the slow moving cortege, sixty uniformed World War veterans of the Central Adirondacks and most of the local population followed the caisson to Stephen's last resting place on a wooded knoll overlooking the Moose River a short distance below the dam. On his modest headstone these words were inscribed:

How sleep the brave who sink to rest
By all their country's wishes blessed.

In 1920 the ancient, honorable and exasperating game of golf made its appearance as a summer diversion in the Fulton Chain country. Chiefly through the efforts of Lyon de Camp a nine hole course was built beside the highway between Old Forge and Thendara, and the Thendara Golf Club was incorporated. Of sporty architectural design and set in a forest environment of rare scenic charm, the course won immediate favor among visiting golfers and the Club has enjoyed exceptional prosperity since its opening in 1921. (In 1920, the name *Fulton Chain,* designating the New York Central Station and the bustling little hamlet surrounding it which had grown up since the coming of the railroad, gave way to the name Thendara. The change was brought about by Mr. de Camp because of the confusion in transportation matters which often resulted from the similarity of names incorporating the word Fulton. *Thendara* is an Indian term meaning "meeting place." Although the aborigines no longer gather in council in that locality, the name is by no means a misnomer. The town hall of the Town of Webb is located at Thendara, and there the members of the Town Board gather in more or less solemn council each fortnight or oftener to transact the official business of their lake- and forest-covered domain).

It was not a growing spirit of contention that encouraged

a lawyer to cast his professional lot with Old Forge. Reasons of family health induced Carroll A. Thompson to begin the practice of law in Old Forge in 1920, and the advent of this learned profession added one more metropolitan touch to the little community. But no village may be properly termed a metropolis unless it boasts a newspaper, and Old Forge could claim no such distinction until the year 1926. On July 3rd of that year, the *Adirondack Arrow* made its appearance, a brisk, woodsy little weekly, originally with an Inlet date line. Its editorial column informed that it was dedicated to the service of the Adirondacks, and it began its life of service with an interesting presentation of mountain news and an attractive display of advertising. Its front page carried a picture of four young people who, according to the caption beneath, had been recently graduated from the Raquette Lake High School. They were Dennis Dillon Jr., Thomas Collins, M. Martha Dillon and Mary Scanlon. Personable, alert and ambitious, they were, like the little newspaper which featured them, just making their initial bow to a great world of affairs.

Jamie W. Stepp, for several years the managing owner of the Clinton Courier and president of the Stepp Printing Corporation, both of Clinton, N. Y., began the publication of the *Adirondack Arrow*. He conducted it with marked success until December, 1928, when the press of his other business interests induced him to dispose of the paper to a group of Central Adirondack business men. Roy J. Dobell, the present managing editor, became connected with the paper in 1927.

XV

EPILOGUE

HARDLY rippling the quiet surface of the lake, a guide boat drew alongside a plank landing-dock that jutted loosely from its moorings of log breakwater at the foot of the Fulton Chain. The deft handling of oars had swung the boat into an easy circle and then straightened it to glide stern forward toward the land. Beside the dock it slowed almost imperceptibly and came to rest in dainty response to the will of the oarsman. From the bow, the rower considered his work, satisfied with the obedient performance of the shapely craft. He was an elderly man—a woodsman—dressed simply in rough, colorless clothes that like himself had stood the test of time. Seventy years or more had seamed his leathery face and fixed his lips in a straight unsmiling line that cut through a stubble of stiff graying beard. But he sat cooly as a youth, his strong figure erect and composed, as one engaged in his accustomed work.

In the stern, his companion, older by several years, tall, gaunt and weather-browned, sat with like composure. For a moment he watched the light dipping of oars that maneuvered the boat shoreward; then his gaze wandered up the lake to where the water narrowed to a gleam of channel and disappeared in the distant gray haze of evening. A motorboat starting suddenly from its anchorage captured his attention. He followed its swift course as it cut the water thirty rods from shore and after dipping sharply to starboard sped up the lake and entered the channel. From its size and shape he knew its keel rode far below the white hull, and idly he watched the swell that rose in its wake and lazied its way in long rolling waves to shore.

The two men drew the guide boat upon the dock, leaving it overturned for the night, and the older man stepped up on the low wall of logs that buttressed the sandy bank. The younger, unmindful of the oncoming succession of waves, paused to gather the oars and duffel which he lifted in a single burden to his shoulder. The dock moved uneasily, then rose and fell in dire agitation before the assaults of the swell that washed across its surface and submerged the flimsy planking in turbulent lake water. Knee-deep, the burdened woodsman staggered to the wall and climbed, profane and dripping, to the safety of an upper log.

"Damn 'em," he snarled. "The white-livered imbeciles aint got gumption enough to pull at a pair of oars! They have to run an engine to haul their lazy carcasses a mile or two upstream and spoil the lakes for men who know how to use them!"

The unpleasant ooze of water in his low-cut boots stirred his anger the more and he glared wrathfully across the lake, and even more wrathfully at his smiling companion. "They've plumb ruined the woods," he growled. "That's what they've done—and you know it damn well! First they wanted a railroad in here, and they got it. Then they wanted steamboats and motorboats, and they got them. Then they wanted automobiles, and they got them. And *now* what have they got? *They aint got nothing!*" His jaws clicked shut, and the square chin set itself belligerently in defiance of possible refutation.

His old friend's eyes continued to twinkle with irrepressible mirth despite the passionate outburst, but he essayed a tone of half-bantering conciliation. "You're getting old, perhaps," he replied soothingly. "I've seen the time when going through the ice didn't rile you half as much. You haven't forgot, have you?" He turned away, as though to leave the irate victim of the swell to nurse his grievance alone, and looked out thoughtfully over the pleasant expanse of water. It had calmed to near-tranquillity. The agitation caused by the speeding motorboat had subsided to a faint pulsing of the dock at his feet, and the reflected glory of leafy ridges appeared again beneath the gleaming surface of the water.

All day the lake had mirrored the blue of a September sky. It had gathered the great bouquets of magnificent autumn foliage that bordered its shores.   Quietly it had gone about the task of picture making—so quietly, in fact, that it seemed to doze at its work; yet in faithful portrayal of Nature astir it had rippled ever so lightly at the frail touch of breeze that murmured across the mountains.

The two friends had spent the day up the lakes as they had often done together during their many years in the woods.   It had been a pleasant day, a cloudless one, the heavens radiant with friendly sunshine that warmed the earth and sparkled on the face of the lake chain.   In flaming rivalry with the sun, the coloring woods had piled their massive gifts of red and gold and russet mountain-high to add to the glory of the day.   The men had watched the rivalry end at the approach of dusk; they had seen the glitter of woods and water dim slowly under the spreading shadows of evening, and now the charm of twilight lay softly upon the forest.   The hills, subdued, were vague in the water.   Far up the lake, clumps of balsam and spruce had supplied contrasts of virile green amid the glowing foliage of day, but now they were no more than shafts of quiet shadow pointing upward from the waterside.

The voice of the gaunt, thoughtful woodsman scarcely disturbed the hush.   He spoke slowly, more to himself than to the man who stood beside him.   "Motorboats can't spoil mountains—and they can't spoil lakes.   Neither can automobiles or railroads.   It's how they're used and what they're used for that can do the spoiling."   He turned to his friend.   "Do you know, it's fifty-five years since I first came here, and the woods are as beautiful today as they were then.   God, it's a wonderful country!"

The other echoed his sentiment.   His emotions, like the once turbulent water, had subsided under the enchantment of the night scene and his normally calm good humor had asserted itself.   "Of course it is.   It's always been a wonderful country.   Always will be for that matter, everyone knows that . . . . but I still say *damn the motorboats!*"   He raised a wet foot and wriggled it gingerly.   Then he chuckled, quietly, contentedly:

so did the older man.

Both knew it was a wonderful country, for it had held them a lifetime. Wisely, neither attempted to analyze its allurement: they could not, perhaps, if they would. But they knew a hundred magnificent ridges that wandered grandly over the mountains, their shaggy backs adorned with the changing finery of seasons, their slopes ornamented in places with broad outcroppings of rock that tore apart the clinging garments of leaf and bough. Rude, amazing cliffs of stone these were that rose boldly to the crests of the hills, some tapestried in fabrics of old moss, some rich in simple gray, all stirring the imagination to fathom the might and power of hidden substance that formed the sinews of the mountains. Many times the men had crossed and recrossed these scenic ridges and tramped the wooded valleys and followed the streams that lay between. Their ways had led to scores of rippling lakes. On their shores they had made open night-camps, complacently as cottagers who latch their doors against the coming of darkness. Penetrating deeper, they had come upon small precious things which the forest had tried to conceal. Shy pools lurked in the dense woods. So gentle they were and so artless their depths, the green woodland had crowded close to behold the beauty of its own reflected face in the clear water. Beside these, too, the men had often made pleasant camp, and there they had known the companionship of small creatures who came unafraid to drink at the shadowed banks.

Truly, the mountains were wonderful in their versatile beauty, and even more wonderful in their immutable strength. They were strong—far too strong, the old friends knew, to be spoiled by motorboats, too strong indeed to be destroyed by any force except that which made them. Venal, stupid men might come among them who were insensible to their grandeur. Such men could work petty evils. They might hack in ruthless greed, or disfigure with garish structures built in shabby ostentation beside the water, or against the clean face of the forest. But such things could not ruin or destroy the mountains; they could only mar them.

Hunger urged the two men homeward. Halfway up the slope which led to the village they paused to look back. The lake was no longer visible. The dark night had descended upon it, and twinkling stars had settled in its waters to mark its place.